Managing in Emerging
Market Economies

---■---

Managing in Emerging Market Economies

Cases from the Czech and Slovak Republics

EDITED BY

Daniel S. Fogel

UNIVERSITY OF PITTSBURGH

Westview Press

BOULDER ▪ SAN FRANCISCO ▪ OXFORD

Copyright © 1994 by Westview Press, Inc.

Published in 1994 in the United States by Westview Press, Inc., 5500 Central Avenue, Boulder, Colorado 80301-2877, and in the United Kingdom by Westview Press, 36 Lonsdale Road, Summertown, Oxford OX2 7EW

Library of Congress Cataloging-in-Publication Data
Managing in emerging market economies : cases from the Czech and
    Slovak Republics / edited by Daniel S. Fogel.
        p.   cm.
    Includes bibliographical references.
    ISBN 0-8133-1792-4. — ISBN 0-8133-1793-2 (pbk.)
    1. Industrial management—Czech Republic—Case studies.
2. Industrial management—Slovakia—Case studies.   3. Privatization—
Czech Republic—Case studies.   4. Privatization—Slovakia—Case
studies.   5. Czech Republic—Economic conditions.   6. Slovakia—
Economic conditions.   I. Fogel, Daniel S.
HD70.C89M36   1994
658'.009437—dc20
                                                                                93-36052
                                                                                CIP

Printed and bound in the United States of America

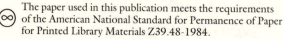

The paper used in this publication meets the requirements
of the American National Standard for Permanence of Paper
for Printed Library Materials Z39.48-1984.

10   9   8   7   6   5   4   3   2   1

Contents

PART THREE
PRIVATIZATION AND MEETING MARKET DEMANDS

PART FOUR
CONCLUSION

Preface

The Czech and Slovak Republics have experienced dramatic changes. Some people know of the peaceful "velvet" revolution in late 1989. Some have a vision of one of the great humanitarians of our times, Vaclav Havel. Others picture a unique experiment in privatization. Still others imagine a region that has an engaging charm and a major significance in world history. Many people see a divided country with lingering hopes of reunification.

My goal in writing this book is to give students, faculty, government officials, businesspeople, and others a glimpse of one of the most historic changes in the world economic scene in decades. I have focused on Czech and Slovak firms and the changes they are making to survive the emerging market economy in the Czech and Slovak Republics. My intent, as is the intent of my colleagues, is to capture significant events in cases that can be used as the basis of discussion.

Thus, one may find the reading here ideal for classrooms and boardrooms. The cases are designed to stimulate discussion and to generate questions about Central and Eastern Europe. Some cases present views of executives trying to survive in an uncertain and somewhat antagonistic world. Other cases are about organizational change and restructuring—how these changes were initiated and managed.

The writing of this book has spanned 1991–1993. The cases cut across the country's name change from Czechoslovakia to the Czech and Slovak Republics. We have tried to present a contemporary view of the two countries, but events are progressing so fast that an accurate picture is only gained by one's physical presence in the two countries.

*   *   *

A book such as this one is not the result of only its authors' efforts. I take this opportunity to acknowledge with heartfelt thanks the persons who have helped me: the U.S. Agency for International Development, the Mellon Foundation, Rockefeller Brothers Fund, the U.S. Information Agency, and the Czechoslovak Management Center for their financial and research support during the case writing periods. Also, much of the detailed editing was done by Heidi Rosenberg, along with help by Kasturi Natarajan at the University of Pittsburgh and with the able involvement of my colleague Suzanne

Etcheverry of the Center for International Enterprise Development. I appreciate the tolerance of the Westview editors, in particular Susan McEachern's. Pat Szekely's help is inestimable, especially her patience as she tried to figure out travel arrangements, ambiguous requests, and inaudible phone connections. Also, I want to acknowledge my loving family—Susan, Cristene, Jessica, and Cathy—with deep and sincere gratitude beyond what my words may express.

Ultimately, a book such as this one is the responsibility of the author. But, if the reader finds flaws in its content, I ask that he or she keep in mind the advice of my hero, Vaclav Havel: "In a world of global civilization, only those who are looking for a technical trick to save civilization need feel despair. But those who believe, in all modesty, in the mysterious power of their own human Being … have no reason to despair at all."

Daniel S. Fogel
Prague, Czech Republic

PART ONE

The Economic Situation of Central and Eastern Europe

CHAPTER ONE

■

Reforming the Economies of Central and Eastern Europe

DANIEL S. FOGEL
SUZANNE ETCHEVERRY

This chapter surveys the issues facing five Central and East European countries (CEECs)—Bulgaria, the former Czech and Slovak Federal Republic (CSFR), Hungary, Poland, and Romania, as they proceed with transitions to market economies. Where possible, the situation of individual countries is discussed.

A general warning is necessary. The quality of data concerning the CEECs is poor. Different sources are not always consistent with each other, which affects the accuracy of the information presented. At the same time, accurate information is often limited and outdated. All data reported in this chapter should therefore be treated with caution and interpreted with these limitations in mind. Furthermore, conditions are changing rapidly and will have changed further by the time this book appears. For example, in January 1993, the Czech and Slovak Federal Republics became two separate countries. Therefore, the general analysis of the policy issues that the CEECs face in making the transition is likely to be substantially more robust than the assessment of how much progress they have made individually.

This chapter has been adapted with permission from the OECD from *Reforming the Economies of Central and Eastern Europe,* Paris, France: OECD, 1992. The material covers the period of transformation until October 1991, but where possible some updated information through the middle of 1993 has been added.

Suzanne Etcheverry is assistant director, Center for International Enterprise Development at the Joseph M. Katz Graduate School of Business at the University of Pittsburgh. She received her MBA and MA in International Affairs from the University of Pittsburgh and her BA in European Studies from Tulane University. Etcheverry recently completed several research studies on U.S.

The broad story that emerges in this chapter is one of great progress made in areas where changes are relatively easy to implement. However, it is far more difficult to make institutional adjustments necessary for a market economy to function properly. Comprehensive reform programs emphasizing macroeconomic stabilization through tight fiscal and monetary policies and liberalization of prices and trade regimes have been implemented in the former CSFR, Hungary, and Poland. Similar but less-advanced programs are also formulated for Bulgaria and Romania.

Complex institutional changes are proceeding much more slowly. State enterprises must be converted to modern business organizations that are adapted to a market environment. Financial institutions must be built to support these new organizations and provide them with the capital to function in the market. Before these changes can occur, both the enterprises and the financial institutions must be separated from the core governments; each institution's role must be redefined and the revenue base secured. When this is completed, private ownership may be introduced and extended to create an incentive structure to yield better results in maintenance and the management of assets. These drastic institutional changes, required for the transition to a market economy, make the problem of the CEECs' transformations quite different from the development problem of raising per capita incomes in poor market economies.

If the CEECs are to make progress with the most difficult aspects of their transitions, they will have to resolve conflicts over constitutional arrangements, the roles of various levels of government, and the relations between them. For example, the former CSFR had problems agreeing on the role of the federal government. Disputes concerning jurisdiction, authority to raise revenues, and property ownership at the local level were, and continue to be, widespread throughout the region. There remains a serious shortage of locally based workers with the right kind of expertise to implement reform programs; people lack specific skills to build and operate market institutions. Many of the most obvious candidates for key jobs are discredited by associations with old regimes or the Communist party. Cultural and psychological change involving an adaptation to a market environment is necessary throughout the region. The gap between aspirations to Western living standards and the reality of what is likely to be achieved in the near future is a source of discontent. Most important, building and maintaining support for the reform process so that governments can see it through to completion must be a paramount consideration in its design. The factor that makes these problems particularly difficult is the large number of ethnic and nationality

investments in Central and Eastern Europe and is currently conducting research on the development of entrepreneurship in the Czech Republic.

conflicts that weaken the cohesion of central governments and delay economic reform.

The two main features of the current economic situation in the region are the sharp declines in output and the high rates of inflation that all the CEECs have experienced. Official data probably exaggerate the output decline. Figures for 1989–1992 for countries for which there is available data indicate approximately a 10 percent decline in output for Hungary, a 12.3 percent decline in Poland, and about a 20 percent decline in Romania. In the period 1989–1991, the figures were 10 percent for the former CSFR and 20 percent for Bulgaria. There is little doubt that the decline in this period was severe.

Annual inflation during 1991 was estimated to range from nearly 40 percent in Hungary to 400 percent in Bulgaria. Poland was successful in reducing inflation sharply after its price liberalization program in early 1990, but there has been slippage, and in late 1991, the situation was in danger of deteriorating. However, the yearly inflation rate for Poland was 44.3 percent in 1992, which was slightly lower than expected. In Bulgaria, the former CSFR, Hungary, and Romania, high inflation rates reflected price liberalization programs implemented in 1991. The authorities in these countries have some confidence that they will be successful in confining the inflationary impact of liberalization to a final adjustment, but this will require that underlying fiscal positions remain under control. This will be a challenge because the reform process may erode existing revenue bases faster than new ones can be put in place. The major contributor to the sharp declines in output and to the high rate of inflation in the period 1989–1992 was the collapse of intratrade, due largely to the compression of Soviet imports to meet debt-servicing obligations and to a decline in investment. However, the most important factor may be that the old planning system has ceased to operate but the new system based on market practices has not yet been firmly put into place.

If the CEECs are to maintain stable economic conditions, each must create an institutional framework for maintaining macroeconomic control. The three items that stand out are (1) establishing a secure government revenue base, (2) creating a strong monetary control regime, and (3) ensuring that a coherent exchange-rate strategy supportive of macroeconomic stability is in place. The most difficult of these will be establishing a secure revenue base. In late 1991, all CEEC revenue bases were heavily dependent on state enterprises. Revenues in the CEECs were buoyant as liberalization programs went into effect, but this may prove to be as temporary as it was in Poland if enterprise cash flow deteriorates. Over the longer term, as reform programs proceed and the private sector expands, the existing revenue base will erode. Introducing reasonably neutral, broadly based tax systems and ensuring that revenues are actually collected will be difficult, but rapid progress is essential.

An important systemic issue that the CEECs face is privatization. All recognize the need to shift the ownership of the majority of state assets to the private sector. Achieving this is proving difficult everywhere. Maintaining support for the process has not always been easy, and defining property rights is proving to be a serious impediment. In spite of the difficulties, however, small-scale privatization is moving forward in the former CSFR, Hungary, and Poland; Bulgaria and Romania appear to be making a good beginning. There is far less progress with large-scale privatization in all the CEECs, which is considerably more difficult because the CEECs have generally failed to develop coherent strategies for addressing the various obstacles that must be overcome, such as resistance from workers' councils in Poland and similar organizations elsewhere.

A second major systemic issue is the need to build a market-oriented financial sector to fill the important role formerly played by the central planning system. This should be done by mobilizing savings and allocating credit. Replicating the more sophisticated elements of international financial markets is not necessary, but building a basic banking system capable of providing an effective payment system is a high priority, and certain nonbanking financial intermediaries could play a positive role.

The transitions in the CEECs are taking place within the broader context of an interdependent global economy. Restrictions on access to markets in OECD (Organization for Economic Co-operation and Development) countries are a serious handicap to the CEECs. Removing explicit trade restraints applying to agriculture, textiles, and steel and avoiding the abuse of instruments such as antidumping are arguably the most important contributions OECD countries could make toward the success of the transition. In agriculture, export capacity in the CEECs is likely to rise, adding to the existing problems of oversupply and low prices on world markets from disposal of surpluses, unless broader policy reforms in OECD countries are put in place. If rural incomes in the CEECs do not benefit from productivity improvements, migratory pressures are likely to be intensified. The interdependence between developments in world agricultural markets and economic conditions in the CEECs reinforces the need for substantial reforms of agricultural policies in OECD countries.

The Main Features of the CEEC Economies

Size and Structure

Tables 1.1 and 1.2 report some economic and social indicators that provide an overview of the size and structure of the CEEC economies. For comparison, figures for the OECD area are also provided. CEEC official figures are suspect because central planning suffered from conceptual limitations and inaccuracy. Furthermore, until recently the exchange rate used to allow cross-country comparisons was arbitrarily chosen. On a purchasing power parity (PPP) ba-

TABLE 1.1 Economic Indicators

	Bulgaria	CSFR	Hungary	Poland	Romania	CEECs	USSR	OECD[f]
GDP ($ billion)[a] (PPP, 1989),	51	124	65	173	103	516	1,858	12,942
commercial exchange rate, 1989)	20	50	29	68	54	221	566	14,459
GDP per capita[a] ($ PPP)	5,710	7,878	6,108	4,565	3,445	5,536	6,500	15,565
($ commercial exchange rate, 1989)	2,261	3,214	2,750	1,807	2,311	2,302	1,981	17,390
Export share as % of GDP (1989)	31	35	33	19	21	25	7	18
Investment share[b] as a % of GDP (1987)	27	26	25	29	30	28	34	20
Sectoral shares in total employment (%) (1989)[c]								
Agriculture	17	12	18	27	28	23	19	8
Industry	49	46	39	37	45	42	39	30
Services	34	42	43	36	27	35	42	62
Energy use per unit of output, relative to OECD (1988)[d]	2.2	1.9	1.3	1.9	2.5	2.0	2.7	1.0
Share of private enterprises[c] as a % of NMP/GDP mid-1980s)	9	3	15	15	3	9	3	70–80

[a]CIA estimates from PlanEcon, September 14, 1990, for PPP-based GDP figures. World Bank and OECD estimates for commercial exchange-rate-based GDP figures. For the USSR, the initial value of the commercial rate established in 1990 is used.
[b]National Statistics.
[c]National statistics and OECD estimates.
[d]OECD Economic Outlook 48, December 1990.
[e]OECD Economic Outlook 47, June 1990.
[f]OECD data are from OECD data bases.

TABLE 1.2 Social Indicators

	Bulgaria	CSFR	Hungary	Poland	Romania	CEECs	USSR	OECD
Population (millions, 1990)[a]	9.0	15.7	10.6	38.2	23.2	96.7	285.9	831.5
Indicators of living standard								
Cars per 1,000 people (1987)[b]	127	122	153	74	11	90	50	385
Telephone per 1,000 people (1987)[b]	248	246	152	122	111	155	124	542
Infant mortality (deaths per 1,000 live births) (1988)[c]	14	12	16	16	25	17	25	8
Life expectancy (years) (1989)[c]	71	71	70	71	69	71	70	75
Synthetic measure (1980)[d]	23	37	24	21	3	20	16	59
Income distribution[e]	–	21	24	24	–	–	26	32
Rate (%) of labor force participation (end 1980s)[f]								
Men	81	82	75	83	83	82	81	83
Women	74	77	62	68	68	69	73	59
Percent of work force with secondary or higher education (1989)[b]	–	29	34	29	–	–	27	61

[a]U.N. Statistical Office, Monthly Bulletin of Statistics, 1990.

[b]OECD The Economics of Central and Eastern Europe. Paris: OECD, 1992, 80.

[c]CMEA Statistical Yearbook, 1989: OECD Health Data File.

[d]Measure of satisfaction of needs combining 13 indicators selected by factorial analysis. Source: Human Development Report. United Nations Development Programme. New York, 1990.

[e]Gini coefficient. OECD data refer to the United States and Western Europe. Source: Branko Milanovic. Liberalization and Entrepreneurship: Dynamics of Reform in Socialism and Capitalism. New York: M. E. Sharpe, 1989. [f]IMF, World Bank, OECD, EBRD. A Study of the Soviet Economy. Vol. 2, OECD, 1991. OECD Employment Outlook, July 1991.

sis, Central Intelligence Agency (CIA) estimates put the size of the gross domestic product (GDP) in the CEECs in 1989 at around $530 billion, similar to that of Canada, and that of the former USSR at around $1.86 trillion, nearly as large as that of Japan. The World Bank estimates for the CEECs based on commercial exchange rates are far lower. These put the CEEC GDP at around $220 billion, similar to that of the Netherlands. On the basis of GDP figures converted at the initial value of the commercial exchange rate established in 1990, GDP in the Commonwealth of Independent States (CIS) is around $570 billion.[1]

Given that the population in the CEECs and the former USSR is nearly half that of the OECD area, even the relatively high CIA estimates suggest low levels of development and living standards. GDP per person appears to be highest in the former CSFR; CIA estimates put it at half the average for the OECD area, and World Bank estimates it at less than 20 percent of the OECD average. The lowest GDP per capita is either in Romania with a GDP at just over 20 percent of the OECD average according to CIA estimates, or in Poland with just over 10 percent of the OECD average according to the World Bank. The indicators of living standards reported in Table 1.2 broadly confirm this picture. Diffusion of cars and telephones is low, infant mortality is high, and life expectancy is short throughout the region. A wider index prepared by the UN Development Program suggests that this is representative of other indicators not shown here. These social indicators confirm that within the region, standards in the former CSFR were relatively high and those in Romania were particularly poor.

Many structural features of the CEECs' economies reflected the emphasis placed by central planning on rapid capital accumulation and extensive development rather than on labor efficiency in industry. Although raising living standards was an objective, priority was given to defense and heavy industry at the expense of consumer goods and of services generally. Furthermore, the incentives to improve farm productivity were poor, so large proportions of the labor force needed to be retained for agriculture. As a result, the economic structures in the CEECs appeared markedly different from those of most OECD countries. In 1987, before the crisis that led to the collapse of central planning became fully evident, approximately 28 percent of the CEECs' share of GDP was devoted to fixed investments, compared to the OECD's average of 20 percent. Employment in industry averaged nearly 40 percent of the labor force, was substantially higher in Bulgaria, the former CSFR, and Romania, and compared with 30 percent in the OECD. In agriculture, employment averaged around 20 percent of the labor force, with wide fluctuations among the CEECs; the employment figure for the OECD was just 8 percent. The figure for employment in services was just over 40 percent in the former USSR and approximately 35 percent in the CEECs, which is low in comparison to the 55–70 percent range of most OECD countries. A feature of the

CEECs that was not unusual by international standards was their openness, as reflected in the share of exports in GDP. However, a large share of intra-CEEC trade was carried out on a barter basis, leaving the region largely insulated from the international economy.

That the planning process failed to be guided by a coherent price structure left a legacy of problems. One is that domestic prices were forced to adjust both to domestic costs and to world prices. Many enterprises appeared not to be viable even if they achieved substantial reductions in staffing levels. Price distortions in the late 1980s were very high. This suggests that if world price levels were allowed to assert themselves, sectors in which input costs exceeded the value of output, that is, value added was negative, would represent 19 percent of the manufacturing output in the former CSFR and 24 percent in Hungary and Poland. If those figures are correct, no exchange-rate policy or strategy toward control of wage costs would have been able to solve the problems that early removal of trade barriers and subsidies would cause in these sectors. A significant part of the manufacturing sector would simply disappear unless rapid changes in production methods were made. There are limitations to the input-output approach on which this study is based, but it is instructive to note that at least one of the few industrial sectors in the region whose main inputs and outputs were subject to a transparent market test, that is, Soviet oil refining, is a concrete case where value added at world prices appears to be negative.[2]

A second problem is that plentiful energy supplies in the former USSR, which were made available to the CEECs on favorable terms, led to a strategy of energy-intensive development and low prices for consumers. Because capital equipment was generally old and often in poor repair and despite high shares of investment in GDP, heavy industry was particularly important, so energy intensity reached very high levels in the CEECs, especially in the former USSR and Romania.[3] This contributed to serious environmental problems. At the same time the CEECs experienced major trade losses as import prices adjusted to world market levels.

High levels of subsidies remained a serious constraint on budgetary positions in most of the CEECs and were an impediment to improved resource allocation despite substantial cuts during 1990–1991. Prices to consumers under central planning were based largely on social considerations, and many basic consumer goods and services, in particular housing, were provided very cheaply. Because these have been fixed for decades, they are increasingly regarded as just prices, which has contributed to the difficulty governments have in allowing some of them to rise significantly.

Some Institutional Features of CEEC Economies

Central planning institutions were designed to carry out, on an administrative basis, most of the functions performed by markets in OECD economies. At the top, state committees (such as Gosplan in the former USSR) made strategic decisions, effectively determining the broad composition of output and performing the main functions of a capital market. Branch ministries or similar institutions, organized along industrial or regional lines, performed the functions of markets for intermediate goods, allocating resources among individual enterprises and deciding where the products should go. This system required that the enterprise be of average size relative to other East European enterprises (although larger than a typical OECD enterprise) and that it be almost entirely owned by the state.[4] Plant closures, where necessary, were likely to involve high social costs, and the existence of a single domestic producer for many commodities has contributed to widespread, although probably unwarranted, concern about exploitation of monopoly power in the CEECs.

Large enterprises in the CEECs were in some respects more like government departments than like the business enterprises of OECD countries. They faced no financial objectives or meaningful budget constraints but aimed, rather, to meet production targets, usually defined crudely in quantitative terms with only limited quality specifications. Cost did not enter into the definition of targets, so there was a strong incentive to hoard labor, accumulate inventories of inputs, and integrate vertically as protection against chronic supply shortages. Because there was no need to monitor and control costs, there was little incentive to develop the requisite accounting and management skills. Furthermore, because the planning agencies performed so many of the functions carried out by markets in OECD countries, skills that Western businesses routinely require in areas such as marketing, quality control, product development, and finance, were not deemed necessary. CEEC enterprises, however, often carried out activities that are normally the responsibility of governments, particularly in the area of social services.[5]

Banks similarly bore little resemblance to those in OECD countries. Their principal role was to act as bookkeepers, monitoring enterprises' success in achieving plan targets and passively meeting financing needs implied by the plan. In the course of performing this role they also acted as tax collectors, transferring surplus funds from enterprises to state budgets. They accepted deposits but they provided only rudimentary payment systems; they did not analyze credit, appraise investment proposals, or manage portfolios. Broader capital markets had no role and hence did not exist.

The concentration of ownership of the enterprise sector and housing was in the hands of the state. This created a situation in which few people had the incentive to concern themselves with the stewardship of assets or the governance of enterprises. Management responsibility for fixed assets and enterprises was overwhelmingly in the hands of managers who were neither owners nor agents acting on behalf of, and hence accountable to, the owners. As a result, mismanagement and neglect led to waste, obsolescence, and disrepair of much of the capital stock and to inefficient operation of the enterprises. Furthermore, because private ownership of fixed assets was largely prohibited, new capital formation was limited largely to that called for by the planning framework.

The Status of Reform Programs

In terms of progress with reform, the CEECs fell into two distinct groups. The first, the former CSFR, Hungary, and Poland, abolished the central planning system and by 1991 implemented comprehensive reform programs. In Hungary, the gradual reform process has been under way since the 1960s and has already achieved a great deal. In Poland sporadic progress toward a more market-oriented system was made during the 1980s. These countries have gone a considerable way, even before the end of 1989, toward dismantling central planning, decentralizing enterprise management, and developing markets for intermediate goods.

The reform programs in the former CSFR, Hungary, and Poland emphasize macroeconomic stabilization through tight fiscal and monetary policies and the creation of market practices through liberalization of prices and trade regimes. Considerable progress has been made in these areas. The more difficult tasks requiring institutional restructuring have also begun to be addressed, although progress is limited.

Bulgaria and Romania make up the second group within the CEEC. Unlike in the other countries, central planning was not abolished in a controlled plan but rather collapsed because the governments' political legitimacy was so fragile that little or nothing was done in the way of market-oriented reforms. Comprehensive reform programs along the lines of the first group were being formulated in Bulgaria and Romania, and implementation had begun; but progress was slower because of its later implementation.

The Situation in 1992

Official information suggests that all the CEECs experienced dramatic declines in output from 1989 to 1991 (see Table 1.3). In the group that has made the most progress with its reform programs, the decline in output between 1989 and 1991 appears likely to be somewhat above 10 percent in the former CSFR and Hungary and approximately 20 percent in Poland. In the second group, where progress is at an earlier stage, the decline is even larger. In Romania, where the collapse in output began first, the decline since 1988 appears to be more than 25 percent; in Bulgaria it has exceeded 30 percent.

These figures may exaggerate the decline that occurred, because there were serious data inaccuracies in the treatment of inventories and the growing private-sector production was probably understated. This exaggeration of data happened most notably in Poland, primarily because the old planning system had collapsed, or in the case of the former USSR, had been collapsing, but a

TABLE 1.3   Macroeconomic Indicators in CEECs

	Bulgaria	*CSFR*	*Hungary*	*Poland*	*Romania*	*CIS*
Output[a] percentage changes from previous year						
1989	−0.3	1.0	−0.2	0.2	−5.6	2.4
1990	−11.8	−1.1	−4.0	−11.6	−8.4	−4.0
1991	−22.9	−10.0	−10.2	−7.0	−13.0	−12.5
1992 (est.)	−6 to −10	−8.0	−5.0	−2.0	−7.0	
Unemployment[b] percentage of labor force, December figures						
1989	0.0	0.0	0.3	0.1	1.6	n.a.
1990	1.5	1.0	2.5	6.1	2.0	1.8
1991	10.4	6.6	8.0	11.8	2.9	n.a.
1992 (est.)	15.0	5.0	12.0	14.0	10.0	
Consumer prices, percentage changes from previous year						
1989	6.4	2.3	17.0	251.1	0.9	7.5
1990	26.3	10.8	28.9	585.8	7.4	10.0
1991	334.0	58.7	35.0	70.3	162.0	300.0
1992 (est.)	100.0	11.0	23.0	45.0	200.0	

[a]Real GDP for Hungary, Poland, Romania and Bulgaria. Net material product for the former CSFR and the former USSR.
[b]Based on registered unemployment figures.
[c]Retail prices for Bulgaria.
Source: National sources, IMF, World Bank, and European Bank for Reconstruction and Development estimates.

new system was not in place. This was coupled with the lack of private ownership, which caused investments to decline sharply.

As a result, open unemployment, virtually unknown in the centrally planned economies before 1991, rose sharply. Estimates of rates of officially recognized unemployment by the end of 1992 were 15 percent of the labor force in Bulgaria, 5 percent in the former CSFR, 12 percent in Hungary, 14 percent in Poland, and 10 percent in Romania. The Romanian figure may reflect underregistration and may therefore understate the problem.

Inflation in 1991 was fueled primarily by price liberalization programs. Poland, which was threatened with hyperinflation at the end of 1989, liberalized most prices and sharply devalued the zloty as part of its "big bang" reform program in January 1990. As a result, the annual inflation rate for 1990 reached 550 percent; the government hoped to hold inflation to around 50 percent in 1991. However, the further devaluation of the zloty in May, together with slippage in monetary control, contributed to inflation that was estimated to be approximately 65 percent. In the rest of the CEECs, price liberalization was nearly complete by the middle of 1991. Estimates show that inflation may have reached 400 percent in Bulgaria by the end of 1991. In the former USSR, prices that remained regulated increased by up to 200 percent at the beginning of 1991. At the time of the attempted coup in the USSR in August 1991, inflation for the year appeared likely to reach 150 percent; but financial control deteriorated, and inflation for that year was about 300 percent.

In general for most of the CEECs, industrial output and the rate of inflation improved in 1992. The decline in industrial output leveled off, and some countries experienced growth. In Poland, the former CSFR, and Hungary, industrial output rose between 2 and 4 percent. Monthly inflation rates in 1992 were 2–4 percent between January and December in the Czech Republic, Slovakia, and Hungary. In Poland, the monthly rate in 1992 declined to under 1 percent in December from 8 percent in January.[6] Depending on the distortions caused by price control in the past and the extent of macroeconomic imbalances, estimated annual inflation rates for 1992 were about 9 percent in the former CSFR, 23 percent in Hungary, 45 percent in Poland, and 200 percent in Romania.

Transition Issues in the CEECs

Constitutional arrangements and the roles of various levels of government and their relations must be established if reform is to succeed. In the former CSFR and the former USSR, economic and political changes have led to demands for greater regional autonomy and efforts to renegotiate federal charters. In the former CSFR, agreement on an acceptable division of powers was difficult to obtain. Even in unitary states such as Hungary, more responsibility is being devolved to local governments, and local elections have given some local authorities greater legitimacy. However, increased responsibilities for subnational levels of government have not always been accompanied by the necessary financial resources, and many local governments are finding it difficult to carry out their new tasks. As a result, disputes have arisen over property ownership and rights to government revenues. These disputes were at the heart of the breakup of the Czech and Slovak federal republics.

Resolution of these conflicts is essential to creating the legal framework that defines the environment in which market relations work. The legal framework must include not only legislation but also an infrastructure to enforce it and to resolve disputes. The CEECs have well-developed infrastructures for handling criminal and many types of civil matters, but in the commercial area much more work needs to be done. Effective definition of property rights will require registries, registrars, and procedures for verifying titles. Because laws in areas such as company law, contracts, and tax are only now being written, court systems to interpret them must be established. Furthermore, lawyers and judges will not only find these areas unfamiliar but they will have no body of precedent to guide them.

Another core of the transition process is the major institutional and structural reform effort, which is needed both to give the authorities adequate tools to maintain macroeconomic stability and to improve resource allocation and capital productivity. Three reform elements can be identified that must be in place if reform is to be successful: (1) the establishment of framework policies, (2) the dismantling of the institutional apparatus of a command economy and the building of institutions adapted to a market environment, and (3) the development of human capital and market-oriented attitudes.

The most important of the "people" problems is the large number of ethnic and nationality conflicts throughout the region. As the Yugoslav experience graphically demonstrates, these weaken the cohesion of the central governments and distract attention from economic reform. With the possible exception of Hungary, not one of the CEECs is free of this problem. There are other serious problems:

1. The reform process must be designed so that governments can sustain the political will to see difficult reforms through in the face of adjustment costs. In some countries, notably Poland, this is an increasing problem.

2. Policies to establish the framework of a market economy and to allow the necessary institutional changes require qualified people to implement them. Most of the CEECs have a thin layer of capable people at the top and little else. There is a serious shortage of locally based, permanent staff with the requisite expertise to implement reform programs. Lack of workers, for example, is a factor in Poland's failure to clean up banks' balance sheets.

3. Institution building and making markets function require a wide range of specific skills that are scarce in the CEECs. The experience of the former German Democratic Republic (GDR) may be indicative. An extensive poll conducted in 1990 of West German industrial and service firms operating in Eastern Germany showed that 75 percent believed management in enterprises lacked dynamism and qualifications and performed poorly. Only 18 percent felt comfortable leaving existing management in place, even after retraining. At the same time, enterprises that were becoming corporations obliged the Treuhand to find 40,000 supervisory board members.[7]

4. Many of the most obvious candidates for key jobs are discredited by association with the old regimes or the Communist party (nomenklatura)

or, in Romania, are suspected of having at least collaborated with the secret police.

5. A cultural change involving an adaptation of attitudes to a market environment is necessary throughout the region. The daily requests that Romanian ministries receive from enterprises for price or output targets despite the freedom to operate in markets illustrate the problem.

Pace and Sequencing Issues

Much has been written about pace and sequencing, but relatively few generalizations can safely be made about these issues. Given the different histories and starting positions of the various CEECs, as well as the variety of institutional arrangements they aim to establish, there is no single blueprint for reform that can be applied in all countries.

Flexibility in program design is limited by three main factors:

1. Problems can emerge that threaten to reach crisis proportions and must be addressed as they arise. The increasing shortages in shops in Poland in late 1989 were in this category.
2. Coherent change in some areas, for example, privatization of large enterprises, involves complex implementation issues that cannot be solved quickly.
3. Expertise to implement reforms is in short supply, and the demand on the time of senior ministers and officials with authority to make decisions and resolve disputes is heavy. Crises take first priority, and addressing important areas must often be delayed.

These constraints make practical discretion over pace and sequencing relatively modest. With regard to pace, a country such as Hungary, which has considerable experience with gradual reform, may find that slow but steady reform best suits its purpose. Where a reform effort is only beginning, however, a rapid and radical program has advantages in terms of establishing the direction of change and the credibility of the reform effort. With regard to sequencing, reasonable macroeconomic stabilization is a precondition for a successful reform effort.

Macroeconomic Policies and Issues

Macroeconomic policy must ensure financial conditions conducive to reasonably low inflation in order to provide a stable environment for the reform process. It must also facilitate the management of external debt, which is a preoccupation of policymakers in all of the CEECs except the former CSFR and Romania. Under International Monetary Fund (IMF) programs that have been put in place, there are three key elements to the stabilization effort.

1. The CEECs must maintain fiscal discipline. The key to achieving this is keeping general government budgets near balance or in small surplus. However, where enterprises and banks are part of the state, the budgetary concepts widely used in OECD countries can be misleading. Implicit subsidies to enterprises in the form of bank credits will ultimately be taken over by the government and are effectively budgetary items even if they are not accounted for as such.
2. Limits are needed on bank credit expansion to strengthen the balance of payments and limit monetary growth.
3. The CEECs need income policies to encourage wage restraint. These appear to be intended not only to play a macroeconomic role in support of monetary policy but also to provide a means for governments to contain production costs in their role as owners of state enterprises. New policies in the Czech Republic, Hungary, and Poland are designed to encourage private enterprise.

Exchange-rate policies are not generally oriented to providing an effective nominal anchor, except in the former CSFR.

In 1992, the authorities in Bulgaria, the former CSFR, Hungary, and Romania had some confidence that inflation was under control, and there is evidence to support this view. Credit ceilings were substantially undershot, and monetary growth was slow because banks took a conservative view on risk; demand for credit was low in view of the uncertainty about privatization and economic prospects. The governments' revenue bases in 1992 were still unstable. On the budget side, the former CSFR budget deficit was the same as the year before, about 2 percent of GDP, most of which accrued in the Slovak budget. Poland's deficit was over 6 percent in 1991, reached 7 percent of GDP in 1992, and is likely to double in 1993; and Romania's budget deficit was about 2 percent of GDP from 2.4 percent in 1991. Bulgaria experienced a deficit of about 5 percent, up from 3.5 percent in 1991.

Hungary's budget deficit was 7 percent of GDP in 1992, up from 5 percent in 1991, and is projected to rise to 11 percent in 1993. It was forecasted to be 70 billion forints (about $9 billion) in 1992. It turned out to be 190 billion. One hundred billion of the shortfall was accounted for by unexpectedly low company and bank taxes. One reason for these low tax collections is that the speed of change is so rapid that the tax system cannot keep up with collections. This fact, coupled with the rapid increase of the private sector, means that most new businesses probably do not pay taxes. Thus, once the tax system develops, the private sector may not be as enthusiastic about its opportunities for new business. Private companies will pay greater amounts of taxes, the government's revenues will increase, yet the private sector may decline in growth.

At the same time, the experience of OECD countries suggests that income policies will give rise to pressures that undermine their effectiveness. These policies are difficult to design without introducing rigidities and distortions to the labor market at a time when flexibility is needed. There might be several months of satisfactory fiscal figures and low monetary growth, followed by two or three months of moderate inflation. These predictions came true. For example, the Czech Republic maintains tight controls on wages and employment policies. In the short term, Poland and perhaps Hungary must take measures to prevent fiscal deterioration. Beyond that, all the CEECs must create and continue to create an institutional framework for maintaining macroeconomic control. Three priority areas stand out:

- Governments must have a stable revenue base adapted to the institutional framework of a market economy.
- A monetary control framework is needed that will allow some flexibility in financing budget deficits without requiring support from income policies.
- A coherent approach to exchange-rate strategy, supportive of macroeconomic stability, must be established.

Establishing a secure revenue base is an urgent task in all the CEECs. In late 1991, the revenue base was heavily dependent on the state enterprise sector (see Table 1.4). The government's ability to collect revenues largely depends on the relations among enterprises, banks, and the central authorities established under the old planning framework. Over the longer term, privatization and growth of new enterprises in the private sector will erode the existing revenue base, particularly as banks evolve into modern financial institutions. This will lead to a phaseout of their roles as tax collectors; time will be required to build effective new tax administrations. Private sectors represent increasing percentages of GDP. In 1992, over 40 percent of Poland's GDP was from the private sector. Thus, government revenues will depend on their abilities to collect taxes.

As inflation stabilizes or falls, as real wages recover, as recession deepens, and as the scope for using inventory reductions as a source of liquidity is reduced, enterprise finances are likely to come under pressure. This is already evident in Poland, where price liberalization occurred a year earlier than in the other CEECs. Not only will this adversely affect government finances but it will lead to pressure to provide implicit subsidies through the banking system or to face the political issues involved in closing down large enterprises; something that the CEECs are just beginning to face.

The CEECs plan to address the problem of establishing a secure revenue base by shifting taxation from enterprises to households and by implementing broadly based and transparent income and value-added taxes with relatively

TABLE 1.4 Level and Composition of General Government Revenues in 1989 in CEECs (percent of GDP)

	Bulgaria	*CSFR*	*Hungary*	*Poland*[a]	*Romania*	*USSR*
Total revenues	57	60	61	47	53	46
Enterprise income taxes and transfers[b]	23	17	14	14	15	18
Social security contributions	9	15	16	7	7	4
Domestic taxes on goods and services[c]	11	18	18	13	19	12
Revenue from international trade	5	1	3	2	–	6
Individual income taxes	4	7	6	1	–	4
Other revenue	5	2	5	9	12	2

[a]For Poland, data refer to 1988.
[b]Including entrepreneurial income from state-owned enterprises and financial institutions and for the USSR, including transfers to extra-budgetary centralized funds.
[c]Product-specific turnover taxes, excises, sales tax, and value-added tax.
Source: George Kopits. "Fiscal Reform in European Economies in Transition." In *Transition to a Market Economy in Central and Eastern Europe.* Paris: CCEET, OECD, 1992.

low and uniform rates. By 1991, Hungary was the only country that had made progress in implementing them, although Bulgaria and Poland proceeded with major reforms in 1992.

Putting these reforms into effect and ensuring that revenues are actually collected will be a major task. Personal taxation often treated different taxpayers arbitrarily; profit taxes were negotiated between individual enterprises and the government and included a dividend component. Accounting systems and standards need to allow for various income measures so that the taxation system is less distortional and more neutral. The ability to use these systems needs to be extended beyond large enterprises into the public sector. The financial skills of tax administrations will have to be strengthened as banks gradually cease to act as tax collectors, and measures need to be taken to safeguard against corruption.

A strategy for public-expenditure control will be required in view of the probable erosion of revenue bases. Prospects for saving in the area of defense are good, especially in the former USSR and the former CSFR, and some streamlining of public administration is possible as privatization progresses. Avoiding pressures from debt servicing, however, is largely a matter of ensuring overall fiscal control. Pressures for increases in several areas are likely to be strong during the process of transition, and four areas in particular merit attention:

TABLE 1.5   Subsidies in CEECs and OECD Area (percent of GDP)

	1985	1989	1991	1992 (est.)
CEECs[a]				
Bulgaria	13	15	4.0	1.7
CSFR	15	19	7.3	5.2
Hungary	21	16	7.4	3.4
Poland	16	17	4.8	1.8
Romania	1	1	6.4	13.6[c]
USSR	9	18	n.a.	n.a.
OECD[b]				
United States	0.6	0.6		
Japan	0.9	0.8		
Europe	2.6	2.3		

[a]General government budgets. Subsidies include transfers to enterprises.
[b]National Accounts definition.
[c]Mid-year.
Source: For CEECs, George Kopits. "Fiscal Reform in European Economies in Transition." In *Transition to a Market Economy in Central and Eastern Europe.* Paris: CCEET, OECD, 1992; and OECD estimates. OECD figures are from OECD data bases. Figures for 1991 and 1992 from European Bank for Reconstruction and Development, *Quarterly Economic Review,* April 1993.

1. Subsidies, which ranged between 15 and 19 percent of GDP in 1989, except in Romania, where they were very low, were cut substantially, but by 1991 they were still high compared with those in most OECD countries (see Table 1.5).
2. The social safety net, which already covered illness, disability, and early retirement, was being extended to cover the unemployed. The CEECs will face limits on how much they can afford for income support.
3. As in OECD countries, the ratio of old-age pensioners to the work force is projected to rise from 15 percent in 1990 to approximately 25 percent in the year 2025 in the former CSFR, Poland, and the former USSR, and from 20 percent to 30 percent in Hungary. To avoid heavy fiscal pressures over the medium term, actuarially sound pension schemes need to be established at an early stage.
4. Poor infrastructure environmental conditions require heavy capital expenditures. Although much of this will fall on the public sector, efforts should be made to find ways in which private capital can be introduced in some of these areas, possibly including telecommunications, water, electricity, and transportation.

All the CEECs have established a monetary control framework based on a two-tier banking system in which the intermediation function of commercial banks is separate from the monetary control functions of the central bank. Central banks use reserve requirements and limits on refinancing credit and are increasingly refinancing rates to assist banks in exercising monetary control. However, given that financial markets are underdeveloped and that neither banks nor enterprises are yet responding fully to market signals, there are limits to the effectiveness of these instruments.

Eventually, central banks need to be given a clear mandate to preserve the value of their currencies, in terms of either general purchasing power or a well-managed foreign currency. The European currency unit (ECU) has been suggested and has the autonomy to do the job.[8] Only in Hungary does such progress appear likely in the near future. The fact that many OECD governments have a major influence on the conduct of monetary policy should not obscure the importance of insulating monetary policies from short-term political pressures. The CEECs lack the stable institutions and track record of political cohesion that the OECD countries built up over many decades, and the economic problems they face are far more severe than anything the OECD countries have had to contend with since the immediate postwar period. In Latin America, weak governments have often found monetary creation to be a politically attractive alternative to addressing difficult fiscal and structural problems; this provides grounds for concern and, it is hoped, will not become a problem for the CEECs.

Exchange-rate arrangements are an integral aspect of the monetary framework. They must be consistent with keeping inflation low. Given the weakness of monetary control frameworks, there is an advantage in designing exchange-rate arrangements to provide positive support. Some CEECs are unlikely to commit themselves to any particular regime or target in the near future, preferring to manage the exchange rate in a more pragmatic fashion. However, even these countries must develop a coherent strategy for this management. By late 1991, the CEECs had chosen a variety of strategies. Poland devalued for large competitive advantage and then managed with a view toward resisting inflation. The former CSFR pegged its currency and used a nominal anchor. Hungary managed pragmatically with a view toward maintaining competitiveness. Romania floated its currency for most transactions before the end of 1991. Bulgaria floated all transactions.

Although the float in Bulgaria and the near float in Romania were largely forced by a shortage of foreign exchange, this strategy has clear advantages where the "correct" exchange rate is unknown in an environment of large and rapid changes of relative prices. However, in such an environment, assessment of domestic monetary conditions is also difficult, as a number of OECD countries discovered. This strategy places the full burden of inflation control on domestic monetary management without the benefit of a clear nominal anchor to assist the monetary authorities. Particularly given the weak institutional framework for exercising monetary control, free-floating currency is a risky strategy. For example, a large devaluation in January 1990 in Poland was rapidly offset by inflation, which left authorities with the choice of restoring a favorable competitive position with another large devaluation or allowing it to erode in order to resist high inflation. In late 1991, they were leaning toward resisting inflation, devaluing only once (by 14.4 percent in May 1991) before announcing that from October 1991 the exchange rate would be adjusted downward on a daily basis along a preannounced path. This strategy is similar to that followed in recent years by Mexico and, if it is adhered to, will put significant downward pressure on inflation. The principal threat to this strategy in 1991 appeared to be the deteriorating fiscal position. Hungary, however, has followed a pegging strategy that gives a high value to maintaining a favorable competitive position. Because this strategy envisages no nominal anchor beyond the short term, Hungary runs the risk of losing control of inflation.

Developing Markets for Goods and Services

All of the CEECs took significant steps to establish a market framework for goods and services. Central planning has been largely or completely eliminated, private property and legal equality between state and privately owned firms is established, and by 1991 prices for 85-90 percent of goods had been liberated. The removal of most nontariff trade restrictions has created the potential for greater competition in domestic markets. At this stage, two key areas need attention: the legal infrastructure to enforce contracts and reduce disputes, and arrangements to ensure an effectively competitive environment in domestic markets.

Improving the legal infrastructure underpinning business activity is essential in all the CEECs. Most antibusiness laws were abolished in the CEECs. Initially these countries turned to old laws from the pre-Communist period, but these are inadequate in a modern environment. Bulgaria, Hungary, and the former CSFR subsequently introduced new commercial codes, some aspects of which are based on European Community (EC) legislation. By 1991 in Poland, however, legislation was blocked in parliament and in Romania it was still under consideration. In November 1992, the Polish government established the "small constitution," which allowed the government to issue legally binding decrees. This has created the beginning of a stable political and legal environment for business development. By and large, throughout the CEECs civil courts have jurisdiction over commercial disputes, torts, and contract enforcement, but these courts are understaffed and their personnel lack the expertise and experience to deal with these complex contract arrangements.[9] In the private sector, legal counsel from lawyers competent to handle commercial matters in a market economy is scarce.

Production of many goods is often concentrated in a single or relatively small number of enterprises, giving rise to concern that effective competition may be absent. Reduction in the number of sectors reserved for the state, which is now largely restricted to public utilities, has helped. Equally important is the rapid progress made in opening domestic markets in the CEECs to foreign competition, especially in the former CSFR and Poland. Quantitative restrictions on imports has largely been eliminated in favor of tariffs, and restrictions on access to foreign exchange for current transactions has also been removed.

Because an open-trade regime ensures that markets for most products are contestable, it is not clear how much more is required to ensure that monopoly exploitation does not become a serious problem. Nevertheless, some CEECs pursued two additional approaches to fostering competition. First, efforts were made to break monopoly firms into smaller units. The initial focus in some countries (Bulgaria, Poland, and Romania) was in the areas of food processing, road transport, and distribution systems. Second, an active competition policy was introduced. Competition laws were passed in most countries and were actively implemented in Poland. These may have been misguided, however, insofar as the laws provided that price controls could be imposed on first entrants into a new market simply because they appeared to have a dominant market share.

Doubts about the viability of many enterprises in the CEECs and the threat of rising unemployment raised the question of how rapidly industry support in the form of tariff barriers and domestic subsidies should be reduced. Border protection had already been lowered substantially, largely through the removal of most nontariff barriers. The issue, therefore, largely related to how rapidly tariffs and various surcharges should be reduced. They were both highly variable and averaged between 8 and 25 percent. Moreover, the CEECs may raise tariffs in order to achieve more bargaining power in negotiations over trading arrangements with OECD countries. Poland had already raised tariffs on agricultural products. Explicit subsidies were largely limited to a few basic consumer services, public transportation, household energy, and housing. Some of these consumer services are widely subsidized in OECD countries also. Apart from energy price subsidies in Poland, and agricultural export support in Hungary, producer subsidies were largely avoided.

The desirability of increased integration in the international economy, a coherent relative price structure, and effective market discipline on domestic enterprises makes it important that the CEECs continue to move in the direction of removing border protection and domestic support for enterprises. In 1992, Hungary, the former CSFR, Poland, and Romania signed agreements with the EC that will improve access for their goods into the EC market. Beginning in January 1993, Hungary, the former CSFR, and Poland have implemented a mutual trade liberalization to establish a free market in industrial goods over the next ten years.

Reforming the Enterprise Sector

Creating a healthy enterprise sector is a key to improving productivity and growth performance over the longer term. Indeed, there is almost unanimous agreement among close observers of developments in the CEECs that privatization is the largest and most important systemic issue that these countries face. There are two main elements in creating a healthy enterprise sector: (1) establishing a favorable environment for the emerging private sector and (2) restructuring and privatizing existing state-owned assets and enterprises.

All the CEECs have made progress in establishing a body of company law, including the recognition of various forms of organization and ownership such as small businesses, partnerships, and limited-liability companies. In this environment, the private sector expanded rapidly in all the CEECs, and particularly in Hungary and Poland. By 1992, private-sector activity reached 40 percent of GDP in Poland and Hungary (if unofficial and nonagricultural activity is taken into account), and between 15 and 20 percent in the former CSFR.

New firms face a number of further practical impediments to their success. Access to credit from the banking system is difficult, and notwithstanding the efforts of competition agencies, vertically integrated state enterprises may be unwilling to supply inputs adapted to small firms' needs or to provide access to distribution systems. A poor transportation infrastructure, difficulty in obtaining access to telecommunications, and a lack of housing for a new work force pose further constraints on new enterprise development.

All the CEECs recognize the need to shift ownership of the majority of state assets to the private sector, although the commitment to moving forward in the former USSR is less clear than elsewhere. Two general impediments to privatization stand out. First, it has not always been easy to maintain support for privatization. In Bulgaria, Hungary, and the former USSR there have been episodes of spontaneous privatization that lack transparency and appear to be inequitable, leading to public resistance to the process. The need to maintain support requires that some sensitive issues be handled carefully. Conflicts of interest during sales must be avoided, final ownership and control must not be given to the former nomenklatura on unduly favorable terms, and some allowance for the interests of previous owners proves to be politically necessary. Another difficulty, which has not yet been faced but is likely to be contentious, is large-scale layoffs in privatized enterprises.

Slow progress in the definition of property rights is also a serious impediment to enterprise reform in all the CEECs. To the extent that land is affected, lack of progress is also a barrier to the emergence and expansion of new private businesses. It is important that property rights be defined given that (1) it must be possible to write a clearly specified sales contract that will satisfy lawyers; (2) buyers must be able to establish title to property to satisfy registrars so that at a later date it may be transferred; (3) the need for buyers to comply with a tax code means that tax inspectors must be satisfied; and (4) the need for buyers to be able to use assets as collateral to raise money from credit markets means that bankers must be satisfied that their rights will be protected.

Several problems with property rights can be identified. The need to settle disputes over ownership in the public sector is closely related to the problem of sorting out constitutional issues. By March 1991 in the former GDR, claims by city and local governments reached nearly 500,000, which is indicative of the potential for problems.[10] The former CSFR, a federal country, largely avoided disputes between the federal government and the republics until recently. Disputes between local and central governments are a problem in Hungary and Poland and are likely to increase in all the CEECs as privatization proceeds. At the same time, the rights of employee representative groups must be clarified. These groups were given significant rights to use state-owned assets in previous legislation, particularly in Hungary, Poland, and the former USSR, and are reluctant to give up control and often block efforts to vest ownership completely in the state. The experience of Yugoslavia suggests that failure to address this issue coherently will be a serious impediment to enterprise reform and will make privatization extremely difficult.

None of the CEECs avoid the issue of restituting property confiscated under Communist regimes to former owners, notwithstanding the confusion such efforts have created in the former GDR. Restitution, however, is not a serious issue in Poland. Most land there was never nationalized, greatly limiting the potential demands for restitution. Although normally there will be no restitution in Poland, former owners may receive compensation in the form of rights to equity in enterprises undergoing privatization. Elsewhere, however, this is a major issue. In Hungary, the government hoped to move in a similar direction to that in Poland, but political pressures for restitution were strong, and the issue was complicated by constitutional provisions prohibiting differential treatment of land and other assets. The former CSFR had undertaken restitution of original properties, and it had a more flexible approach than did Germany, where claims could be denied. Bulgaria and Romania were working rapidly to restitute agricultural land.

Despite the difficulties described, small-scale privatization was moving forward. Poland appeared to be most successful. By 1992, up to 70 percent of small state retail shops were either owned privately or were leased. By 1991, the former CSFR had begun auctions, but after the sale of over 12,000 of the estimated 100,000 shops, the pace slowed because of uncertainty created by the restitution issue. In Hungary, sale of small enterprises was delayed by the enforcement of contracts that entitled state-owned companies to continue to run small shops. By the middle of 1992, less than 3,000 of the 10,000 shops that were candidates for sale were sold to private owners. In early 1993, the Hungarian government embarked on a new initiative to speed up small-scale privatization and to give special incentives to Hungarian buyers. The government aims to transfer over 50 percent of business activity to the private sector by 1994. In Bulgaria, it is estimated that the private sector composed about

15–25 percent of GDP in 1992. In Romania, about 30 percent of the retail units and tourist locations have been leased to private concerns. In 1992, the urban private retail sector accounted for about 4 percent of Romania's work force.

There was far less progress with large-scale privatization of enterprises sold as going concerns. Ambitious programs fell far short of their objectives. In Poland, privatization of state-owned enterprises has gone much more slowly than expected, and in March 1993, the parliament rejected the government's Mass Privatization Plan. By the beginning of 1993, over 1,000 parastatals and 100,000 retail businesses had been privatized. How much progress the mass privatization plan will have in transforming Poland's 600 state-owned enterprises that are up for privatization remains to be seen. For Poland and the other CEECs, there are three broad sets of issues that need to be addressed to develop a coherent strategy for privatizing large enterprises.

First, governments must balance a large number of considerations when carrying out a large program of privatization. Speed, obtaining high prices, equity, placing control in the hands of experienced management, ensuring good corporate governance, extending share ownership as widely as possible, and limiting (or encouraging) foreign participation need to be seriously considered. These considerations, however, are not always taken into account consistently.

Many large enterprises in the CEECs also require some degree of reorganization in order to be sufficiently well-defined as business entities. This is necessary so that the enterprises may write sales contracts and attract positive prices through positive net present values. There is a wide range of practical problems that must be overcome if successful privatization is to proceed:

- Physical assets, financial assets, liabilities, and broader rights and obligations must be identified sufficiently well to allow satisfactory contracts to be written.
- If liabilities are too high, net worth will be negative.
- Obligations that do not appear on the balance sheet, such as environmental liabilities or long-term contracts, may be too difficult to assess for buyers to place a valuation on the enterprise.
- Responsibilities to provide social services or limit freedom to manage an enterprise implied by obligations to employ an excessively large work force can make the net worth of an enterprise negative.

Private sectors have little in the way of accumulated savings except for their claim on state property. As a result, financial means to pay a fair price for state assets must largely be borrowed, come from abroad, or be obtained illegally. Illegally obtained funds are a sensitive issue in the CEECs and clearly cannot provide the financial basis for a large privatization program. However, the amount of foreign participation is likely to be limited both by lack of interest and by resistance in the CEECs.

The former CSFR gave priority to rapid privatization and planned to limit restructuring to the bare minimum. An effort continues to be made to transfer at least some of the social service obligations, such as kindergartens, to the state. However, the government will not take over debts, and there is no provision made to change management structures in order to improve operating performance for fear that this will delay progress. It remains to be seen whether this will be sufficient to get the process moving, given the problems that are posed by restitution claims and the desire not to sell to those who obtained their money illegally. On the positive side, workers' collectives are less forceful and more pragmatic in their approach to foreign ownership.

Hungary and Poland were planning more in the way of restructuring, so that enterprises would be more focused on commercial objectives and would be capable of complying with company law before they were privatized. In Hungary, some debt restructuring was envisaged. However, neither country had a clear strategy for separating social responsibilities from commercial activities.

Despite these problems, some progress was being made in Hungary and Poland. Hungary took a pragmatic approach of management-initiated privatization but was attempting to speed up the sale by tranches of twenty to forty enterprises to investors in Hungary and abroad who were able to introduce new capital, technology, and management. Investor-initiated privatization was also allowed, permitting foreign investors to bid directly for individual firms. Procedures to "privatize the privatization" by putting the privatization of a group of firms up for bid was also being explored. Poland planned to offer large blocks of shares of larger firms to potential investors, particularly in industries requiring large injections of investment and technology. Greater emphasis was placed on smaller enterprises that could be sold outright. These could be liquidated, allowing the assets to be used to form a new company, or the assets could be leased to a corporation with worker participation. Approximately 150 smaller enterprises appeared to have been dealt with by these methods. Nonetheless, it appeared unlikely that existing procedures in these countries would significantly increase the pace of privatization without some loss in standards of transparency and equity. Lack of domestic expertise to prepare privatization was a serious problem in all countries, and drawing on foreign firms proved costly in relation to the revenues from sales.

A vouchers system overcomes the problem of finding financially capable buyers. This was proposed in the former CSFR, Poland, and Romania. Vouchers would be widely distributed to the general population and would be used to purchase shares directly or through holding or investment companies. The voucher approach was appealing from an equity standpoint and dealt with the lack of accumulated savings in the private sector by transferring equity directly.

Transferring the vouchers to investment or management funds, each holding a range of firms in its portfolio, may help to resolve some of these difficulties related to the spread of risks and governance. Both Poland and the former CSFR proposed to introduce variants of these schemes. However, in both countries, the use of vouchers appeared to be reserved for the middle-quality companies; the best firms would be floated at the highest price. These companies were probably most in need of equity injections and new technology that could come only from abroad. However, in the absence of control, foreign investors were unlikely to be interested. Vouchers may, therefore, be best-suited to facilitate the purchase of minority shares in firms where a single large stockholder is able to exercise control.

Building a Financial Sector

Apart from privatization, building a market-oriented financial sector is the most important systemic issue the CEECs face. Formerly, the central planning system encompassed the major roles that financial sectors play in market economies. As decisionmaking is decentralized to households and enterprises, new institutions will be necessary to carry out these roles. They are necessary to mobilize savings, facilitate payments in an effective way, and encourage improved investment and resource allocation decisions by making credit available on the basis of expected profitability and ability to repay. Furthermore, healthy financial sectors are preconditions for other key elements of the CEECs' transitions. They provide a source of noninflationary finance for governments' borrowing needs, which permits some separation of monetary and budgetary policies. This allows monetary policies to be directed more easily toward inflation control. Equally important, the private business sector, including both new firms and privatized state enterprises, will require financing opportunities and other financial services if it is to prosper. Building a basic banking system capable of offering savings instruments that pay positive, real interest rates and providing an effective payment system are critical. Certain nonbank financial intermediaries may also play a positive role.

Two-tier banking systems with monetary control separated from intermediation are established in all the CEECs, but banks are poorly prepared for a competitive environment. A major difficulty is poor-quality loan portfolios, often with a heavy concentration of an enterprise or sector. Banks are generally undercapitalized, and if their assets were valued realistically, many would probably have a negative net worth. As a consequence, their willingness to recognize loans as nonperforming is limited. This encourages continued lending to weak enterprises rather than enforcement of greater financial discipline and redirection of credits to more promising borrowers. In view of this problem, banks have been told to be more careful in their loan policy, and extension of credit tends to be below IMF program ceilings, which may have aggravated the declines in output.

In most of the CEECs, there is likely to be little alternative to some restructuring of banks' balance sheets by the government before banks can be privatized or obliged to operate in a competitive environment. There is some concern about the apparent fiscal impact of recapitalizing them, but this will largely be a bookkeeping adjustment with no direct impact on the net worth of the public sector, given that most banks are state-owned. Impediments to restructuring portfolios include the difficulty in evaluating loans to enterprises that are themselves in need of restructuring and the lack of qualified workers to do the job.

Skills are seriously limited or nonexistent in accounting, prudential control, portfolio management, commercial loan appraisal, management of payments, and data processing. Until these shortages are adequately addressed, progress in building even basic modern financial institutions will be slow.

As enterprises are subjected to effective budget constraints and pay more attention to cash management, development of efficient payment systems will become a primary priority. This is also important from a macroeconomic perspective because improvement in payments systems is required to stimulate the development of money markets, which will allow monetary policy to rely on market-oriented control procedures. Until this occurs, monetary policy has to depend on administered credit ceilings, which limit the degree to which credit allocation can be placed on a market basis.

Capital markets are primitive in CEECs. Even though stock exchanges have opened in Hungary and Poland, their capacity to mobilize savings or to play a monitoring role is extremely limited without a constant flow of standardized and accurate financial information, and an adequate number of investors or listed companies.

A number of broad policy issues must be addressed in order to clearly define the environment of financial institutions. Until this is done, these institutions cannot become operational. An infrastructure of laws and accounting standards and practices, together with supervisory arrangements and mechanisms, must be put in place to ensure the closure of bad financial institutions before problems become so large that there are systemic repercussions. The CEECs must decide what role they wish foreign financial institutions to play. These institutions have much to offer in the way of capital, financial expertise, management skills, and the capacity to increase competition. At the same time, policies toward entry and participation in different types of activity must be defined. The thrust should encourage competition and avoid obstacles of portfolio diversification by lending institutions. Liberal policies toward international capital movements will encourage integration in the international economy.

Labor Market Policies

Labor market adjustment is an important aspect of the transition process. Major shifts of labor are needed to fill jobs in expanding areas while phasing positions out of declining sectors. These shifts will often require retraining and relocation of personnel. Rising unemployment in some countries, most notably in Poland, already strains the consensus for reform. In addition, the wide dispersion of market-clearing wages—which is implied by the existence of large skill mismatches, that is, where employees are over- or underskilled for the jobs that they are required to perform—creates problems because income differentials in the CEECs have traditionally been smaller than in most market economies.

The most important institutional reforms to encourage smooth labor market adjustment are those needed to build healthy enterprise sectors in profit-oriented businesses that face stricter budget constraints. Until these are in place, employers have little incentive to insist on wage settlements consistent with the overall economic environment or realistic levels of staffing. In 1991, the incentive structure for employers remained poor, and this is likely to necessitate continued reliance on income policies.

All the CEECs introduced some form of incomes policy, in part to support the weak macroeconomic control framework. Even if the monetary framework is strengthened to permit reliance on market-oriented control procedures, a broad policy toward the determination of income covering the public sector is still necessary because principal-agent relations between governments and enterprise management are not sufficiently well-structured to allow governments to rely on decentralized bargaining between employees and management.

However, income policies inevitably create tensions that make them difficult to sustain over long periods of time. As noted, real incomes have fallen sharply in all of the CEECs, which is likely to create pressures for relaxation. In Poland such a relaxation occurred during 1990, leading to a recovery in real wages of 20 percent during the latter part of the year. In Hungary, inflation expectations, associated with failures to achieve announced inflation targets, were reflected in wage pressure, and fringe benefits were increasingly substituting for cash compensation. Perhaps more important, income policies often lead to rigidities in relativities. Although relativities in the CEECs were generally narrower in 1991 than those found in market economies, they were still significant. However, relativities are an inappropriate measure in many cases because they often reflect political, rather than economic, considerations. Therefore, substantial changes are likely to be necessary. Income policies threaten to make these adjustments to market conditions more difficult.

Even if we allow for increased availability of goods, economic hardship in the CEECs has increased significantly as real wages fall and unemployment rises. All governments introduced unemployment insurance systems and by and large are attempting to reduce negative incentive effects. In addition, most countries also have a social assistance system. If unemployment continues to climb, however, the budgetary costs of such programs may make them unsustainable.

Education and training were among some of the most important social responsibilities assigned to enterprises under central planning. CEEC governments need to pay increasing attention to training programs for the unemployed and new labor market entrants with an emphasis on skills that are likely to be in demand in the burgeoning service sector.

The housing situation is adversely affecting labor market flexibility in CEECs. Shortages in housing restrict labor mobility where regional unemployment differences are high, as in Poland, the former CSFR, and Hungary. As noted, some countries are moving to sell housing stock. However, controlled or heavily subsidized rent, limited access to finance, and lack of incentives or financial capacity to undertake housing construction are impediments to improvements.

Transition Issues:
The International Dimension

The transition from central planning to market economies in the CEECs is taking place within the broader context of an interdependent global economy. The prospect for a successful transition is influenced by developments in the rest of the world, especially in the OECD countries, and developments within the region impact elsewhere. This interdependence raises a wide range of issues in both the CEECs and the OECD countries. The most obvious of these, not discussed here, relates to the size and use of prospective peace dividends following the relaxation of East-West tensions in recent years, particularly following the failure of the coup d'état in the former USSR. However, four other particularly important areas that are addressed and discussed provide some background information about the situation in CEECs and about the major policy issues that are on the agenda for both CEECs and OECD countries. These four areas are external financing prospects and the role of assistance, trade and trade arrangements, the environment, and migration.

Most of the issues surveyed concern problems facing the CEECs such as constraints on their freedom of action and limitations on their opportunities, which exacerbate the difficulties inherent in making the transition to a market economy. The most important of these follow:

1. All of the CEECs have problems managing external debts, except for the former CSFR and Romania. Hungary has succeeded in servicing its debts in a timely way, but Bulgaria has not, Poland is renegotiating, and the problems in the former USSR appear likely to worsen.

2. As of 1992, Hungary, and to a lesser degree the former CSFR and Poland, had attracted significant amounts of direct investment. These three countries enjoyed only limited access to international financial markets, and the other CEECs were almost entirely cut off due to creditors' perceptions of economic and political risks. External financing for the region is still largely limited to assistance from official sources.

3. The problems the CEECs have in compensating for the collapse of trade with the former USSR are only partly attributable to the difficulty of adapting production to technical and quality standards of other markets. External factors such as the Gulf crisis, which had particularly adverse effects on Bulgarian and Romanian trade, and restrictions on access to markets in OECD countries are also important.

4. Restrictions on access to markets in OECD countries continue to be most severe in those areas where CEEC prospects appear to be best, notably agriculture, textiles, apparel, and steel.

5. The CEECs must integrate into the multilateral world trading system and establish strong trading partnerships. Most still need to obtain full membership in the GATT (General Agreement on Tariffs and Trade) without special protocols that reflect the former state trading nature of their economies. Only the former CSFR has full membership without protocols. The CEECs' trading relationships with each other must be redefined following the demise of the Council for Mutual Economic Assistance (CMEA), and open trading arrangements must be established with OECD countries.

6. Environmental degradation is severe in some areas, with adverse repercussions for human health and agricultural production. Availability of water for home and industrial purposes cannot be taken for granted. Environmental issues are an important part of the public policy agenda in the CEECs, and environmental considerations need to be integrated into the economic policy framework in order to achieve objectives in both areas simultaneously.

7. From the perspective of the CEECs, an orderly flow of outward migration toward OECD countries would be beneficial given that migrants provide substantial remittance income, and if they return, their home countries will profit from their work experience in a market environment. However, the market for skilled labor is international, and barriers for migration are relatively low and remuneration levels high compared with those that have prevailed in the CEECs. This may pose problems. Attracting and retaining people with important skills will necessitate adjustments in relative incomes in CEECs, which may not be consistent with income policies now in place. If this is achieved, it may create a politically difficult situation in that the majority might believe that a small group of people is benefiting at their expense.

8. Differential progress in transitions across CEECs, political upheavals, and ethnic tensions are potential sources of intraregional migratory pressures. Some of the CEECs, therefore, will have more immigrants than they are will-

ing to accept. They will need to develop policies regarding issues that are similar to those of most OECD countries.

Transition covers a broad range of issues. Perhaps the only generalization that can be made about policy implications for the CEECs is that persevering with the policies necessary to facilitate a successful transition is key to solving many of their problems. Managing external debt and restoring international creditworthiness in the CEECs are largely problems of ensuring sound fiscal and monetary policies while implementing systemic reforms that will lead to attractive returns on investment. Even without an active environmental policy, these countries will need to consider the problem of air pollution and other environmental hazards to make a successful transition to a market economy. In the future they will have to comply with comprehensive industrial modernization and increases in energy prices toward world levels. They will also need to facilitate expenditure on remedial measures; higher growth will generate the means to respond more forcefully to environmental concerns. Finally, the economic benefits of a successful transition will reduce potentially disruptive migratory pressures.

Notes

1. For two comprehensive surveys of the policy issues that CEECs will face, see OECD, *Reforming the Economies of Central and Eastern Europe,* Paris: OECD, 1992; and *World Bank Country Studies.* These studies are updated frequently. Write to the World Bank, Washington, DC, for a list of the most current studies.

2. See *PlanEcon Report,* Washington, DC: PlanEcon, August 18, 1989, pp. 22–23.

3. This reflected failure to scrap or modernize old plants, inattention to maintenance, and long gestation periods for large projects, so the amount of capital tied up in unfinished projects was high.

4. See OECD, *Employment Outlook,* Paris: OECD, July 1991, Chart A3, p. 18.

5. For example, the *International Herald Tribune* (June 4, 1992) reported that the Azoty chemical works provides the town of Kedzierzyn Kozle, Poland, with an indoor skating rink, swimming pool, a culture center, a laundry, a thousand free apartments, and 80 percent of its heating needs.

6. "Eastern Europe," *Economist* (March 13, 1993): 21.

7. See OECD, *Economic Survey of Germany* (Paris: OECD, 1991), Part 4.

8. Peter Bofinger, "The Role of Monetary Policy in the Process of Economic Reform in Eastern Europe," *Discussion Paper, No. 457,* London Centre for Economic Policy Research, 1990; John Williamson, "Convertibility, Trade Policy and the Payments Constraint," in *The Transition to a Market Economy in Central and Eastern Europe* (Paris: CCEET, OECD, 1992).

9. In the former USSR the administrative courts have partly taken over this role.

10. See OECD 1991a, Part 4.

CHAPTER TWO

■

Economic and Social Reforms in the Czech and Slovak Republics

DANIEL S. FOGEL
SUZANNE ETCHEVERRY

In the 1930s, Czechoslovakia was one of the fifteen most developed countries in the world. It survived World War II relatively unscathed, with most of its property, plants, and infrastructure intact, and by 1948 it had more or less regained its prewar income level. With the strong industrial tradition of a country that had been the economic backbone of the Habsburg empire, and close trade and financial links to the remainder of Western Europe, Czechoslovakia was well-placed to realize its potential and become once again one of the richer countries in Europe. Yet, forty years of central planning and close political and economic ties with the Soviet Union led Czechoslovakia to relative economic decline.[1] Three developments during those forty years are important for understanding the present reform effort: the long-term decline of GDP growth, the protection of living standards, and the reduction of the income gap between the Czech and the Slovak republics.

From 1950 through 1987, growth of net material product declined from 8 percent in the 1950s to 2 percent in the 1980s; the strategy of "extensive growth" could deliver fewer and fewer additions to output. Figures on inflation and growth were often exaggerated, but it seems that this growth slowdown accelerated in the 1980s, and output stagnated. By then, total factor productivity was also declining,[2] and labor productivity was growing at only 1.5 percent per year, compared to 4.3 percent between 1970 and 1980.

Growth also declined in relation to OECD growth. As a result of this performance gap, per capita GDP in 1989 (at PPP exchange rates) was lower than the OECD average of $15,563 or the Austrian per capita income of

$13,407: estimates range from $7,800 to $11,000.[3] This put Czechoslovakia at about the same level as Greece, Portugal, and Spain, whereas in the 1930s, Czechoslovakia had a higher per capita income, similar to that of Austria.

The decline of growth was not equally reflected in living standards, which, according to official data, continued to rise more rapidly than output. In the 1970s, consumption was shielded from declining growth and the terms-of-trade stock after the oil prices increased by borrowing abroad. In the 1980s, consumption continued to increase despite a reduction in domestic absorption overall as the investment ratio declined substantially. As a result of these slowly but steadily improving living standards, the Czech and, particularly, Slovak citizens have taken a cautious attitude toward radical reform.[4]

The virtual elimination of the income differential between the Czech lands and Slovakia during these forty years is another factor that will play a role in the unfolding of reforms. This equalization, however, will cease now that the two republics have become separate countries. Slovakia's per capita income rose from 60 percent of the Czech per capita income in 1948 to 87 percent in 1988, boosted through a deliberate policy of rapid industrialization and fiscal transfers. The 1990 per capita income was $3,180. Many of the newly created industries were in heavy industry, mining, and armament production, often dependent on the Soviet Union for raw materials and as a market for their products. Economic reforms and shrinking export markets in the East are making many of these industries inviable. The impact of a rapid switch to a market economy was therefore bound to be felt much more strongly in Slovakia than in the Czech lands. This differential impact increased the friction between the two republics and was a factor leading to the 1993 breakup. A related factor that led to the breakup was that in December 1992 Slovakia was experiencing 11 percent unemployment; the Czech Federal Republic was at about 5 percent.

In the past, deteriorating economic performance and obvious inefficiencies of the economic system led to several radical attempts at reformation. The most far-reaching attempt at political and economic reform in the 1960s was brought to an abrupt end with the events of the Prague Spring of 1968. During the following two decades, "normalization" was reintroduced with strict central planning. Inspired by perestroika in the Soviet Union and by reform attempts in Poland and Hungary, various measures were taken after 1986, some of which helped lay the groundwork for the far-reaching reforms that Czechoslovakia embarked on in 1990: The State Enterprise Act of 1988 laid the basis for breaking up enterprises into smaller units; a new joint-venture law made majority holdings possible and allowed for repatriation of profits; the Law of External Economic Relations (July 1988) increased the possibilities for companies to engage in foreign trade and abolished the monopoly of the fifty to sixty foreign trade organizations that had controlled trade before; and the creation of a two-tier banking system out of the former state bank in

January 1990 provided the framework for the further development of financial markets.

After the Velvet Revolution of November 1989, Czechoslovakia abandoned the inefficient system of central planning and aimed to create the systemic and macroeconomic conditions for the return to a path of economic growth that would allow it eventually to catch up with the industrialized countries. To this end, it dismantled the central planning apparatus, strove to reintroduce a market economy, and initiated a process of forging close links with the international economic and financial community. In several respects, the initial conditions for systemic transformation in Czechoslovakia were less favorable than in some other Central and East European countries:

1. The private sector at the beginning of 1990 was almost nonexistent. Less than 0.5 percent of nonagricultural output was produced in the private sector; employment in nonagricultural cooperatives and self-employment constituted less than 3 percent of total employment.

2. The legal and institutional basis for a market economy was missing, and little preparatory work had been undertaken except in a few areas such as joint-venture and banking laws. There was no legal basis for private enterprises; it had to be created in May 1990.

3. Economic activity was still concentrated in large units, with large-scale enterprises dominating the industrial landscape and monopoly trade organizations organizing the distribution of goods. The average number of employees in state-owned enterprises in 1989 was over 2,000.

4. The closed character of the economy and the tradition of tight central planning were also reflected in the low number of joint ventures active in Czechoslovakia. At the end of 1989, only 50 joint ventures were registered, against approximately 500 in both Hungary and Poland.

5. Prices were almost completely controlled in 1989, except for a few luxury items, on the wholesale as well as on the retail level. Contract prices had not yet been introduced. A system of export and import taxes and subsidies isolated domestic producers from world market changes and provided little incentive to export. A foreign exchange retention system, long used by other centrally planned economies, had only just been introduced.

6. Czechoslovakia was more dependent on socialist trade than were other Central and East European countries except for Bulgaria. Exports to and imports from socialist countries made up more than 60 percent of total exports and imports. Czechoslovakia was therefore more vulnerable to the collapse of CMEA trade than was Hungary or Poland.

7. Available statistics were based on reporting by state-owned enterprises and cooperatives and were published according to the material product system. They were clearly inadequate to cope with the rapid structural change that started in 1990 and have not been able to provide an accurate picture of economic developments. This is particularly true of output, where newly

emerging enterprises are not adequately captured by existing systems, and of foreign trade, which was based on reporting by foreign trade organizations. But monetary, balance-of-payments, and budgetary statistics were also not available in international terminology.

Thus Czechoslovakia was, at the outset of its systemic transformation, an economy almost completely dominated by central planning, with little experience of markets and almost no legal and institutional basis for a market economy. In contrast to Hungary and Poland, Czechoslovakia could not build on substantive earlier reforms but had to tackle the complete transformation of a centrally planned economy into a market economy. Nonetheless, this task was made somewhat easier by the absence of serious macroeconomic imbalances that have plagued other Central and East European countries. The following are several favorable macroeconomic conditions of the Czechoslovak economy that made reform somewhat easier than in Hungary and Poland:

1. Inflation never emerged as a serious problem, averaging less than 2 percent from 1980 to 1989. This can partly be ascribed to setting prices administratively; conservative fiscal and monetary policies also ensured that the consumer goods market was more or less in balance. Inflation was down to about 3 percent in the second half of 1991 and never got over 2 percent in 1992. Hidden inflation is estimated at about 2.5 percent per annum from 1988 to 1992.
2. The monetary overhang in Czechoslovakia in 1989 was relatively small. Some indication of the possible overhang is given by the increase in monetary holdings since 1980, a year in which the overhang is believed to have been negligible. From 1980 to 1989, broad money increased by 18 percentage points of GDP, of which two-thirds took the form of increases in household deposits.
3. At the end of 1991, total debt outstanding and disbursed amounted to $11 billion, 91 percent of which was in convertible currencies, comparable to Portugal and Thailand. Taking into account reserves and claims on developing countries, the net position was close to zero. This was the result of a deliberate policy of reducing net debt in the early 1980s, and limiting borrowing thereafter. The current account closed with a $700 million surplus in 1991, or 2 percent of GDP.
4. As the government budget had been close to balance for many years, net government debt in 1989 was small, less than 1 percent of GDP.

The basic challenges that the two independent governments now face in pursuing economic reform may be summarized in four points:

1. The countries' legal frameworks and basic institutions, defined by strict central planning, must be completely overhauled so that a market economy may emerge and function. New laws and regulations must be developed and implemented with the help of the inherited bureaucracy. At the same time,

these new laws and regulations must be agreed upon quickly, and in a democratic manner. To make this system work the countries must change their "centralized, controlled" attitude to one of responsibility for making these necessary changes for a decentralized, market economy.

2. Macroeconomic stability must be maintained. On the domestic level, this entails the implementation of tight fiscal and monetary policies and controls on wage increases. This will prevent a one-time adjustment in the price level, which results when price liberalization becomes embedded in the underlying rate of inflation. On the international level devaluations must be consistent with the increase in price levels while keeping a current account deficit within limits that can be financed.

3. The reform program must combine structural transformation and macroeconomic policies in such a way that the switch to a market economy costs as little as possible if the program is to gain and maintain broad public support. The difficulty is that some structural reforms of legal and institutional frameworks take more time than others. Liberalization of prices and the opening up of trade leads to external imbalances and inflation if the basic elements of a market economy are not in place, especially if competition is inadequate and economic entities do not face hard budget constraints. In this case, a tight macroeconomic policy may not be fully effective in restraining prices and wages before output falls substantially and unemployment mounts.

4. The Czech and Slovak republics must deal with the move to privatization. The coupon system developed prior to the split of the countries is working moderately well in the Czech Republic but has been slowed in the Slovak Republic. This differential effect will further separate the two countries' economic and social ties.

This chapter will provide the necessary background to better understand this book's cases. The reader is given glimpses of what transpired after the beginning of 1992, a story that is still unfolding. Yet, our focus is on one of the most exciting periods of modern history—1989 through 1991.

Macroeconomic Developments and Policies

The main task of macroeconomic policy is to maintain macroeconomic stability. During the early stages of the transformation process, this task was complicated by a weak institutional environment where wage-bargaining institutions were lacking, competition was limited, the financial sector was underdeveloped, and the enterprise sector was unresponsive to market signals. Macroeconomic control is precarious in these conditions, calling for a somewhat more cautious macroeconomic policy stance than would otherwise be necessary. The former Czechoslovak government prudently chose to maintain a tight policy stance in 1990 and 1991, and monetary and fiscal policies were successful in preventing the price-level jump that followed price liberalization.

In this section we first describe macroeconomic developments in 1990 and 1991. We then turn to questions of fiscal and monetary policies and review some developments in 1992.

Demand and Output

GDP declined by 1.1 percent in 1990 and then by 16 percent in 1991.[5] Industrial production decreased by 25 percent in 1991. Three main factors contributed to this consistent decline. Export demand fell due to the weakening of CMEA trade; reduced oil deliveries by the Soviet Union decreased inputs to the fuel and petrochemical industry and constrained economic activity in general; and the beginning of industrial restructuring was reflected in output declines of several industries, most notably in mining and armaments.

Domestic demand did not decline in 1990. On the contrary, it increased by 4.7 percent in real terms, with the diverging paths of demand and output reflected in a corresponding deterioration in the trade balance. A main factor behind the increase in domestic demand was a scramble by enterprises and households to convert financial assets into goods. This occurred especially in the final quarter of 1990 in anticipation of currency devaluation and large price increases resulting from price liberalization. Stock building by enterprises contributed 3.4 percentage points to demand growth for the year. Fixed investment (including unfinished construction) declined, mainly due to cuts in government capital expenditure as part of the austerity budget of 1990, but nevertheless remained high relative to international fixed investment at 26 percent of GDP. The relatively strong growth in personal consumption took place despite a fall in real wages of 5.8 percent. Continued consumption growth was made possible in part by higher government transfers, mainly due to the universal income support introduced in July to compensate for the phasing out of consumer subsidies; but the sharp reduction in saving by the population was the main factor.[6]

Due to problems in gathering statistical data, economic developments in the first half of 1991 are very difficult to read. Net material product is recorded to have declined by 13.8 percent relative to the same period one year earlier, and real GDP by 9.2 percent.[7] These estimates probably overstate the actual decline because statistics in 1991 cover only enterprises with more than 100 employees, and private-sector activity is not captured at all. The number of private entrepreneurs rose from 86,000 in 1989 to 921,000 in June 1991.[8] It is estimated that the private sector in August 1991 accounted for 1.2 percent of industrial production, 13 percent of domestic trade, and 5 to 6 percent of construction. Statistical problems are even more acute when it comes to analyzing the reasons for this decline in output for two reasons. Changes in the methods of collecting foreign trade statistics make this data presently unsuitable for year-to-year comparisons. This may be a source of inconsistencies between national accounts data, which suggest that declining exports to CMEA countries were largely offset by increased exports to other regions, leading to the conclusion that falling exports were not a major factor accounting for weak output.[9] Second, the large price changes associated with devaluation and relative price changes make it difficult to distinguish between price and volume changes. This is a problem with regard to inventories because stock-building estimates presented in the national accounts, such as trade numbers, may be subject to particularly large margins of error.

It is impossible to assess with any precision whether the decline in output in the first half of 1991 was driven by demand factors or supply problems. Both played significant roles. The maintenance of nominal government spending plans in the face of higher-than-anticipated price increases implied a significant cut in real government spending. Tight credit policies contributed to weak investment. This was further complicated when enterprises spent their money on higher taxes rather than on investment when high valuation gains were placed on their inventories. More important, however, was the financial distress placed on enterprises when larger-than-expected wage cuts occurred, which adversely affected consumption. The large changes in relative prices associated with liberalization led to declining production. The increasing uncertainty facing state-controlled enterprises as they waited to see what their role would be was further complicated by the slow implementation of privatization and market disciplines. This led to a large decline in investment irrespective of financial conditions. Finally, the collapse of traditional export markets to Eastern bloc countries, even if compensated for by increased sales to Western markets, implies a fall in output because the terms-of-trade costs led to lower real incomes for the population, and hence squeezed consumption. Overall, the decline of 9 percent in GDP recorded in the first half of 1991 appears not to be excessively large given that it was an unavoidable transition cost of the first phase of systemic transformation.

Unemployment

Unemployment did not exist until 1990; however, authorities estimate that overemployment was at least 15 percent of total employment. Since the second half of 1990, unemployment has risen rapidly. By the end of 1992, it reached about 6.0 percent of the work force.[10] Three developments will compound the unemployment problem in the future. First, 1991 unemployment in the Slovak Federal Republic was much higher than in the Czech Federal Republic—10.3 percent in October as compared with 3.9 percent in the Czech Federal Republic. Not only was the level of unemployment in Slovakia much higher, but unemployment was increasing more rapidly and continues to do so.

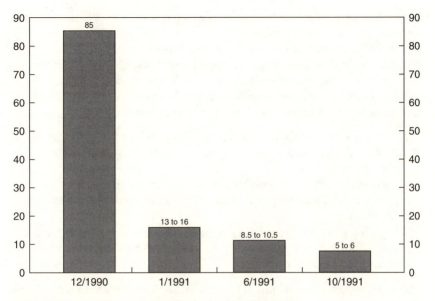

FIGURE 2.1   Regulated Prices in Czechoslovakia, 1990–1991.
Source: Czechoslovakia Federal Statistical Office.

Second, restructuring seemed likely to increase redundancies faster than workers could be employed elsewhere. The private sector was still too small to be able to absorb all the workers from the state sector.

Third, unemployment has increased due to a large influx of graduates. The working-age population increased by approximately 100,000 people per year from 1989, when it was 57.6 percent, to 1993 and is expected to increase another 100,000 per year, reaching 60.3 percent in 1995.

Prices and Wages

In the past, prices were stable in Czechoslovakia as a result of prudent macroeconomic policies and price regulation. From 1971 to 1991, consumer prices rose by about 1 percent annually. Even taking into account hidden and repressed inflation, the authorities estimate true inflation at around 3.5 percent in 1993.

Most prices were deregulated in January 1991. The percentage of GDP under price regulation was reduced from 85 percent in 1990 to 13–16 percent in January and was further reduced to 10 percent or less in June 1991. By October 1991 only 5 to 6 percent of GDP remained subject to price regulation, comparable to OECD countries (see Figure 2.1).[11]

During the course of 1990, consumer prices increased by 10 percent. The lifting of price controls on January 1, 1991, led to a jump in the price level of 25.8 percent in January as devaluation fed into domestic prices. Small monetary overhang was eliminated, relative price adjustment took place, and some monopoly positions were exploited.

Tight fiscal and monetary policies provided the conditions to bring inflation under control quickly. Import competition played a lesser role in the initial stages of price liberalization because of the strong devaluation and import surcharge of 20 percent. In addition to instituting tight macroeconomic policies, authorities took three actions to restrict price increases:

1. Price caps were set for some key consumer goods such as potatoes, pork, milk, and eggs, and mandatory maximum trade margins were put in place for others.
2. Industrial sectors with a high degree of market power were obligated to give prior notification of price increases and subject to time-related price regulation.
3. Price increases for household energy were delayed until May for fuels, central heating, and hot water and until October for electricity; rent increases were deferred until 1992.[12]

An income policy was also used to reduce the burden placed on fiscal and monetary policy instruments, though its effective role in curbing inflation was small. In a tripartite agreement, the government, employers, and unions sought to determine, ex ante, the maximum allowable decrease in real wages. This allowed the necessary fall to take place but provided, at the same time, a floor for the decline in living standards. The real wage was targeted to decrease by 10 percent in real terms between December 1990 and December 1991. Maximum allowable wage increases in nominal terms were defined on this basis for the first quarter of 1991, with provisions for subsequent adjustments reflecting actual inflation developments. To enforce this agreement, an excess wage tax was introduced with penalty tax rates of up to 750 percent.[13]

Nominal wages grew less than expected on average. During the first quarter of 1991, they fell compared to the estimated December level, partly because of seasonal factors, and wage growth remained sluggish in the second and third quarters. There was, however, considerable differentiation between sectors. Nominal wages declined in construction and agriculture but increased substantially in telecommunications, health, and internal trade, in part reflecting differences in financial viability between sectors.

External Debt and the Balance of Payments

Czechoslovakia's hard currency debt was manageable. In 1989, external debt was only 15 percent of GDP and 109 percent of exports; debt service was 19 percent of exports. This was small in the international perspective and put Czechoslovakia about on a par with Portugal, and not far away from countries such as Thailand (see Table 2.1 and Figure 2.2). In this respect, Czechoslovakia was in a favorable position relative to Hungary or Poland.

TABLE 2.1   External Debt Ratios: Cross-Country Comparison, 1989

	External debt total (bn$)	Total debt service (bn$)	External debt (% of gross domestic product)	External debt (% of export goods & services)	Debt service (% of export goods & services)
Czechoslovakia	7.9	1.4	14.9	108.7	18.8
Portugal	19.9	3.0	45.0	115.9	17.5
Thailand	24.1	3.1	36.4	88.0	11.4
HICs[a]	501.4	69.2	44.7	282.7	39.0
Poland	41.5	3.9	58.8	475.8	44.5
Hungary	20.4	3.5	71.3	239.8	40.6

[a]Highly indebted countries.
Sources: The Institute of International Finance, Washington, DC, 1991; State Bank of Czechoslovakia, 1989.

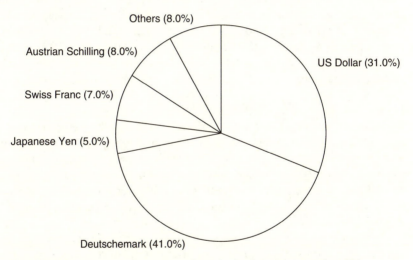

FIGURE 2.2   Currency Composition of Czechoslovakia's Foreign Debt, 1990.
Source: State Bank of Czechoslovakia.

Balance-of-Payments Developments in 1990   Three features dominated Czechoslovakia's external balance of payments in 1990: the announcement that summer of a large devaluation of the koruna planned for January 1991, the changing attitudes of private banks following Bulgaria's and the Soviet Union's debt-servicing difficulties, and the decline of intra-CMEA trade. By far the most important event was the announcement of the large devaluation, which occurred months ahead of the event. Enterprises with foreign exchange retention accounts rushed to import machinery, equipment, and other goods from Western Europe, and importers decided to forgo trade credit and pay immediately, or even prepay imports. As a result, convertible currency imports increased by 35 percent in value terms in 1990, three times as much as exports.[14] The deterioration of the trade balance explains almost all of the deterioration of the current account from $.4 billion in 1989 to −$1.1 billion in 1990.

In addition to the reduction of net trade credits related to devaluation expectations, Bulgaria and the Soviet Union's debt-servicing difficulties led banks to reevaluate their lending policy toward Central and Eastern Europe in general. In mid-year, these banks withdrew substantial amounts of short-term deposits from Czechoslovak banks.

The disintegration of intra-CMEA trade led to a large reduction in nonconvertible currency imports and exports. Export values in nonconvertible currencies declined by 29 percent in 1990.

Balance-of-Payments Developments in 1991   Developments for the first half of 1991 are difficult to interpret not only because of the exaggeration in statistics but also because of the shift from nonconvertible to convertible currency trade. If we bear these difficulties in mind, the data for 1991 indicate that the convertible currency deficit was better than was expected at the beginning of the year.

Macroeconomic Policies

Fiscal and monetary policies in the first half of 1991 were tighter than the authorities had planned. A mid-course correction in June provided a fiscal stimulus of several percentage points of GDP while keeping the original target for the budget surplus in nominal terms. Monetary growth also picked up in the second half of 1991, and the targets for credit expansion were raised somewhat. A real devaluation of the koruna of more than 7 percent relative to 1990 was maintained.

Fiscal policy in the former Czechoslovakia has always been conservative. In the past, the budget was in surplus or showed only small deficits. During the five years before 1990, the general government deficit averaged 1 percent of GDP.[15] Prior to 1989, accumulated government assets were financed by drawing down previously accumulated government assets with the State Bank. After 1989, the government became a net debtor as a result of taking over export credits from the State Bank,[16] and its net asset position reflected mainly the takeover of devaluation losses of some of the banks' hard-currency liabilities. The initial budget for 1990 prepared in December 1989 again provided for a small deficit in the general government account. Yet, the new government chose to adopt a more restrictive policy stance as part of the preparation for economic reform and restructuring of the economy. Thus, a revised budget was submitted in March 1990, calling for a budget surplus of 0.7 percent of GDP as compared to a deficit of 0.8 percent in 1989. This target was achieved.

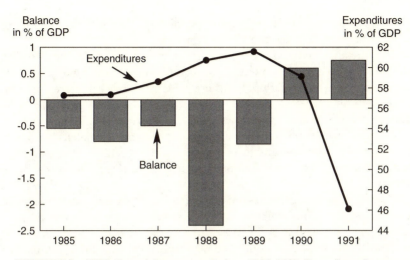

FIGURE 2.3   CSFR General Government Budget, 1985–1991. Expenditure figures for 1991 include mid-year budget revision. *Source:* Czechoslovak Federal Ministry of Finance and OECD estimates for GDP in 1991.

Tight fiscal policies were maintained in preparing the 1991 budget in order to prevent the development of an inflationary spiral in the wake of price liberalization (see Figure 2.3).[17] A surplus of 0.8 percent of the GDP was programmed into the budget. Perhaps more significantly, this implies a reduction of expenditures by 12 percentage points of GDP to approximately 47 percent of GDP. This reduction of expenditures was matched by an almost equal decline of revenues. The structural changes implied by such a demand shift of 12 percentage points of GDP away from the government to households and enterprises are likely to be quite contractionary in the short term. With an inflexible supply side dominated by the state-owned industry, reduction of government demand in one sector led to immediate output losses, whereas much of the relative increase in demand by enterprises and households was directed either toward imports, thus contributing little to supporting domestic production, or toward other sectors of the economy. It will take some time to respond to the increased demand if there is not significant spare capacity with which to begin.

For 1992, the critical question was the development of a tax base. Enterprise profits in 1991 were largely accounting profits related to the revaluation of inventories and to unrealized profits due to inventory increases. The resulting tax liabilities were financed by running up interenterprise credits and by keeping wages low. These developments did not extend into 1992. A shrinking tax base could make expenditure reductions necessary, which were difficult to implement after the large reductions in 1991, especially in an election year and in times of increasing social expenditures. The budget continues to be under pressure, as it has been in Hungary and Poland.

Given the absence of effective competition within the banking system and underdeveloped money markets, interest rates do not yet serve a market-clearing function. Monetary policy therefore cannot rely on interest-rate instruments alone to regulate overall financial conditions but still must rely on administered quantitative guidelines. Also, the shortage of instruments associated with the generally underdeveloped state of financial markets has meant that possibilities for smoothing monetary conditions have been extremely limited, though this situation is improving progressively with the privatization program.

Whatever the appropriateness of the initial monetary objectives, there can be no doubt that at the beginning of 1991, monetary stringency was substantially greater than had been intended in view of economic developments in the first half of 1991. This, combined with the slower than projected growth of money, a substantially larger rise in prices than had been expected, and a weaker performance of output, greatly affected the implementation of monetary policies.

Table 2.2 provides information on the development of the principal money and credit aggregates until September 1991. The weakness in the aggregates in the first three months of 1991 stands out. In the face of a price increase of 41 percent, net domestic assets barely grew, and broad money declined. These developments raise three questions: Was the slow growth of money and credit demand- or supply-induced? To what extent did it contribute to the weaker-than-projected performance of the real economy? How did it come about? Only partial answers are available.

The strongest piece of evidence to suggest that the weakness of the aggregates was not a result of weak credit demand is provided by the increase in unpaid interenterprise bills at the beginning of the year.[18]

Banks, the Czechoslovak Commercial Bank in particular, ceased lending. Three separate explanations for this can be cited.

1. It is possible that the banks held a virtual monopoly over bank credit—assuming that banks refrained from lending at 10 percent interest but would have at 24 percent—and that additional lending was undertaken only by dropping below the allowed ceiling rate. Although the banks could not exercise price discrimination among customers, they could restrict credit to the point where all loans would be contracted at the ceiling rate.

2. The State Bank advised large commercial banks to reduce their market shares to enhance competition. Commercial banks, in particular, overreacted to the contraction of credit advice when they attempted to ter-

TABLE 2.2 Monetary Survey for Czechoslovakia, 1985–1991 (billion koruny)

	12/31/85	12/31/86	12/31/87	12/31/88	12/31/89	3/31/90	6/30/90	9/30/90	12/31/90	3/31/91	6/30/91	9/30/91
Net foreign assets	-1.1	1.2	-0.8	4.0	17.8	13.4	10.7	0.9	-9.2	-19.1	-16.2	-0.8
Foreign assets	39.4	44.2	46.7	58.4	37.8	39.8	30.6	19.1	22.8	30.0	40.2	57.4
Foreign liabilities	40.5	43.0	47.5	54.4	20.0	26.4	19.9	18.2	32.0	49.1	56.4	58.2
Net domestic assets	432.0	446.4	475.4	525.4	530.0	521.6	536.0	538.4	559.9	566.7	604.0	629.7
Domestic credit	459.6	483.0	505.9	542.6	583.6	559.5	579.9	590.4	640.2	656.0	667.3	695.6
Net credit to government	-81.1	-70.2	-65.3	-46.4	5.9	-9.4	-0.5	1.6	54.2	37.9	8.6	11.6
Credit to enterprises	502.5	514.3	529.8	543.8	530.8	522.3	533.5	541.6	536.0	567.8	611.3	642.6
Credit to households	38.2	38.9	41.4	45.2	46.9	46.6	46.9	47.2	50.0	51.2	51.6	53.1
National property fund			0.0	0.0	0.0	0.0	0.0	0.0	0.0	-0.9	-4.2	-11.7
Broad Money	431.0	447.6	474.6	529.4	547.8	535.0	546.7	539.3	550.7	547.6	587.8	628.9
Money	260.3	261.3	270.7	309.5	311.1	288.0	303.3	294.5	291.2	279.9	294.3	324.7
Currency outside banks	53.9	56.2	58.6	62.5	68.0	70.0	72.4	73.2	73.7	72.9	76.2	80.7
Households	49.4	51.8	54.3	57.9	62.8	64.3	66.4	69.1	69.0	70.3	70.3	74.7
Enterprises	4.5	4.4	4.3	4.6	5.2	5.7	6.0	4.1	4.7	5.5	5.9	6.0
Demand deposits	206.4	205.1	212.1	247.0	243.1	218.0	230.9	221.3	217.5	207.0	218.1	244.0
Households	98.4	101.3	104.0	105.7	107.5	109.9	112.2	113.2	103.3	95.7	92.0	92.0
Enterprises	108.0	103.8	108.1	141.3	135.6	103.7	115.2	100.8	111.4	106.4	121.0	146.1
Insurance companies	0.0	0.0	0.0	0.0	0.0	4.4	3.5	7.3	2.8	4.9	5.1	5.9
Quasi-money	170.7	186.3	203.9	219.9	236.7	247.0	243.4	244.8	259.5	267.7	293.5	304.2
Time & savings deposits	170.0	185.4	202.9	217.5	232.5	240.3	233.7	233.4	231.7	240.2	254.0	259.1
Households	120.5	133.6	147.7	159.9	170.2	170.1	168.8	166.9	167.4	171.3	180.1	188.1
Enterprises	5.3	5.0	5.3	5.9	6.6	12.9	14.6	13.8	10.5	15.1	19.7	16.8
Insurance companies	44.2	46.8	49.9	51.7	55.7	57.3	50.3	52.7	53.8	53.8	54.2	54.2
Foreign currency deposits	0.7	0.9	1.0	2.4	4.2	6.7	9.7	11.4	27.8	27.5	39.5	45.1
Households	0.3	0.4	0.5	0.9	1.7	2.7	3.5	4.1	9.8	13.5	18.1	22.4
Enterprises	0.4	0.5	0.5	1.5	2.5	4.0	6.2	7.3	18.0	14.0	21.4	22.7
Other items (net)	27.6	36.6	30.5	17.2	53.6	37.9	43.9	52.0	80.3	89.3	63.3	65.9
Memorandum item												
Interenterprise credit	13.0	32.3	46.3	26.2	7.2	10.6	13.8	27.8	53.6	76.4	123.4	65.9
Change in household financial wealth		18.5	19.4	17.9	17.8	4.8	3.9	2.4	-3.8	-1.6	12.6	16.7
End-year velocity of broad money	1.5	1.55	1.50	1.40	1.39	1.45						

Source: State Bank of Czechoslovakia, various years.

minate "perpetual inventory loan" clients, forcing the government to step in to provide recapitalization for the banks.[19]

3. It is also possible that the banks, under the guidance that they should be prudent and take into account credit risk, simply decided that in the case of many of their clients, even large borrowing-lending spreads were insufficient to cover the risks. The banks moved sharply to impose hard budget constraints, perhaps more sharply than authorities would have desired.

Czechoslovakia was the only country in Central and Eastern Europe to have managed a real devaluation on a sustained basis without having engaged in further nominal devaluations to offset domestic inflation. This was an important achievement because it contributed to strong export performance as well as to price stability. This achievement gave Czechoslovakia the option of using the exchange rate as a credible nominal anchor for 1992—provided macroeconomic policies remained geared toward stability—and was an ideal framework for the ambitious privatization and restructuring program planned for 1992.

In light of this background, we can better understand what happened in the years after this book's cases were written. Based on data for the first half of 1991, and partial indicators through October, Czechoslovakia managed the macroeconomic stabilization and liberalization phase of the transformation rather well. Prices are now determined by demand and supply; the trade regime is a relatively liberal one; and macroeconomic stability has been achieved. Structural changes and tight macroeconomic policies led to a fall in production in the first, and to a lesser degree, in the second quarter of 1991; this decline, however, was a level adjustment, and industrial production stabilized in the third quarter yet dropped 9 percent in 1992. GDP declined by 12 percent; it dropped by 4 percent in the first quarter of 1993 compared with the first quarter of 1992. Unemployment, at about 7 percent in December 1991, is in 1993 at about 3 percent in the Czech Republic, one of the lowest unemployment rates in Europe. Consumer prices have been flat since July 1991, but electricity prices increased in October and some increase of demand at Christmas increased the price level by approximately 5 percent in the fourth quarter, bringing the total increase from December 1990 to December 1991 to 5 percent. Strong exports to the OECD and lower-than-expected oil prices contributed to a lower-than-expected current account deficit in convertible currencies for the year, at approximately $0.5 billion. The current account in nonconvertible currencies is likely to show a surplus because of the credit financing of Czechoslovak exports to former CMEA partners.

The outlook for the future is more difficult to assess, and uncertainties are considerable. The projections given here are therefore best seen as an attempt to quantify judgmental evaluations of scenarios and risks, and not as precise point estimates.

On the supply side, much will depend on the fate of the large-scale privatization program. If privatization is successful in the sense that not only is ownership transferred but also effective managerial control is established quickly, liquidation of unprofitable business units may proceed rapidly. This will reduce production early in the program; more profitable lines of business will turn around and begin growing again.

On the demand side, uncertainties loom large as well. The basic question is whether hard-won stability can be preserved. There are at least three pressure points that put it at risk. First, wage growth could accelerate if wage earners try to recapture partially the losses suffered in 1994. This danger could become real in newly privatized companies if no effective ownership control is established, and if managers and workers try to distribute the available cash flow before restructuring is carried out. This is especially possible because wage control in the nonstate sector was abolished in 1992. Second, the tax base is likely to erode. There were not huge accounting profits to tax in 1992; import competition will reduce margins with the phasing out of the import surcharge; and generally low activity depressed sales tax revenues. Expenditure cuts may be necessary for creating a balanced budget yet may be difficult to achieve in times of increased pressures for social expenditures. Third, if privatization does not lead to effective control of former state companies, banks may find themselves in a position where it is difficult to refuse credits to newly privatized companies awaiting restructuring. Concerns about the consequences of not doing so would indeed be well-founded. These three pressure points highlight that preservation of macroeconomic stability in the former Czechoslovakia will necessitate continuous efforts.

Overview of Structural Reform

Structural reform is above all a change in the role of government, withdrawing progressively from the detailed management of economic activity to a focus on supporting the growing private sector with the laws and institutions of a market economy.

The Division of Authority Between Different Levels of Government

Long-suppressed Slovak national aspirations surfaced in the wake of the November 1989 events. The federation has long been seen by many Slovaks as a tool of Czech domination, imposing economic and political outcomes that do not take into account Slovak preferences. The federal constitution of 1968 divided the formerly unitarian state into two administrative units and devolved some central powers to the republics. For the following twenty years, however, the central authorities continued to dominate decisionmaking at all levels of government under the direction of the Communist party hierarchy. With the breakdown of Communist rule, demands for decentralization of economic power and greater self-determination came together and set in motion a process of devolution of power.

This process has been reinforced by different attitudes to reform, with Slovak citizens showing a more skeptical attitude toward economic reform. In an opinion poll the Group for Independent Social Analysis carried out in November and December 1990, 71 percent of respondents in the Slovak Federal Republic thought that reform would lead to great social injustices, against 53 percent in the Czech Federal Republic. Forty percent in the Slovak Republic saw reform as the beginning of a "wrong" development, against 23 percent in the Czech Republic.[20] This difference on the impact of the reform program between the two republics, and the Slovak Republic's cynicism over the outcome, has its roots in the disparate state of their economies: Unemployment, for example, is rising far more rapidly in the Slovak Republic than in the Czech Republic.

The competence law, which the Federal Assembly adopted in December 1990, decentralized economic decisionmaking power and devolved control over state-owned enterprises to the republics. Many areas of economic policy were defined in this law as the joint responsibility of the republics and the central government; others such as central banking and customs were assigned to the federal government. The vague formulations of this competence law served as the basis for agreement on the economic reform program and its implementation at first. Over time, however, disagreement over direction and speed of implementation of the economic reform program increased, and fundamental flaws in the competence law became apparent. In the areas of taxation and prices, the federal government was in charge of policy, but execution of these policies was in the hands of the republics. As divergences of opinions widened, necessary policy coordination became increasingly difficult.[21] The result was the split of the country into two independent republics.

Privatization

The ultimate objective of market reforms is to increase welfare through higher income and the availability of goods that correspond to the preference of the population. This requires the existence of enterprises that are geared to achieve high productivity to respond flexibly to consumer demand. Privatization is seen as a means to this end by rapidly bringing private initiative and entrepreneurship into the process of transforming enterprises. This also creates an entrepreneurial class. Because the private sector in Czechoslovakia accounted for less than half a percent of nonagricultural output in 1990, pri-

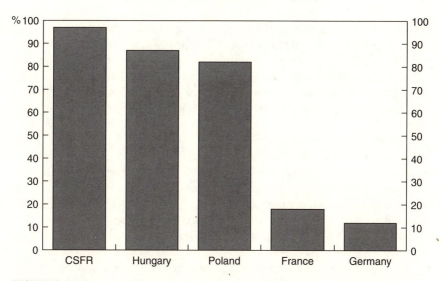

FIGURE 2.4   State-owned Sector in Czechoslovakia as Share of Value Added, Mid-1980s.
Source: B. Milanovic. *Liberalisation and Entrepreneurship: Dynamics of Reform in Socialism and Capitalism.* Armonk, N.Y.: M. E. Sharpe, 1989.

vate-sector development was linked more closely to the success of privatization than in either Hungary or Poland, where the private sector accounted for more than 10 percent of GDP at the outset (see Figure 2.4). Thus, the government made privatization the cornerstone of its structural policies. This section first provides an overview of the balance that Czechoslovakia's privatization program struck between efficiency, social fairness, and fiscal considerations; the privatization program is then described and evaluated.

Efficiency, Fairness, and Fiscal Considerations

The contribution privatization makes to increasing the average income of the population is the main criterion by which to judge its promise. At the same time, privatization is politically feasible only if the process is perceived as fair. Finally, fiscal considerations may limit available options.

With respect to efficiency and costs, the aim of privatization is to maximize the net present value of the future flow of value added (in a competitive environment) from the enterprises being privatized. These costs include the establishment of institutions such as the National Property Funds and Privatization ministries; the hiring of experts to help evaluate enterprises' worth and determine limitations on enterprises' property rights; and the evaluation of privatization projects by the founding ministries and the ministries of privatization. Czechoslovak authorities initially estimated that approximately 120,000 small business units and more than 4,000 large enterprises would be privatized. Standard approaches to privatization such as sales or placement with foreign investors will take years. Delay, however, will reduce the net present value of the future stream of value added because the longer an enterprise is not placed under effective management and control, the longer higher productivity and conversion to more promising product lines will be deferred. The likelihood is greater that markets will be lost and production will decline further.

From these considerations the government concluded that a speedy implementation of privatization was necessary, even if this meant that decisions had to be made with imperfect information. In the case of small privatization, published valuations were based on book values; in the case of large privatization, the voucher method was designed to render an ex ante valuation, unnecessary if there was no foreign participation.

The use of incentives is the most important requirement to attain efficiency. Managers of privatized enterprises must be motivated to use assets in the most practical and efficient way. Effective monitoring and control by owners over managers is needed for this.

The privatization process must be perceived as socially fair to be politically acceptable. In the state enterprise sector, housing was virtually free, workers received other amenities, and low production rates were normal. With the breakdown of the command economy and the transition to a market economy through privatization, there will be an inevitable redistribution of wealth. To be acceptable, this redistribution must increase overall growth prospects so that losers can be compensated, and the redistribution process itself must follow rules that people consider fair. Four rules have been followed in the former Czechoslovakia: transparency through the use of auctions, prevention of undue gains by the nomenklatura through regulations inhibiting spontaneous privatization, wide distribution of ownership through the voucher method, and partial compensation of those who suffered losses under the socialist regime.

The most problematic of these is compensation in the form of restitution because it may slow down the establishment of clear property rights and lead to a freezing of privatization until claims of former owners are known and settled. Moreover, eligibility rules and cutoff dates for compensation became a matter of debate that was resolved by the courts, as has been the case in Hungary. The Czechoslovak authorities tried to balance political pressures and economic efficiency by a judicious choice of cutoff dates that limited the total amount of property that was restituted, especially in the enterprise sector, and by combining large privatization and restitutions in such a way that restitution became an integral part of the privatization process, handled by the same authorities. The regulations contained in the large restitution law ensured that most restitution in the enterprise sector would take the form of financial compensation.

Fiscal considerations were not a constraint on the mode of privatization in Czechoslovakia. The government had practically no internal debt, and the external debt was small. Thus, the government did not need to use the privatization process for raising revenue in order to cover budget deficits or to reduce the internal debt.[22]

Privatization Programs

Privatization can be divided into small and large scale. The former involves the auctioning of small business units, primarily to domestic investors, and proceeded at a rapid pace. Between January and August 1991, more than 12,000 units were sold. Large-scale privatization is pursued through a complex program combining several forms of privatization, including outright sales, foreign investment, and the extensive use of vouchers. Three-quarters of state-owned enterprises were slated for large-scale privatization; the remainder would stay, temporarily at least, in state hands or would be liquidated. More than 50 percent of the enterprises to be privatized were scheduled for privatization by the summer of 1992.

Enterprises included in the large-scale privatization prepared privatization projects that were subjected to a multistage approval process. These projects defined the mix of modes of privatization, for example, sale, foreign investment, or privatization vouchers. The distribution of state enterprises to the population through vouchers played a central role. Debates on restitution slowed through the privatization process, although initial difficulties were overcome mainly by limiting the extent of restitution and by making it part of the overall privatization process.

Effective Management and Control

The issue of effective management scarcely arises for enterprises with foreign participation. Here, the foreign partner can be expected to provide effective monitoring and management expertise, together with much needed technological know-how and access to Western markets, even if the company holds only a small amount of equity. But the issue is relevant for those enterprises that were or will be privatized through the voucher method only. Will a concentration of shareholders develop who take an active interest in management and restructuring the firm? And will those enterprises in which a major shareholder takes control develop management and marketing expertise quickly enough to survive and thrive in a competitive environment? The government hoped market solutions to these questions would develop in a spontaneous manner. One such method was the rapid development of mutual funds that offered attractive incentives to investors to join a particular fund. Also, the government encouraged the development of effective control mechanisms, for example, through investment funds managed by domestic and foreign banks in cooperation with consulting companies to provide business expertise and management. Such funds were allowed not only to invest and trade shares but also to take a managing interest in companies. At the same time minimal rules and supervision to prevent fraud and protect investors are urgently needed.[23]

The use of vouchers was expected to result in a slower increase of foreign investment than achieved with other methods. If an enterprise could find a foreign partner quickly enough for its participation to be included in the privatization project of the enterprise, foreign investors needed to rely on buying shares in companies. In this case, the development of a stock market becomes all the more urgent.

Some control of enterprise management may also be achieved by way of falling share prices and subsequent takeovers as owners exit. This mechanism is unlikely to be very effective initially, however, and even in the medium term should be supplemented by other control mechanisms. One reason for the limited effectiveness of falling share prices and takeovers is that financial markets are thin. This reduces the usefulness of price signals. But the main reason is that effective control and management skills are a scarce resource in the former Czechoslovakia. The sale of shares by domestic owners will lead to an improvement if there are foreign investors to bring management and accounting skills or better overall governance. In the case of a purely domestic takeover, some improvement in enterprise performance may be achieved but will remain limited as long as accounting, controlling, marketing, and management skills remain extremely scarce. Technical assistance in these areas therefore deserves high priority.

The Legal and Institutional Framework

In a market economy, the government provides the legal and institutional framework for the development of the private sector. In many countries, this framework has taken decades to develop. Czechoslovakia had to create quickly the institutions and laws for a market economy. Progress as of late 1991 is reviewed in this section.

Protection of Competition   The elements of a market economy depend on the existence of functioning enterprises in a competitive environment. As Czechoslovak state-owned enterprises were privatized and began to react to market signals, it became important that the government ensured that companies were subject to the disciplinary force of competition. This was the objective of the Competition Protection Act, which became effective in February 1991 and which was modeled largely on European Community legislation. It established or recognized three competition offices: the Federal Office for Economic Competition; the Office of the Czech Republic for Economic Competition; and the Slovak Antimonopoly Office.

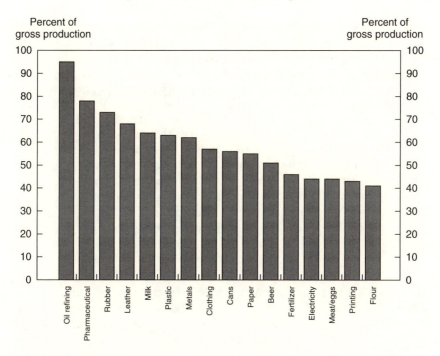

Percent of gross production

Percent of gross production

FIGURE 2.5   CSFR Five-Firm Concentration Ratio, 1989.
Source: CSFR Federal Statistical Office, 1990.

Many sectors in Czechoslovakia were highly concentrated. Figure 2.5 shows those sectors where the five-firm concentration was above 40 percent in 1989. These sectors accounted for 48 percent of industrial production in 1989, and for 39 percent of employment for the same year. Since then, some deconcentration has taken place; nevertheless, the degree of concentration in 1989 suggests that the protection of competition will be an important policy area. The law regulates cartels, mergers, and monopolistic or dominant market positions. A dominant market position is defined as a market share exceeding 30 percent. Not covered are state monopolies that are subject to special laws, such as railways and salt and tobacco manufacturing. Public utilities such as gas and electricity are covered. The task of the competition offices is to ensure that dominant or monopoly positions are not abused.

The strength of the law is that unlawful actions are defined clearly, as are instances in which approval by the competition offices is required. In particular,

- The law lists seven elements of cartel contracts that are against the law.
- Mergers are subject to approval if the merging enterprises have, together, a dominant market position; contracts that were not approved ex ante are void.

- Enterprises must report when they achieve a dominant market position in the relevant market. The law lists four specific kinds of behavior that are considered misuse of market power.
- During privatization, the privatization ministries must set up conditions that guarantee that the monopolistic position of privatized firms will be eliminated.

There are, however, some aspects of the law that are not well-suited to the present situation. The definition of dominance may be unduly restrictive, especially when applied to sectors where foreign competitors are in a position to contest the market. Perhaps more important, the law fails to distinguish between competitive horizontal agreements and vertical agreements such as one between a firm and its suppliers or distributors. Such vertical agreements are not necessarily anticompetitive, but they are prohibited unless the competition authority gives specific approval. This may generate wasteful bureaucratic delays.

Any company that believes its rights have been violated by illicit restriction of competition may ask the competition offices to set up an inquiry and can pursue claims through the court system. The competition offices can also open investigations on their own initiative.[24] They are independent of government ministries and are authorized to fine entrepreneurs for actions against the Competition Protection Act up to an amount of 5 percent of the sales value of the previous year.

With the Competition Protection Act and the competition bureaus, Czechoslovakia gave itself the legal and institutional means to promote and protect competition. Yet it will take some time before the offices are fully operational. They are in the process of building their staffs, establishing internal procedures, and finding their places in the changing institutional landscape. There are at least two aspects of the law that are not conducive to effective protection of competition:

- Three competition offices were set up for a rather small country, which is likely to lead to problems of communication and coordination. The Federal Bureau of Competition has authority only if the market position of an enterprise in the relevant market exceeds 40 percent.
- The supervision of the impact of competition on state subsidies to enterprises was vested with the republics' bureaus rather than with the federal bureau. As most subsidies and credit guarantees are likely to be given by the republics' governments, the possible lack of de facto independence of these bureaus could lead to the ineffective protection of competition, especially if the competing enterprise is located in the other republic.

Bankruptcy Law   Bankruptcy rules have a number of functions; the threat of bankruptcy during the transition is especially important to speed the process of privatization and the restructuring of enterprises so that none remain in state hands. However, in the face of the large external shock to Czechoslovakia and the complete restructuring of the rules upon which the economy is built, the criteria for a declaration of bankruptcy are difficult to define. If payment difficulties are used as the criterion, more than 80 percent of former Czechoslovak enterprises would be technically bankrupt, as illustrated by the rapid growth of involuntary interenterprise credit during 1990 and 1991. If solvency is used as the criterion to define bankruptcy, one faces the problem of asset valuation; again, at present the value of many enterprises appears low. Despite these difficulties, a bankruptcy law is important in the present circumstances because it enables the restructuring of enterprises that are not yet privatized, or are not intended for privatization. As the private sector develops, it will become even more important as one of the key institutions of a functioning market economy.

The Federal Assembly approved a bankruptcy law in July 1991 (adopted by the Czech Republic in 1993). Two procedures are envisaged in this law. The first applies to enterprises that are insolvent; these are, as a rule, to be liquidated, and control over their assets is taken from management. The second applies to enterprises that are illiquid because of delayed payments by customers. These enterprises will be restructured and maintained as going concerns.

During a transitional phase, the law is to be applied selectively. Given the technical insolvency of much of the industry, this is probably unavoidable. It makes bankruptcy a very visible political decision, however, and there is a risk that this could undermine the effectiveness of the law.

Support for the Development of Private Entrepreneurship   The government reckoned that the development of small- and medium-sized companies would be an essential element in its move toward a market economy. The Scenario of the Economic Reform states that "market-based economic, small-scale and medium-scale enterprises function as one of the most important sources of permanent and intensive change. They function as a source of economic growth." In 1990, the Federal Assembly passed a number of laws to support the development of the private sector:

- A constitutional amendment granted equal status to the owners of private, cooperative, and state property.
- The law on private business activities gave all citizens the right to establish their own businesses, subject only to registration, in almost any sector of the economy. No limitations on the number of employees or the amount of property of the enterprise are contained in this law.
- The foreign trade law was amended to allow all economic units, including private entrepreneurs, to export their own products and to import products for their own production.

- The law on cooperatives was amended to establish the right of a member of an agricultural cooperative to get back the land originally contributed, subject to the condition that the land continue to be used for agricultural purposes.
- The joint-stock companies law reestablished joint-stock companies as a legal form in Czechoslovakia.
- A law regulating the taxation of small enterprises was also adopted.

Two further measures that are important for private-sector development are scheduled to be implemented soon. A new accounting law, which took effect on January 1, 1993, will make accounting practices meet international standards, in conformity with EC legislation.[25] The new commercial code and the establishment of commercial courts provided the civil law infrastructure for business based on freedom to contract. The code was adopted in November 1991 and was implemented on January 1, 1992. Policies of active support for the development of small- and medium-sized enterprises are under consideration.

Regulation of State Enterprises   One of the most difficult policy areas to legislate is the management of enterprises that will remain in the state sector. These comprise public utilities and enterprises in strategic sectors that will remain in state hands for the foreseeable future, enterprises that will eventually be liquidated, and enterprises that are to be privatized later on. Even if privatization proceeds at a rapid pace, the two governments will have to manage a large number of state-owned enterprises for many years. Import and domestic competition will help change the behavior of these enterprises, but the questions of hard budget constraints, incentives, and corporate control must be solved. By 1991 the government had hardly begun to address these issues. Instead, it focused its limited resources on ensuring the success of the first wave of large-scale privatization.

The basis for the commercialization of state enterprises was established with the enactment of the law on state enterprises in 1990. This law transferred control over management from the founding ministry to a supervisory board. This board was made up equally of ministry representatives and elected workers' representatives. The right to appoint and recall the director, however, remained with the ministry. Plan targets and restrictions on the use of enterprise funds were abolished. Under the new rules, enterprises were supposed to make their own decisions on investment, production, and marketing. This led, in the short run, to a management vacuum because enterprise directors were suddenly lacking directives but did not have the necessary incentives and skills to manage the enterprise in a rapidly changing economic and financial environment.

Efficient management of state enterprises is a challenge in the best of circumstances. It is especially difficult without the presence of a strong private
sector to provide a yardstick of efficiency and management know-how based
on experience. As the relative size of the state sector shrinks, this task will become more manageable, and the experience of other countries will become
more relevant.

Direct Government Policies

As Czechoslovakia moved toward a market economy, the government's direct
involvement in the economy declined. This does not mean, however, that the
independent governments' roles will become less important. As the governments withdraw from the direct management of the economy, their tasks will
become increasingly to provide the legal and institutional frameworks that allow market economies to thrive, to ensure macroeconomic stability for the
private sector, and to provide the necessary infrastructure. Although such indirect support of the economy becomes more important, the governments
continue to influence the economy directly in a number of spheres. Most important are their expenditure and tax policies, and the organization and financing of social security. The governments may also employ more direct
structural and sectoral policies. This section reviews developments in and
plans for expenditures and revenues, social security, and structural and
sectoral policy. These plans have been adopted by the Czech Republic.

Government Expenditures and Revenues   The Czechoslovak government
made substantial progress in 1991 with the restructuring of its expenditures.
Three main changes distinguished the 1991 budget from previous years. (See
Figure 2.6.) First, greater autonomy of the republics was reflected in new
budgetary procedures that increased their responsibility for revenues and expenditures. Second, the size of the public sector was greatly reduced. Third,
the structure of expenditures and revenues changed. In particular, subsidies
declined substantially. The Czech government introduced a major tax reform
on January 1, 1993.

Subsidy Reduction   The most important change in the structure of government expenditures was the reduction of subsidies and their partial replacement with transfer payments. The 1991 budget envisaged a decline of subsidies by 9 percentage points of GDP (see Table 2.3). Most consumer subsidies
in the form of negative turnover tax had already been phased out in July 1990,
and heating subsidies were eliminated in January 1991.

Budgetary subsidies to enterprises were also cut significantly. The 1991
budget envisaged a cut of 2 percentage points of GDP, to 4.2 percent of the
originally projected GDP. The largest reductions were to be achieved in agriculture. Even so, price support for agricultural products will remain the most

60

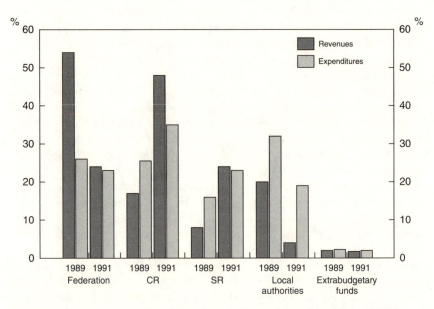

FIGURE 2.6   The structure of the CSFR General Government Budget, 1989 and 1991.
Source: Czechoslovak Federal Ministry of Finance and OECD estimates.

TABLE 2.3   CSFR Budgetary Subsidies, 1985–1991 (billions 1990 koruny)

	1985	1986	1987	1988	1989	1990	Budget 1991
Total subsidies[a]	80.0	85.4	88.7	96.1	122.1	111.8	45.2
As % of GDP[b]	11.8	12.3	12.5	13.0	16.1	14.0	4.2
As % of general government expenditures	20.9	21.7	21.6	21.6	26.4	24.1	9.1
Subsidies to enterprises	40.8	39.2	41.1	47.7	59.2	51.9	45.2
Agriculture	23.9	23.7	22.5	26.3	35.0	30.0	23.9
Subsidies to households (negative turnover tax)	26.6	28.6	29.8	29.8	49.1	49.2	0.0
Dairy	8.9	9.1	9.6	9.4	13.0	13.1	0.0
Meat	4.3	4.4	4.5	4.5	11.9	12.0	0.0
Coal & Gas	5.5	6.8	7.3	7.5	7.1	7.2	0.0
Foreign trade subsidies	12.6	17.6	17.8	18.6	13.8	10.7	–

[a]Total budgetary subsidies include subsidies paid by national committees (residential heating, housing, and urban transport) as well as transfers to enterprises from the state budget.
[b]The GDP ratios in 1991 refer to projected GDP with assumptions of real GDP growth of 12 percent and inflation of 55 percent.
Source: CSFR Ministry of Finance, various years.

important part of enterprise subsidies, accounting for more than half of the total. The next most important items were housing subsidies, which were split into approximately half for low-interest loans for housing construction and support to the operation of state apartments and half for public transportation.

Tax Reform By 1991, Czechoslovakia had not yet restructured its tax system. Instead, it focused on overhauling taxes that were dependent on the previous system of controlled prices and on reducing direct taxes on enterprises in order to increase incentives.[26]

The main unresolved issue in fiscal reform in 1991 was the apportionment of tax bases to different levels of government. This issue is clearly linked to the constitutional question and can be solved only in combination with it. For the effective functioning of different levels of government, it is important to establish clear tax bases for each level, and not to rely on fragile transfer arrangements. This can be done by assigning individual taxes or by a fixed apportioning of tax bases to different levels, or by a combination of both.

Social Protection The Czech and Slovak Republics have comprehensive and well-developed social safety nets. The intention of the authorities is to protect certain levels of social security but at the same time to introduce more market elements in order to improve efficiency and allow individuals to determine their insurance coverage individually. The guiding principle is that the state should provide a minimum standard of social protection to every citizen. Above that, individuals must purchase additional coverage from the market. The main programs are unemployment benefits, sickness benefits, pensions, universal income support, family allowances, and free health care.

Expenditures for social security are high as a percentage of GDP (see Figure 2.7). Social security expenditures were funded out of the general state budget, and there were no social security contributions by either employers or individuals. The payroll tax of 50 percent and part of the wage tax are sometimes interpreted as constituting contributions for social security, but these revenues are not earmarked and thus there is no direct link between them and social security expenditures. For the administration of benefits, the government has relied in the past on trade unions and enterprises, as have other Central and East European countries. The government began in 1990 to introduce decentralized social security administrations to take over these functions from the trade unions and enterprises.

Social Security Reform The government plans to overhaul its social security system. Social security funds are, according to plans under discussion, to be introduced by 1993, grouping pensions, basic health care, and sickness benefits. Financing will be through compulsory contributions of employers

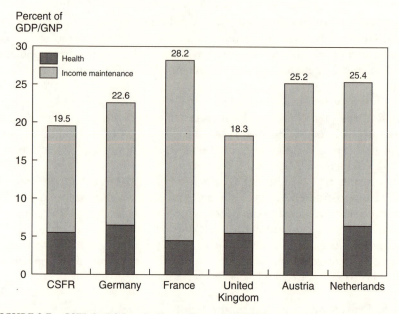

FIGURE 2.7   CSFR Social Security Expenditures, Late 1980s.
Source: H. Oxley et al. *The Public Sector: Issues for 1990s,* OECD Department of Economics and Statistics Working paper no. 90, 1990; and OECD estimates for CSFR in 1990.

and employees.[27] Health insurance will provide only basic coverage and will be complemented by private insurance schemes. The health sector will be opened for private providers, and fees for services and materials will be introduced.

Structural and Sectoral Policies   Czechoslovakia's microeconomic policies were based on three pillars: allowing market-determined relative prices to guide economic decisions, creating the incentives for enterprises to react to these prices through rapid privatization, and providing the legal and institutional frameworks for a market economy to develop. The difficulty was that although price liberalization and macroeconomic stability can be achieved fairly rapidly, the development of the legal and institutional frameworks, privatization, and the buildup of enterprises' capacities to function effectively in the new environment take more time. In the meantime, output has declined. Structural and sectoral policies have been proposed to fill this gap.

The Scenario of the Economic Reform that the Federal Assembly adopted in September 1990 contains a special chapter devoted to structural policy. It identifies seven goals: (1) an increase of the share of light industry in total industry, (2) reduction of the resource intensity of production, (3) strengthening of the tertiary sector, (4) revitalization of economic growth and entrepreneurial activity, (5) development of tourism, (6) increased information and communication in society, and (7) environmental protection. The government proposals translated these general goals into a concrete program that was rejected by the Federal Assembly. It judged that the proposal was too ambitious and was a step backward toward traditional planning. The debate is continuing. The republics' governments are now working on their versions of structural and sectoral policies.

In a broad sense, structural policies encompass the policies that provide the legal and institutional frameworks for the functioning of the market as well as those mechanisms that help improve resource allocation in areas of market failure. In this sense, structural policies are the essence of the transition to a market economy. Two forms need to be distinguished: across-the-board policies and sectoral, or industrial, policy. There is no doubt that structural policies in the form of across-the-board measures for all sectors are urgently needed to support and accelerate the transition.

Across-the-board structural policy encompasses environmental protection. The environment has been neglected under centrally guided policies of rapid industrialization and because of the underpricing of raw materials and energy, especially coal. As a result, air pollutants such as sulphur dioxide are among the highest in Europe and are linked to adverse effects on human health. Half of the drinking water does not meet the government's own standards; a third of the forests are damaged, and a majority of animal species are considered endangered. If greater efficiency were encouraged, the removal of subsidies and proper pricing of inputs could reduce some forms of pollution by a quarter. The benefits of economic restructuring would be reinforced by establishing and strictly enforcing realistic standards and by introducing a comprehensive scheme of environmental taxes. However, these efforts are held up by interministerial conflicts. These problems should be resolved soon to ensure that economic restructuring takes place on a sound environmental basis.

The sectoral-industrial policies are quite different forms of structural policies. Such policies are designed either to support a sector or to reduce its activities and thus influence the structure of the economy directly.

On a normative level, the objective is to increase overall growth by reallocating resources to sectors with better growth potential, and withdrawing resources from sectors with a lower potential. The question then is whether governments have the necessary information to identify "winners" and "losers" better than do enterprise managers and investors. In general, the CSFR government did not show itself to be more adept at this than the market, partly because there was only limited analytical support to make such decisions. Areas of comparative advantage as revealed by studies based on domestic resource costs may be of only limited help in identifying sectors that are promising once resources have been reallocated. Cross-country comparisons provide hints but give little guidance to what should be done, and the same is true of other means of analysis. Foreign direct investment by firms with extensive knowledge of market trends is likely to identify promising companies in certain sectors, but in the remaining tier, it will be difficult for the government to identify enterprises with promising prospects.

Industrial policy can be pursued with two types of instruments, direct and indirect. Direct intervention in enterprises and sectors occurred throughout decades of central planning under Communist rule. This system runs counter to the thrust of reforms to decentralize economic decisionmaking power and has been discredited. Indirect means such as taxes and subsidies are preferable. However, the Czechoslovak government made its expenditure and tax system rule-based, transparent, and uniform. To use this system, inherited by the new independent governments, simultaneously for purposes of industrial policy would overburden administrative capacity and make the structure of expenditures and taxes less transparent.

Considerations of political economy may be the most important ones to keep in mind when devising industrial policies. The availability of policies generates pressure to grant special treatment to sectors and enterprises with political muscle even in market economies. Often, such policies become substitutes for social policies, or they slow structural change instead of promoting it. Once introduced, such policies prove difficult to phase out and tend to become permanent. In the Czech and Slovak republics, an additional consideration is that such policies could be used by the bureaucratic apparatus to prolong direct intervention in enterprises' economic decisionmaking. This would, however, run counter to the thrust of market-oriented reform. Already such pressures are being felt, not just from domestic enterprises but also from foreign investors. In some cases, foreign investors have tried to make their investment conditional on protection from competition or on the granting of monopoly positions in government procurement contracts.

These arguments do not go so far as to say that sectoral policies should not be pursued at all. They suggest, however, that extreme care must be taken and that at the present stage, the case for industrial policy is weak and resources put into sectoral policies are likely to be wasted. Sectoral policies should nevertheless be considered in a few areas of national interest where market reactions would be either too slow or not forthcoming at all. Obvious examples are the conversion of the armaments industry and energy.

Notes

1. In some respects the planning system in Czechoslovakia was more flexible than in other centrally planned economies. For example, material supply was carried out by wholesale trade organizations and was not under the supervision of a specialized ministry.

2. See Alena Nesporova, "The Influence of Total Factor Productivity on the Growth Performance of Czechoslovak Economy in the Eighties," paper prepared for the Fifth World Congress of the Econometric Society, Barcelona, 1990.

3. The lower bound of this range is the CIA/PlanEcon estimate; the upper bound is the PPP estimate of Czechoslovak studies and Alan Heston and Robert Summers, *A New Set of International Comparisons of Real Product and Price Levels, Review of Income and Wealth* 34 (1988). Valued at the commercial exchange rate, per capita income in 1989 was only $3,200 (and $2,500 in 1991).

4. See, for example, the results of a poll in *Hospodarske noviny* 22 (May 30, 1991).

5. Net material product (NMP) differs from GDP primarily in that it excludes from output so-called nonproductive services (i.e., services not linked directly to the production of goods) and also measures investment net of depreciation charges.

6. Negative household savings are overstated in the household appropriation account because this does not take into account foreign currency holdings. A cross-check with the monetary survey is shown in Table 2.2. In 1988 and 1989, differences between the two sources were minor. Foreign-currency holdings started to become important in 1990, especially in the fourth quarter in expectation of the devaluation.

7. This estimate of the change in real GDP between the first half of 1990 and the first half of 1991 is the first real GDP number released by the Federal Statistical Office.

8. About two-thirds pursue private business as a part-time activity.

9. More details on the statistical problems related to foreign trade data are provided in Chapter 4.

10. This outcome would not have compromised the 1991 budget allocations for employment compensation.

11. This apparent low weight of regulated prices may have been to some extent misleading. Because housing rents were still controlled at very low levels, their weight in total expenditures was unrealistically low.

12. Seasonal factors alone cannot explain this decline, because the wholesale prices did not change much. It is also worth noting that prices in parallel markets were lower than in the state distribution system.

13. In the first half of 1991, only two enterprises actually paid the excess-wage tax.

14. Of the total import increase of $1 billion, $220 million is due to payments in hard currency for Soviet oil deliveries in the fourth quarter.

15. The general government budget comprised the budgets of the federation, the two republics, the local authorities, and the extrabudgetary funds. The Czechoslovak budget presentation was like those of other Central and East European countries, not consistent with international definitions. Among other variations, borrowing was recorded as revenues, and amortisation payments were recorded as expenditures. The presentation here follows standard international conventions and was later also published by the Federal Ministry of Finance.

16. In 1991, the government paid interest at a rate of 3.5 percent on most of its debt to the State Bank. Until July 1991, this was negative in real terms. The implicit subsidy to government, however, was very small because net debt of government in 1990 was less than 7 percent of GDP and declined in absolute terms in 1991, amounting to about 1 percent of GDP at the end of the year. Proposals under discussion would increase the interest rate to equal the discount rate minus 3 percent.

17. Introduced changes in the structure of the budget are described in Chapter 3.

18. Until March 1991, the underlying data reflect a fairly complete picture of inter-enterprise arrears. The reason for this "high-quality" data—generally not available for other countries in Central and Eastern Europe—is that until March the banks were required to accept all bills presented for payment against an enterprise that held an account with that bank. If the relevant account had insufficient funds, these bills were put into a queue, to be paid off when funds became available. The relatively high degree of computerization within the banks made it possible to maintain such a system, and indeed the periodic settling of accounts

was also undertaken. That is, a situation in which Company A owed Company B, Company B owed Company C, and so on until Company N owed Company A was periodically consolidated by the banks to leave only net indebtedness on the books. As of March 1991 the banks were no longer required to accept bills for payment in this way. Since then, banks have been free to choose whether to accept unpaid bills, and in practice do so for their "good" customers only. The decline in recorded interenterprise credits since then is judged by the authorities to be "statistical" rather than reflecting any fundamental easing of pressures.

19. These so-called perpetual inventory loans, which totaled about 110 billion koruny for the banking system as a whole, were relatively unattractive to the banks because they had no fixed maturities and paid a low rate of interest, 6 percent. In early 1991, the banks sought to convert these loans into short-term credits. Resulting enterprise distress forced the government to step in. Eighty percent of these loans were taken off the books of the Commercial Banks and placed in the so-called Consolidation Bank run by the government. These loans were subsequently recontracted with enterprises to have an eight-year maturity, and to carry an interest rate of 13 percent. The liability side of the Consolidation Bank was constituted in part by shifting State Bank refinancing credits from the commercial banks, and for the rest by shifting savings bank deposits and insurance fund deposits from the commercial banks to the Consolidation Bank.

20. Jiří Pehe, "Opinion Polls on Economic Reform," *Report on Eastern Europe* (January 25, 1991).

21. The reform of local government is an example. Under the previous regime, national committees, conceived originally as local bodies that were to combine elements of both self-government and state administration, had functioned as the municipal branches of the central government. In 1990, the national committees were replaced by a system of local self-government, for which the legal framework was established in September by the Czech and Slovak national councils. The main element of local self-government was elected municipalities with a large degree of independence. First elections for municipal assemblies were held in November 1990.

22. However, the republican governments planned to use part of the receipts that would accrue in the privatization process, especially from foreign investors, to clean up the enterprises' balance sheets. National Property Funds assets could be used to fulfill obligations of the privatized enterprises, that is, to pay back part of their outstanding debts to the banking system. In this way, governments could achieve financial restructuring of enterprises at the moment the enterprises were privatized in a self-financing operation.

23. Such funds could be set up in a rather informal manner, requiring approval only by the (understaffed and overburdened) privatization ministries subject to minimal requirements including a minimum capital of 1 million koruny, a description of investment policies, and a listing of board members. It was planned to regulate these funds later under the investment fund law, which became effective in July 1992.

24. For behavior that was regulated by the Competition Protection Act, the civil courts had authority; decisions by the competition offices could be challenged in civil courts, but this was later transferred to administrative courts; it was planned that unfair competition would be handled by commercial courts after the commercial code was passed by parliament.

25. Especially EC directives IV and VII.

26. Turnover tax rates were unified to only four rates of 0, 12, 22, and 32 on January 1, 1991, and were reduced further to 0, 11, 20, and 29 in May 1991. Also in January, the profits tax was reduced from 65 to 55 percent. Private enterprises paid 55 percent of profits, too, but the rate for the first 200,000 koruny was only 20 percent to support small enterprises and to reduce tax evasion.

27. A trial run took place in 1992 within the budget. Part of the payroll tax is earmarked for this purpose.

PART TWO

Managerial Behavior and Entrepreneurship

CHAPTER THREE

■

Transformation Management
in Czechoslovakia

In 1918 Czechoslovakia was established as an independent state of Czechs and Slovaks. In the 1980s it had a population of 15.5 million, of which two-thirds were Czech and one-third were Slovak. Hungarians formed a significant minority of 0.7 million; other minorities of Germans, Poles, Ukrainians did not exceed 0.1 million.

Prior to World War II, Czechoslovakia was known for its industry. Slovakia, however, was primarily an agrarian society.

Communist rule began in 1945 after World War II and lasted until November 1989, when through a peaceful revolution, the Communist government was overthrown and a transformation process began in Czechoslovakia.

In this chapter, we attempt to understand the political and economic changes that occurred in Czechoslovakia after the November 1989 revolution. In order to do this, we must understand the country's political economy prior to that event. The comparative management framework included in Appendix 3.1 was used to develop an understanding of the management system and its environment in the period prior to the Velvet Revolution as well as the period following the revolution. Based on the framework, a series of interviews were conducted in November 1991 in both the Czech and Slovak republics with stakeholders of the political economy: deputy ministers and advisers to various ministries of the government, top managers of large state-owned firms, top managers of leading associations of industry and management, labor union leaders, and top managers of banks and export trading corporations.

First, we will discuss the management system and the general political and economic environment prior to November 1989. Second, the changes made

Raghu Nath of the Katz Graduate School of Business at the University of Pittsburgh and Jaroslav Jirásek of the Czechoslovak Management Center prepared this case.

after 1989 will be described. Finally, the management system and its environment as it prevailed in November 1991 will be discussed.

The Management System
Prior to November 1989

Management Philosophy

During the Communist regime, top managers in large state-owned enterprises were subservient to the party. This obedience to the party and its ideology was one of the most pervasive values governing management philosophy. There were, however, other values that played important roles within the system.

One prevailing core value was "economic egalitarianism," which implied relatively small differences in the economic arena between the top management and workers. The salaries of top management were no more than six to seven times the salaries of average workers. This is still true in large state enterprises. In one of the most successful state enterprises visited, the salary of the general manager was only six times the salary of the average worker.

Another significant core value was an emphasis on "good and broad education." Most large organizations had their own vocational centers to train skilled workers. All of the executives interviewed stressed this aspect.

Opportunism took root after 1968, when many competent professional managers were purged for expressing views against the party. Because the selection process for top managers was dominated by the party, a number of mediocre people with party connections came to power in the state enterprises. These CEOs were not well prepared for their jobs. Their primary role was to maintain a position of privilege they did not deserve. However, approximately one-half of the top managers still continued to be selected on the basis of prior training and professional competence. Thus, a "double-faced culture" developed in the large enterprises. One aspect of this culture was obedience and submission to the party's ideology to maintain the top position, although there were top managers who yearned for professional competence based on good education and training.

Collectivism was the stated ideology of the party, that is, "We are all together as a family." In practice, however, once promoted to the top position, most managers tried to preserve their jobs and, therefore, acted out of self-interest rather than in the interests of the organization.

Men and masculinity were most valued; however, there was consideration for all workers and their welfare. Ideas put forth by the women's committees in organizations were listened to by the Communist party representative and brought to the attention of the general manager, who usually acted on those concerns.

Organizational Structure and Processes

The organizational structure was centralized and formalized. In addition to the management hierarchy, there was a party hierarchy in the enterprise. Also, there was usually a youth committee and a woman's committee, and in some cases other committees such as a committee of scientists and engineers. All of these groups were actively involved in the affairs of the organization. For example, in the selection of the top manager, candidates were proposed by the general manager, the party representative, and the youth committee. Though the final selection was made by the general manager in consultation with the ministry, the party usually confirmed the final candidate.

There was a clear, well-established hierarchy from the ministry to the top manager to his deputies and department heads. The ministry would usually send directives to the top manager each year regarding the volume of production, the product mix, the productivity targets, cost targets, and innovation targets such as the building of a new plant or the development of new products. The top manager would then call his deputies and ask them to develop programs to meet these targets. The top manager played the role of watchdog and enforcer. A command type of management system resulted, with a large power differential between top management and the workers.

The communication process was from top to bottom as well. Because ministries sent the target directives, there was little planning in its proper meaning at the enterprise level. Operating decisions and implementation of these decisions did occur at the organizational level.

Enterprises performed few sales activities. The ministries dictated how much to supply to whom. Export trade was handled by the large trading companies, which had monopolistic power. The advantage of these large monopolies was their great bargaining power vis-à-vis foreign customers. One of the trading companies, for example, handled more than two-thirds of the total export from Czechoslovakia of machine tools. Therefore, the trading company could bargain and get better prices from foreign buyers. These monopolies became bureaucratic and inefficient over time and at the time of our study were being dissolved.

Union-Management Relations

There was usually a harmonious relationship between the labor unions and management because both were subservient to the party. In case of any major conflict between the two, the party was able to resolve it or effect a compromise. The labor unions were active at the enterprise, industry, and national level. They negotiated wage and salary (including benefits) contracts at the enterprise and industry levels. In practice, unions exercised little power at the national level because the party mediated differences between unions and management.

Unique to Czechoslovak unions is that they owned property. Much of this was resort property in Czechoslovakia and abroad. As a result, unions provided subsidized vacations to their workers. In addition, each large company usually provided subsidized vacations to its workers at its vacation properties. There was an emphasis on management's social responsibility in terms of providing secure jobs as well as good benefits including free or subsidized vacations. In the case of hazardous industries such as the nuclear industry, workers were given one additional month of free vacation after working for two months at a hazardous site.

This sense of social responsibility prevailed after the revolution. Industrial production fell by 25–35 percent in 1991, yet only 5 percent of the work force was laid off.

The Political and Economic Environment Prior to November 1989

The institutional framework was dominated by the party hierarchy, which permeated every facet of Czech life. Not only did it dominate the political arena but, through its representatives in each enterprise, the party also dominated industrial and economic activity.

The Economy

The economy was characterized by low inflation, full employment, and a stable currency. The standard of living for the population was within an acceptable range. There was subsidized housing, and one out of four families owned their own vacation homes. Czechoslovakia had the healthiest economy among Eastern bloc countries.

The economy could be described as a command economy. Prices, rents, and currency were strictly controlled by the government, which in turn was controlled by the Communist party.

The Legal System

The legal system in Czechoslovakia was patterned after the normative law of Western Europe rather than after U.S. common law. It was dominated by the concept of state ownership. All enterprises were owned by the state. No private ownership except personal property was allowed.

Technology

The state of Czech technology was acceptable but fell far below Western European standards. However, among the Eastern bloc and developing countries, Czechoslovakian products enjoyed a good reputation.

After the 1960s, there was some introduction of modern technology, such as numerically controlled machinery, in the large enterprises. There was little development in the areas of communications and computer technologies.

The Infrastructure

The transportation system was dominated by railroads and trucks, and generally there were adequate road and railroad systems. However, as previously mentioned, the state of communications technology was relatively poor. Telephone systems worked poorly, and there was little introduction of telefaxes or other modern communication systems. TV and radio were controlled by the party. There were some independent newspapers, but it was dangerous to publish anything against the party, and they usually did not.

The Industry Structure

Manufacturing was dominated by large firms. There were also large farm cooperatives and service sectors. There were approximately 120 to 130 large manufacturing firms and forty large export trading companies. An example of a large firm is VKD, which employed about 27,000 workers and produced locomotives, turbo compressors, streetcars, power semiconductors, and heavy electrical machinery for power generation. In the area of locomotives alone, it produced about 600 locomotives a year prior to 1989.

Changes After November 1989

In November 1989, what is now popularly known as the Velvet Revolution occurred in Czechoslovakia. A spontaneous outpouring of millions of people in the squares of Prague demanded the ouster of the Communist regime. There was absolutely no violence, not even a single window was broken, yet a great political transformation occurred because the Communists simply gave up and retreated from the scene. Elections were held in that same month for two-year terms, and a newly created party of independent people called the Civic Forum came to power. Vaclav Havel, a playwright and poet, was elected as the president of the newly independent country.[1] Thus in a short period, power was transferred from the Communist party to the independent party of the people, the Civic Forum.

The Civic Forum was a movement comprising people united by their desire for independence. Yet they had wide differences of opinion in terms of economic and other policy matters. These differences began surfacing soon after they came to power. As result, in early 1990 the Civic Forum split into three factions that later became independent parties. The first was the Civic Democratic party headed by Václav Klaus, the minister of finance. The second was the Civic Movement, headed by the minister of international affairs, Jiří Dienstbier, and the third was the Civic Democratic Association, headed by

Vladimír Dlouhý, the minister of the economy. In addition, the Social Democratic party was formed by Komàrek. These parties had different views as to how to transform the economy. Thus, there was a wide diversity of ideas and little consensus.

In a public opinion poll conducted in October 1991, the Civic Democratic party received 22 percent of the votes; the Communist party was second with 10 percent of the votes. The Social Democrats placed third with 8 percent of the votes, and the Civic Movement received 6 percent. All other parties (there were 65 parties registered in early 1990) were under 5 percent. According to the new laws, any party that did not receive at least 5 percent of the votes could not have representation in either of the two houses of parliament. Thus, at the time of this study Klaus and his party were providing the leadership for economic transformation.

The Economic Transformation Concept

In early 1990, Klaus and his party developed what is now known as the "economic transformation concept." This concept comprises the four following elements:

1. Devaluation of currency. The koruna was devalued from 14.5 koruny per dollar to approximately 30 koruny per dollar.
2. Internal convertibility of currency. This involves free access to hard currency by entrepreneurs and firms; each private citizen could receive a maximum of 5,000 koruny per year.
3. Privatization. This has two components. Small privatization covers small- to medium-size firms; large privatization deals with large state-owned companies.
4. Price deregulation. Consumer prices were completely deregulated except in the areas of energy and rent.

Klaus declared that privatization would be total. In order to effect this, the Ministries for Privatization and State Property Administration were formed. It was presumed that after privatization was complete, the Ministry of Industry would lose the basis for its existence. Klaus emphasized the following elements of privatization:

1. Privatization would be total, that is, all property would be privately owned.
2. Privatization should be complete in a short period of time, no more than three years.
3. Vouchers worth 1,000 investment points would be issued to each adult citizen over eighteen years of age for 1,000 koruny. Each citizen would then be entitled to exercise these vouchers for buying common stock in

one or more companies. It was estimated that each citizen's vouchers would buy 60,000 to 80,000 koruny worth of property.

The program for privatization was declared in the middle of 1990. The first phase of this program was implemented in November 1991. The last date for submission of proposals for privatization by firms was October 31, 1991. Interviews indicated that several organizations had submitted such plans and that others were confused about the whole affair. The Ministry of Industry and the Chamber of Commerce tried to assist enterprises in preparing these plans. However, officials at the Ministry of Industry believed that there should have been options other than privatization by vouchers and had concerns about the speed with which the scheme was being implemented. In response to questions from his opponents regarding the speed of implementation, Klaus replied that people who do not believe without reservation in advantages of the market economy—want the government to lead us into market economy gradually and want to place it under surveillance of bureaucrats and scientists.

After January 1991, prices for consumer goods except for fuel and power were deregulated. Thus, from the middle of 1990 through the beginning of 1991, the economic transformation concept was implemented in terms of devaluation of currency, internal convertibility of currency, price deregulation, and the first stage of privatization by vouchers. Plans for privatization submitted by many firms were evaluated by the relevant ministries, and the privatization by voucher of these firms began in January 1992.

The implementation of the economic transformation concept had a significant impact on the economy and industry of Czechoslovakia. We will now discuss this impact.

Impacts of the Economic
Transformation Program

Fall in Industrial Production The major impact of the fall in industrial production was the deceleration of the economy. Estimates differ; it was generally believed that industrial production fell 25–35 percent by the end of October 1991. According to an estimate by a well-informed general manager, production fell almost 40 percent by the middle of November 1991. Because the effects were unevenly spread, some areas of the country were decimated. Many people described the conditions as akin to those of the 1930s depression.

Unemployment Unemployment went from almost zero in 1988 to approximately 5 percent of the total working population of eight million people in 1991. In Slovakia unemployment was 10 percent; in Bohemia it was the lowest at 3.5 percent.

Remarkably, unemployment increased much less than the fall in production. This was due to many factors. First, there was a sense of social responsibility on the part of the enterprises and their general managers. As a result, a large number of workers were kept on when there were no jobs for them. According to a very high-level adviser in the ministry, "This is like a time-bomb which may explode any minute, and the country may experience massive unemployment and layoffs."

Consumer Prices   Consumer prices had risen by 60 percent by June 1991. After that, prices stabilized, and there was zero inflation.

Interest Rates   Interest rates rose from 4 percent in 1990 to approximately 20 percent by October 1991. They were estimated to be in the 17 percent to 18 percent range in January 1992.

Liquidity Crisis   Large industry also experienced a liquidity crisis. One of the general managers of a successful organization indicated that although his receivables were more than payables, his customers were unable to pay. Therefore, he was experiencing heavy cash-flow problems. Other general managers agreed and indicated that they were managing cash flow on a daily basis. In fact, cash-flow management had become the top priority of general managers at large enterprises.

In order to manage the cash flow, enterprises were going to banks for short-term credits; many expressed the belief that "banks are now our bosses, and the ministries can't help us anymore."

Foreign Trade   Foreign trade increased slightly and was generally balanced by 1991. Light industry, which was export-oriented, benefited from devaluation; heavy industry, which depended upon a large import of raw materials, was suffering.

Foreign Debt   Czechoslovakia's foreign debt increased from $4.5 billion in 1989 to $8.5 billion in October 1991 and increased to $9 or $10 billion by the end of 1991. IMF provided a bridge loan of up to $3 billion, and a further loan from IMF for the same amount was negotiated in November 1991. As usual, the IMF set forth conditions for its loan; wages had to be kept low and inflation had to be in check. In general, IMF praised Czechoslovakia for its economic transformation plan.

Positive Impacts   The emergence of an extensive network of economic services such as restaurants, shops, travel agencies, and exchange offices was a positive aspect of the economic transformation. Foreign travel increased, and all kinds of foreign goods were available in stores. In addition, the appearance of small shops improved as they were taken over by private entrepreneurs. Someone who had returned to the country after an absence of a year commented that he had seen a remarkable change in the way the shops displayed their products: "They're much cleaner, aesthetically appealing, as compared to the drab shops of before."

The economic transformation also attracted foreign capital, although not in quantities hoped for. The table in Appendix 3.2 gives a picture of foreign investment in Czechoslovakia in 1991. The head of a foreign consulting firm indicated that his firm alone brought in $400 million of foreign direct investment and was currently negotiating another $400 million.

Foreign investors were showing a great deal of interest in investing in Czechoslovakia. A new law allowed foreign entrepreneurs to own 100 percent equity. This was very appealing, particularly for large multinational companies, many of whom were engaged in serious negotiations. However, voucher privatization had introduced a good deal of uncertainty. Therefore, these firms were waiting to see how this evolved before making their final decisions.

In summary, the effects on the economy were encouraging, but there was a great deal of concern and uncertainty about the future. Foreign experts were being asked frequently what they thought as to where the country was headed and what would become of it.

Also, opposition to Klaus's policies was becoming stronger; he was forced to respond to this criticism in the local media. No viable alternatives have been proposed by his opponents, and he remains in power.

The Management System in November 1991

Management Philosophy

Because domestic markets within Czechoslovakia had shrunk drastically, the prevailing management philosophy was survival. In that spirit, external markets were being sought. At the same time most governments were preoccupied with privatization and were developing privatization plans; thus there was no long-range business planning implemented as of 1991.

Organizational Structure and Processes

In order to attract foreign partners, large companies were breaking up into autonomous divisions. Plans were to create holding companies for these autonomous divisions. The belief was that although the entire company might not be attractive to the foreign partner, the individual division would be.

Within each newly formed division, there remained a predominant functional structure. However, accounting and finance departments would be strengthened while the production department was downgraded and reduced. Unnecessary departments and functions would be either reduced or totally eliminated. These changes would affect the security guards, the internal party hierarchy, and liaisons with ministries and planning. Also, a number of levels would be reduced. New ties would be developed with the banks, and several organizations would set up their own distribution systems.

Communications between functions and levels were impeded due to lack of new information and because old indicators were obsolete. Thus, the organization was managed on a crisis basis. A few enlightened general managers held more frequent meetings with their staffs to pull together whatever information was available and share it. This mode of communication, however, was rare. Out of several general managers interviewed, only one indicated that he had resorted to this practice.

Decisionmaking within the organization became more personalized and centralized. In most organizations, general managers, with the advice of only a few people, were preparing privatization plans. Also, the general managers dealt with the banks in order to keep the liquidity crisis in check. Again, only one general manager indicated that he brought together all his staff in a group setting to manage the cash-flow crisis.

Strategies and Policies

Because the focus was on day-to-day survival, there was very little long-range planning. Because the general feeling that the ministries could not help and that the bank was the boss, most of the focus was on cash management and staying solvent.

There was a great emphasis on acquiring financial as well as marketing skills; less emphasis was placed on production. There was also an increase in subcontracting. The introduction of high technology into production processes had been put aside for the time being because of a shortage of funds.

The overall emphasis was on finding foreign markets and foreign partners. Yet a general manager, when interviewed, indicated that he found alienation between ministries and foreign companies. According to him, ministries were like academics with theoretical knowledge and no practical experience. This theme was repeated by most of the general managers interviewed. There was no bold strategy being formulated because of the fear of losing one's job. There was also an attempt by general managers to involve a lot of people in developing proposals for foreign partners, so that they were not blamed for pushing their own agendas.

Due to shrinkage in the domestic market, there was a need to lay off a large number of people. This was being done judiciously due to the prevailing social values. Thus, many people were being kept on when there was no work for them. Also, legislation in the area of unemployment required providing two months of lay-off notice as well as five months of severance pay.

In the area of development and training, there was an emphasis on on-the-job-training. The rationalization was that "we cannot spare people to send to seminars." However, some people were being sent to seminars in the areas of marketing and finance. The prevailing belief in the area of training was that the basic need was to *focus on context* rather than on function, that is, on environmental dimensions such as political economy rather than on functional areas such as production. It was more important to work toward managing transformation rather than toward a "quick fix."

The Political and Economic Environment in November 1991

There was strong emphasis on entrepreneurship. One million, out of a total of ten million adults were registered as entrepreneurs. At the same time, there was a low level of business ethics; many people wanted to make a quick profit. Individualism was now valued over the former Communist egalitarianism and collectivism, and differences in economic status were encouraged. There was also a decentralization and localization of power. Therefore, the power distance between leaders and workers decreased. Risk-taking for entrepreneurship was encouraged by the leadership, but people were uncertain and often unwilling to take risks.

After the breakdown of Communism, there was a rise of nationalism in Slovakia, and there was discussion of a Czech-Slovak split. President Havel went to Slovakia several times but was rebuffed. During one visit, people threw eggs at him. Havel asked for the power to rule by decree, and thus there was a good deal of political uncertainty, which had an impact on foreign direct investment.

Because the Communist party structure no longer existed, organizations such as the Confederation of Industries, Chamber of Commerce, and educational institutions such as the Czech Management Center, the School of Economics, and a variety of consulting firms had sprung up to replace governmental roles in regulating business. The government was still particularly active in nominating and approving top management and in the arena of economic transformation.

The policy for economic transformation was being spearheaded by Klaus, the minister of finance. A tripartite committee comprising government, labor, and industry representatives had been set up to deal with problems regarding implementation of the economic transformation program in areas such as wages, employment, trade, and industrial policy.

Banks and insurance companies were gaining power because of the liquidity crunch being experienced by industry. It was felt that financial institutions with development funds would play an increasingly important role. Industry profits were under a squeeze, but banks were making huge profits; some estimates were as high as 1,000 percent.

Labor unions, occupied with internal organization, were not actively participating in industrial planning. As well as the organizations mentioned previously, regional organizations were emerging to provide the missing links. For example, town councils were setting up partnerships with industry.

The Economy

There was a strong emphasis on establishing a free market. In order to achieve this, price controls had been lifted, devaluation of currency had occurred, and the voucher scheme to privatize industry had been implemented. There was a romantic belief that government should completely stay out of the industrial system, neither setting industrial policy nor taking part in planning. Many people complained about government interference. Yet at the same time Czechoslovakia had opened its markets to both the United States and Europe, who practice protectionist policies.

There was a plan for Czechoslovakia to become an associate member of the European Community and later attain full membership. Programs were being implemented to achieve this objective. Among these, foremost was the opening of the market.

The Legal System

Major changes were taking place in the legal system. In a relatively short time, since 1990, a number of new laws had been enacted. These laws pertained to such areas as foreign exchange, foreign direct investment including joint ventures, voucher privatization, and internal convertibility of currency.

Technology

The hope in Czechoslovakia was that foreign direct investments and joint ventures would facilitate a technology transfer from Western Europe, yet at the time there had not been much change. However, an interview with a general manager of a planned joint venture indicated that there was a great expectation of not only technology transfer but also transfer of management know-how. This would be accomplished by sending technical people to the parent company's operations in Western Europe; at the same time, engineers from the parent company would come to Czechoslovakia to provide on-site education. An engineering expert from a Western European parent company conducting training sessions at a factory site said in an interview that although the factory's technology was outmoded, the workers were skilled and management was promising. Therefore, it would not be difficult to retrain the work force as well as management in ways that would help to modernize the factory and produce a product of high quality comparable to that in the West. It was planned that after five years the joint venture would export a large portion of its production to the West.

The Infrastructure

There was not much change in the transportation system. Railroads and major roadways were in good condition; secondary roads needed work. The air transportation system also needed to be modernized.

The communication system was not very reliable. There were very few telefaxes and a lack of computerized systems. A new joint venture with Western telecommunication companies had been formed to improve the communication system.

Though independent media had sprung up, they were reluctant to criticize the government's policies on economic transformation. An interview with a leading media person indicated that media would not criticize the present economic transformation concept but present various alternatives in a broad framework of economic transformation and privatization.

The Industry Structure

Large companies were disintegrating, and at the same time, small- and medium-sized enterprises were springing up. These enterprises tended to be mostly in the service sector. There was an underreporting of income and profits, and hence a parallel economy was on the rise.

Prior to November 1989, the USSR was Czechoslovakia's most important trading partner. By 1991, Germany was the most important trading partner, followed by Austria, and then the former USSR. A number of large companies were facing bankruptcy. It was estimated that one-third of the present organizations were doing well and that two-thirds were endangered.

Notes

1. In his plays, Havel ridiculed obedience to the party hierarchy. This made him a popular figure.

Appendixes

APPENDIX 3.1   An Open-Systems Framework for Comparative Management

Systems	Subsystems	Some Elements
Environment	Cultural Milieu	Cultural values and belief systems (Hofstede's dimensions), social norms and mores, myths and stories
	Sociopolitical	Political parties, business/government relations, political/economic groups, policymaking bodies, unions, and other advocacy
	Economic System	Stage of economic development, economic philosophy, banking system, capital markets, fiscal policy, factor endowment, income distribution, parallel economy
	Legal System	Nature of society, legal framework, type of laws, enforcement of laws
	Technology	Level of technology development, scientific/technical manpower, R&D expenditure, type of technology, developer versus copier
	Communication and Transportation	Communication (press, telephone), transportation (highways, air system)
	Industry Structure	Urban/rural, small versus large organizations, sectoral distribution
Business and Management	Management Philosophy	Prevailing management ideology, managerial style and orientation
	Organization Structure	Type, degree of centralization and formalization
	Organization Processes	Decisionmaking and communication processes
	Human Resource Management	Attitudes, practices, and policies
	Other Policies	Production, marketing, financial, etc.
	Union/Management Relations	Conflictual versus cooperative, labor legislation
	Unions	Type, affiliations
	Other Groups	Consumers, church, environmental groups, etc.

Source: R. Nath, ed. *Comparative Management: A Regional View.* Boston: Ballinger of Harper and Collins, 1988.

APPENDIX 3.2 Joint Venture Investment in Czechoslovakia in 1991

Foreign Partner	Country	CR/SR Partner	JV's Name	Sector	Status	Foreign Capital [Kčs 000m]	Total Amount [Kčs 000m]
Volkswagen	Germany	Skoda	VW-Skoda	autos	operating	6,630.0	9.6
Glavabel	Belgium	Sklo Union	Glavunion	glass	operating	–	1.9
Linde	Germany	Technoplyn	–	industrial gases	operating	106.0	1.6
Volkswagen	Germany	BAZ	–	truck components	approved	incl.abv	1.1
Alusuisse Lonza	Switzerland	Kovohute Decin	Aluminum Decin	aluminum processing	finalizing	–	1.1
US West/Bell Atlantic	USA	CR/SR govts	Eurotel	telecom systems	operating	60.0	1.1
Cabot	USA	Deza	–	coal processing	–	80.0	–
IKEA	Sweden	Danubia	–	furniture manufacture	–	76.5	–
CBS	France	Tourinvest	–	hotels	–	175.0	–
Siemens	Germany	Tesla Karlin	Tescom	telecom equipment	approved	15.0	–
Otis	USA	–	–	elevators	–	–	–
Cofumin	Belgium	–	–	–	–	–	–
Cementarie Belge Reun.	Belgium	Cementárny a V.	–	cement	finalizing	–	–
Procter & Gamble	USA	Rakona	–	detergents, washing powders	operating	20.0	–
Bata	USA	CR govt.	–	shoes	approved	–	–
Voest Alpine l'bau	Austria	VSZ	Linkomet	steel making	–	–	–
Cannon Eng.	USA	VAB	–	–	–	–	–
ABB Stotz Kontakt	Switz./Austria	Slov.Electro.Zav.	–	–	approved	–	–
Lafarge Copée	France	Cizkovicka cement.a V.	–	cement	approved	–	–
Diversified Global	USA	Pilzenski Prazdroj	–	bottling plant, theme parks	finalizing	–	–
Total	France	Benzina	–	petro distribution, gas statn	–	–	–
Management Inv. Grp.	Netherlands	Slovnaft	–	truck repair, motel	approved	3.4	–
SBS	France	–	–	construction	approved	–	.025
Tetrapák	Sweden	Grafobal	–	packaging	approved	–	–
Coca-cola Amatil	USA/Austria	Nealko Kyje	–	bottling plant	finalizing	est 10.0	–
Cengas	USA	Kamenohelne doly	–	gas extraction	finalizing	–	–
Henkel	Austria	Palma	–	detergents, washing powders	finalizing	–	–
Besize/Steigenburger	Belgium/Germany	Interhotely	Carlon Hotel	hotel and office block	operating	–	–
–	–	Pivovar ZB	–	brewing	sale pending	–	–
–	–	Benzinol	–	petrol distribution, gas statn	post-priv. sale	–	–

APPENDIX 3.2 Joint Venture Investment in Czechoslovakia in 1991 (*Continued*)

Foreign Partner	Country	CR/SR Partner	JV's Name	Sector	Status	Foreign Capital	Total Amount [Kčs 000m]
Hiag AG	Switzerland	Tuplex	–	–	sale pending	–	–
–	–	Prior	–	department store chain	sale pending	–	–
Heidelberger Zement	Germany	Kralodvorská cementarná	–	cement	negotiating	–	–
Heidelberger Zement	Germany	Pragocement	–	cement	negotiating	–	–
Holderbank	Switzerland	Cementárny a.V.	–	–	negotiating	–	–
Voest Alpine Stahl AG	Austria	Ferona Praha	–	steel distribution	letter of intent	–	–
Voest Alpine MCE	Austria	CKD Slany	–	–	negotiating	–	–
Metropak	Denmark	Stroj Obal	–	packaging	negotiating	–	–
Marius Pedersen	Denmark	municipal council	–	waste disposal	signed	–	0.01
Cagiva Varese	Italy	Zav. Motorcyclové /CZS	–	motorcycle production	letter of intent	–	–
Deutsche Babcock-Borsig	Germany	CKD Kompresory	–	–	letter of intent	–	–
–	–	Skoda Pilzen	–	energy/transportation	negotiating	–	–
Cemapol/Petrimex B.	Netherlands	Slovnaft	–	sheet polythene	approved	–	–
Triplex Lloyd intl.	Britain	Motorlet	Walter Dreitland	precision steel castings	approved	–	0.08
Ralston Energy Systems	USA	Batteria Slany	Ralston Batteria	batteries	operating	26.0	–
Alcatel SEL	Germany	Tesla L.H.	–	digital switches, power supplies	operating	9.2	–
AmCzech Holdings	USA/Britain	Prefa Praha	Eurocast	prefab housing materials	approved	–	–

Source: Adapted from *CMU*, November 1, 1991, Appendix I.

CHAPTER FOUR

■

Ferox Manufactured Products and Air Products and Chemicals: A Joint Venture

Ferox Manufactured Products

November 1989, the Velvet Revolution

It was unusually cold for that time of the year, and the several hundred employees of Ferox Děčín who gathered in the yard could see their breath. Facing them, standing on an unloaded railroad wagon, was the managing director, Radek Malec.[1] The time was exactly noon. Millions of people in Czechoslovakia stopped working that noon. Just as in Děčín, people gathered in meeting rooms, corridors, cafeterias, classrooms, and factory yards and went into the streets with one thing on their minds: making this the very last week of Communist rule in Czechoslovakia.

But few managing directors shared this goal, and even fewer were able to face their subordinates at this critical moment. Many of this elite group knew that it would be better not to show up. However, Radek Malec did face the volatile crowd at Ferox. After decades of mistrust between workers and managers, Malec knew that what he was going to say would be decisive for his own future, as well as for the future of Ferox.

October 1991

Radek Malec, managing director of Ferox, a gas and chemical company, has just read the Czech Republic's public announcement of Ferox's proposed

This case was prepared by Professor Jone Pearce of the Graduate School of Management, University of California, Irvine, and Dr. Michal Čakrt of the Czechoslovak Management Center. It was supported by a U.S. Agency for International Development grant. The material is intended for discussion purposes and is not intended to serve as an example of either good or poor management practices.

privatization plan. Before proceeding with his plans, Malec had to wait for the U.S. company Air Products and Chemicals (APCI) to purchase controlling interest in Ferox and to allow for competing proposals to be brought forward. Although he has had little time to marvel at the monumental changes he and Ferox have experienced, he has devoted considerable energy to planning for the acquisition of Ferox by APCI.

Background

Ferox is located in Děčín, a northeastern industrial city near the German border. The company was founded during World War II to produce chemicals and chemical equipment for the military. At the end of the war it was confiscated as Nazi property by the Czechoslovak government and began to produce simple agricultural chemical products.

Until 1989 Ferox was a component of one of the biggest Czechoslovak industrial trusts. In 1991, as a result of the first phase of the privatization process, it became a separate joint-stock company with stock held by the government. By October 1991, Ferox was governed by an operating board that included people from the company (the chairman of this board was the deputy director for engineering), from other companies, and also from the government ministries. It was anticipated that in the second phase of the privatization the state would offer its shares to potential buyers.

At the time of this study, Ferox had three main product lines: cryogenic equipment, chemical equipment, and air-cooling systems for the chemical industry's long-distance pipelines. In January 1991, Ferox began selling gas, and this line was assumed by its joint venture with APCI. In 1991, the company was working with APCI on a new gas-manufacturing joint venture.

Ferox's customers have been many and varied. Before the 1989 revolution, 40–45 percent of the company's market was dependent, either directly or indirectly, on the Soviet market. In 1991, only 1.5–2 percent of their sales came from that market because their former Soviet customers did not have the convertible currency to pay for Ferox purchases. In October 1991, Ferox had 1,350 employees organized into six functional departments: production services, production, commerce (included purchasing and sales), economics (accounting), personnel, and engineering (see Figure 4.1). Ferox had annual sales of approximately $15 million.

In October 1991, Ferox formally submitted a privatization project to the Czech Republic Privatization Ministry and awaited approval. In accordance with the law, the proposal stipulated that 3 percent of the shares would be set aside for a reserve fund for restitution to the original owners of companies. In addition, Ferox's proposal reserved 3 percent of the shares for employee purchase and 52 percent for purchase by APCI, with the remaining 42 percent of the shares allocated for purchase by Czech citizens through the government's voucher program. Shares purchased through vouchers must be held by the

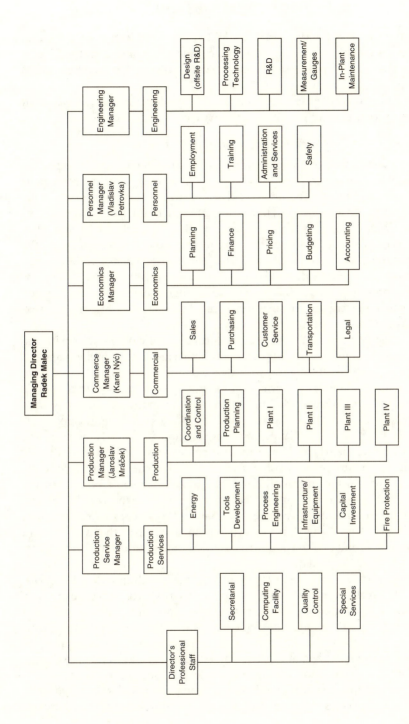

FIGURE 4.1 Functional Departments at Ferox.

original purchasers for two years, until after the privatization of the entire economy is completed, before they can be traded. Revenue from the 55 percent of shares to be purchased by employees and by APCI would go to the National Property Fund.

Several Ferox employees were interviewed regarding the changes as a result of Ferox's joint venture with APCI. Some excerpts from these follow.

Radek Malec, Managing Director

In other companies, the whole management was changed after the revolution, and those companies have had a lot of difficulties. Oftentimes they put researchers and design engineers in charge who are smart but don't really know how to run a company. They believed that all of the old contacts and relations would be useless, that people needed to be replaced because they could not change their behavior. The people expected big changes. We changed the government, why not change the management? They wanted to see blood. We at Ferox devoted a lot of energy to this transition. There was strong opposition to retaining top management, but people recognized quickly that we were playing an honest game. I believe our continuity was well chosen, and we have been able to change.

Since the very beginning of the revolution, I had close contact with the Civic Forum committee, the umbrella antiregime movement, in this plant and we agreed to share information with each other. I kept emphasizing that we didn't want the different political factions fighting here. We have to cooperate at work. If two individuals who must work together in the production process are fighting, the work cannot go on. After the purges following the Soviet invasion of 1968, working relationships were disrupted for nearly ten years and cooperation was damaged. I knew that the company would bear the most unpleasant results for years to come if we had fighting here. I met frequently with the Civic Forum and emphasized the damage that would be done by the clashes here. I met often with the company's branch of the People's Militia and I tried to persuade them to remain calm and to accept that the situation had changed. I emphasized that everyone needed to respect that we were here for production and that the political changes should not destroy the company on which we all depended.

Certain people tried to use the political changes to advance their own positions. They really didn't care about the political changes or the company, only themselves. They tried to take advantage of the situation. Because the Civic Forum was a broad umbrella movement, anyone could say they were a member. We agreed to involve the Civic Forum in the operation of the company by giving it a seat on the operating board of the company and by inviting its representatives to trade union-management meetings, but because the Civic Forum was participating in the running of the company, it had to be responsible for the behavior of its members. In this way we were able to prevent these opportunists from taking over the company. We even had a bulletin board that the Civic Forum could use. It once posted a notice that was very critical of management, and a foreman took the notice down. I put it back up; I felt that if we agreed to let them have a bulletin board we had to live with whatever they put there. Later, we banned the participation of all political parties in the company. So, when the Civic Forum itself broke apart into political parties, it eventually lost its seat on these management committees too.

Even during the most uncertain period of the revolution, we were able to keep production going with relatively little loss. People would start work a little later because they were busy exchanging news with each other when they arrived at the plant, and their breaks were a little longer for the same reason. But we had to be reasonable and couldn't take a hard line with them.

Not once have we in top management been caught lying. That was very important. People saw that management was working to protect the company from attacks. We had to show our people that we are here to protect their future. No one had to leave the company, and with the exception of one of my deputies, no one has left. I have had a job offer for more than double my salary here, but we all have a sense of responsibility to the company. When we had a problem with an order about one year ago, many people worked extra hours to save the good name of the company even though the problem was not their fault.

I first brought in CAPA Consulting back in 1988 because I wanted to change two attitudes in my managers: The system is perfect and problems are only created by people failing to carry out their jobs, and things don't change. I wanted them to know that the structure may change. Thanks to this cooperation (between CAPA and Ferox), we were able to anticipate, well before the revolution, the changes now being required of all companies.

Under our old system, the scope of responsibilities for a company's managing director were much wider than in the West, but the authority was much narrower. We have different tasks to do every day. We are a typical Czech company: We have a kindergarten; we own and maintain apartments for our employees; we have canteens. Up to five years ago, we were also responsible for our seventy-ton quota of dry hay.

Ten to fifteen years ago, the local authority discovered a shortage of hay. All companies in its region were made responsible for a quota of hay. Our assigned meadows were inaccessible for heavy mowing equipment, so we had to select those people from Ferox who understood how to work hand scythes. Our managerial problem was how to choose people who knew how to cut hay. Which employees were needed least that day? Who knew how to use scythes? Even our lawyer went out to cut hay. We had to provide lunches and transportation for them. Then the local authority decided that yields were too low, so we were invited to purchase a quota of fertilizer each spring. Later, the local authority decided that because we were contributing something of economic value to the agricultural cooperative, they should "pay us" for this work. So they paid us 40 koruny per ton—but our own cost was over 150 koruny per ton. After that, we bought a specialized machine to cut on these steep hillsides. A couple of years ago, this responsibility ceased, so now our problem is, who do we sell this equipment to?

Now we can laugh at it. It is the same as looking back on your experience as an army draftee: You look back and only see the comical aspects, you remember the amusing things. It was too crazy. We are here to produce chemical equipment. But then it was different—it was impossible to quarrel about it. It was horrible.

We have to spend a lot more energy to find new customers now. Someone from your system really cannot understand us. Five years ago, this was a strictly planned economy. The main problem was to organize production under conditions in which we were overloaded. The sales forecast was known two years in advance because the only customer was the state. The major problem was to meet the state's special requests for exports—through which the state hoped to make some extra hard-currency profits. Now, we have to find our own customers. Before, we had to take gifts to our suppliers in order to secure deliveries; now, we take gifts to our customers. The procurement problem was much bigger than the sales problem. It was a dictatorship of the suppliers; now, this system is gone. We need to increase our sales department by two or three times, and we lack sales methodology and experience. At present, the situation in our country is still very unstable. Even trying to understand all of the information that comes out each week is hard. Nobody knows what will happen tomorrow. But we are firmly committed to the belief that this company will survive. We believe in our capability to find solutions to our problems. This belief has three pillars.

The first pillar is improvisation. Every day brings new information. One example of how we have improvised is our management of the internal debt problem. Today, we owe our suppliers about 60 million koruny, and our customers owe us 150 million koruny—this latter is the value of over three months of our production. Most of our suppliers retire their debt within the ninety-day period. We have only about five customers who have not paid us within ninety days. They are all big state-owned companies. One is the national railroad. It is impossible to know whether these are bad debts. We cannot imagine that the country will let the state-owned railroad go bankrupt. But we do not know whether a Western partner will come in and help any of these companies to become profitable. Everything is uncertain right now. Recently, we invoiced about 77 million koruny but received only 37 million koruny. Compared to the rest of Czechoslovak industry, we are in good shape.

Another example of how we have learned to improvise started with one of our suppliers. Our stainless steel supplier wrote us a letter saying, "You owe us five million koruny, so we have decided to postpone your next delivery for two months because you haven't paid us." When this letter arrived, we had to solve that problem immediately. So we discovered that we have knowledge of which companies owe money to other companies. We discovered that the steel mill is a supplier of pig iron to the stainless steel manufacturer, and the steel mill is one of our customers. We found a complete circle of debt. So we got all of the economics deputies for all three companies together and we agreed to simultaneously cancel as much of this circle of debt as possible. Each controller crossed the debt off the ledger and sent a fax to confirm.

This was so successful that we have tried to find other complete debt circles—some involve four parties, some even more. We have now hired one person whose sole responsibility is to try to clear debts in this way. But if there had been a computer network connecting us with all our customers and suppliers—which is not the case yet—we could be much more efficient. It is estimated that the entire Czechoslovak industry has 100 to 150 billion koruny of this internal debt, equal to one-third of the country's gross domestic product.

The second pillar is privatization. There are several reasons we believe privatization is the most important precondition for reaching our long-term goal. First, we need investment money, and it is simply not available from local sources. We need new technology to modernize and to reach European technical standards. We need to improve our physical infrastructure to be more efficient.

Second, we need know-how. What I mean by know-how is how to organize. We need information about how to conduct successful sales activities, to overhaul the financial and accounting systems, and how to manage. The smallest difference between us and the West is the difference between our shop floor workers. Our welders are highly skilled. We need injections of knowledge, but we don't want to copy the West thoughtlessly. The West is the source of information, but it is up to us to use the information properly to reach our goals.

I feel that the biggest difference is in sales activities. Before I thought it was just a matter of selling. Now, after working for a year with APCI, I see that it is much more than that. The main thing is to get customers who will be able to pay, and helping potential customers find the means to pay.

The third pillar for our survival is our long-term strategy. Our long-term goal is to become one of the most prosperous companies in the country by European standards. Privatization is our next objective but not our ultimate goal. It is not why we are here. It is a conduit, a tool to help us reach our goal. Privatization has taken a great deal of our time and attention, and we hope it will end soon. Now, we must wait for final approval. We don't want any agitation that might disrupt or slow down the government's approval of privatization.

At present, there is a coalition government and there is a great deal of political jockeying, as well as uncertainty about future political stability. We have an interim postrevolutionary parliament to guide the nation through the immediate postrevolutionary turmoil and develop a new constitution. Because we are a government-owned company, there is always the risk that the politicians will want to use us for political purposes. However, we are not very worried about this because we are in relatively good shape economically and have a good privatization plan, and they have enough other things to worry about. We are trying to get away from political interference and be fully independent as quickly as we can, and we must be privatized to do that. Until we are privatized, we cannot do anything—we cannot sell property or reorganize.

As part of our privatization agreement, we have had numerous discussions with APCI about what we should do to reach our long-term goals. The agreement covers the training they will provide for our people in their facilities, know-how transfer, and so on.

We found APCI two years ago, before the revolution. As part of our 1988 strategic plan, developed with a consulting company, we began to look for Western companies with which to form a joint venture. Of course, we were too modest and vague at the beginning. We were just looking for someone to talk to us. We didn't know enough then. You can't create big plans without information. Before that, we had a bad experience trying to make contact with a Russian company, so we began to look for a Western company. We contacted the major companies in the industry. Only APCI was willing to sit with us then. During a conference in the United Kingdom, several of our researchers had an initial confidential discussion with several people from APCI. We offered them certain opportunities.

Then the revolution arrived and we realized very quickly that we would be facing economic reforms. We have been a monopolist supplier for most of our customers. We felt that this monopoly was neither sustainable nor desirable. Now we could see that the currency becoming convertible would not only allow foreign competition here but would also allow us to go international. We saw that we would soon be facing a normal market, and we did not have the know-how.

Of all the major companies we approached, APCI seemed the most flexible. About January or February 1990, we started our first real discussions. One of APCI's Western competitors had formed a joint venture with one of our customers. APCI expressed its interest in our gas separators and cryogenic units. In April 1990, I visited the company, but still not openly; it would have been dangerous to release information at that time.

In July 1990, we signed a letter of intent for the first joint venture, scheduled for the second quarter of 1991. This joint venture involves the new business, gas production, as well as the transfer of our existing cryogenic business to APCI.

In January 1991, we began our own gas business. We wanted to show APCI that we could get it started without them. We have only about 10 percent of the market, but because many of the customers who depended on us for necessary equipment also buy gas, we thought we would be able to influence more of them to do business with us in the future. Because our containers are 30 percent cheaper than any they can get elsewhere and are just as good, we hoped to retain and even increase our market share for both gas and equipment.

After more months of discussion we created the joint venture with APCI, which came into formal existence in April 1991. APCI owns 51 percent and Ferox, 49 percent. The joint-venture agreement also covers the distribution and sales of cryogenic equipment and liquified gases in Central and Eastern Europe, over which the joint venture has exclusive dealership.

Now we are working on the second joint venture, a large refinery that the first joint venture will need to produce the gas. It is a $70 million project that involves Ferox, APCI, and another Czechoslovak company. We signed the letter of intent in March 1991.

Finally, we agreed to the marriage of Ferox with APCI through the privatization program. They have controlling interest because they like to control what they are paying for. We had to show APCI that we were a good prospect. We have established markets. There is some synergy in the cryogenics area.

Sometimes they don't understand how it is here. I was describing to Heinz Hoffman, the European vice president, and Bill Stoughton, the U.S. chief engineer, how we would use the dependence of our tank customers to influence them to buy gas from us. Stoughton put his head in his hands; he was horrified by the rough way we do business here. But Hoffman, who fled East Germany years ago, said, "Good, good." He understood the situation and got the point right away. You in the West have developed an excellent system for yourselves over the years; you are used to shooting with a silencer on your guns. But we live in the real Wild East during this period here. You Americans can afford to be all polite and honest. If you act like that in this environment today, you won't get anywhere. It's a lot of trouble to explain.

Right now, neither APCI nor Ferox can pull out. This is a marriage with no possibility of a divorce. We are proud that we were able to get a company from the West, that we found the right worm for the hook. U.S. companies often appear too lazy and afraid. The Germans are the most aggressive here; they know the market, the territory, and our mentality.

APCI feels that we are a large company; Ferox will be its biggest manufacturing facility. APCI has 250 people in its U.S. plant and 250 in its UK plant. Its target is to increase our efficiency. We wonder what will be the effect on the other parts of our company, where APCI has no product expertise. Our agreement with APCI says employment will be kept at a reasonable level based on profit in all of the product lines. There is also another uncertainty: After privatization, what will we do with our service work? Some of it may be more efficiently provided by us, but each case has to be examined in detail. APCI wanted me to hire a security service. We have them now in Czechoslovakia, but they usually have only lazy, young people. These pensioners we have now are the cheapest, best solution for us.

For each of these services I will want to review options such as retaining it or leasing it. After privatization, I want to create a steering committee made up of high-level managers from APCI and Ferox to study these areas—people with sufficient knowledge to go through it all and to indicate our weak points. The chief of APCI's manufacturing facility told me, "Don't copy us."

APCI managers are very slow and careful. They evaluate projects step-by-step. They evaluate, then they estimate the finances; they check and check again. I can see how deeply interested the Americans are in the finances, so that even if an order is canceled it will still make money. Before, Ferox was a core manufacturing facility. All of the other kinds of tasks were done by others, for example, the foreign trade companies handled foreign sales. Now we are free to do this work ourselves, but we don't have anyone who understands how to write these contracts, issue letters of credit, conduct currency transfers, and so on. Today, we know about 50 percent of what it takes to make a good deal.

Now, I can see that a successful company is cautious, and why. What is the customers' ability to pay? Sometimes I have been disappointed in the cautious, slow progress in negotiations with APCI. It is their natural style. They must be sure of success. APCI has an entire system of making offers: stages one, two, and three. They protect their power and capability. Even after a U.S. group said that our second joint-venture plant was financially sound, the European Bank for Reconstruction and Development (to whom we have applied for a loan) requires yet another group of Western financial experts to examine the project. This project will have a firm base. Before the 1989 revolution, getting investment money was a grammar exercise. Who could paint the rosiest future? Or an important minister might have a pet project, and then after it was built, someone had to find a market for its production.

To inform the employees about the privatization program, we had to respond to their natural reaction: What will be the future of the company? In the spring, we started to organize meetings of employees, and we explained it to them—all that we knew and our intentions. We have been lucky to retain the trust of our people. We don't have any problems with public disobedience like they sometimes do elsewhere. Of course, the people here have mixed feelings about the relationship with APCI. Many are afraid of losing their jobs. APCI expects us to strictly reduce our staff because productivity is very low here.

There are different levels of employee interest in the privatization program. Some employees would like to talk about it all night. When we had our April meeting to explain the privatization project, we filled our largest canteen to overflowing. We always have our meetings right after the first shift. This was a very good turnout, almost a third of those who were not required to be at their stations.

Many employees still take things lightheartedly. Management's job is to see that employees give 105 percent (the 5 percent is overtime for some extra income; employees don't want more overtime than that because it would cut into their free time). Many believe their only job is to show up at the start of the shift. Quality? Well, everyone makes mistakes. But most here have a sense of responsibility. If they are caught stealing or drinking on the job, they are fired immediately. The trade union supports this policy. APCI agreed to respect the trade union in the privatization agreement.

We are confident that we will have our approval for privatization by the end of 1991. Then we can begin to implement our privatization plan: restructuring the company and selling the support services and equipment we don't need. We need to provide a stable environment in the next three months. We want the image of a smoothly running company. The next couple of months is going to be decisive for many years to come.

Karel Nýć, Commerce Manager

In the past, we negotiated only delivery date and price. Now we negotiate much more. For example, we have added penalties for late payment. One of the ways I try to tell whether we are going to have trouble collecting payment from a potential customer is if they want to negotiate over the penalties. In addition, if it is a customer I don't know well, I ask our economics department to use its good connections with the banker to find out whether the company is in a good financial position.

Now, we have some completely new customers, but Ferox is unknown in the West. One new customer, a Japanese company, is making a purchase from us. Its representatives have just made their ninth visit to the plant in four months; they come twice a month. This Japanese company has very detailed rules for technical requirements. They require sixteen different checks on a flange. They require more detailed production plans and want these plans to be provided very rapidly. I have to put more pressure on the technical department to get us information quickly to make a proposal. Western customers want a quote back in ten days and will not even look at it if it comes in after that. Pressure from my department affects all areas. There is more pressure on the pricing department to provide information more rapidly. For this big Japanese project, after we had a firm order I called a meeting of all of the directors. Previously, this was completely unheard of. I wanted them to know that this was an important order.

We have not made these same changes for our old customers—we treat their orders as we always have. So far, we are closely tracking new accounts only because this still requires a lot of effort. But these new customers force us to make gradual changes in purchasing, planning, production, and control. We are not as computerized as APCI; we have many workers in purchasing and only two terminals. They must do their spreadsheets and economic analyses by hand. Due to these changes, other departments are under more pressure. There are lots of new activities emerging; many people have to do new things to change their jobs, and they complain. Under the old system, everything was petrified; everything was done the same way for decades. People do not know how to change, and they are reluctant. I know very well that they should get some training, but for the time being, we have to change on the go. Later, perhaps when APCI gets in, there will be more opportunity to work in a more structured fashion.

Another difference is that we have to make our own sales directly. Before the revolution, for foreign sales we went through one of the foreign trade companies. You know, before there was this almost insurmountable barrier between us and the outside world. In about six months we are going to have to establish a Ferox office in Prague because we cannot get people with foreign-trade skills to move here. For some sales business, it is easier for customers to fly into Prague and for us to meet them there.

All of these changes take time and money. I have to find a real manager for each activity. It's not easy to ask a fifty-year-old to learn German and to master a computer. Before, we were so overloaded with orders that the customers came to us. Now, the sales people have to visit the customers, and they don't like to travel. All of that has to change.

We cannot know what our focus should be in three years. Nowadays our best customer can change into our worst customer in six months. For example, Poland has changed its customs duties six times in the past year. Even the banks do not know what is really happening in the companies. For the next few years, the winners will be those who survive.

Jaroslav Mráček, Production Manager

We have one goal: to survive the next two years. We sacrifice everything for this goal. There are multiplying pressures for quality of production, especially for the blue-collar workers—the exempt workers were already working at a high standard. I will need two or three more managers in production. Some of my managers held party posts and were members of the so-called People's Militia. The new law forces me to remove them from management positions for the next five years.

Unfortunately, production has traditionally had a lower status than other areas; therefore, it has always been difficult to attract good people. It's a high-pressure job; managers have to resolve conflicts every day. They would rather escape to the laboratories.

The blue-collar workers are often so naive. They don't understand that if they want the same living standards as the Germans, they have to accept the whole package. The way I let them know that standards are higher now is by fully supporting the head of quality control. This is a big change. Previously, quality control was the enemy of the production department. I really need to support the quality-control manager because his people are even worse. Quality is the production supervisors' responsibility; they have the ultimate responsibility for quality. Now, the pressure on them is more accentuated. I have been in this job for a year, and my first and most important goal is to improve production quality.

Many of the employees understand, but some do not; it depends on their maturity. Some are much too self-confident. They agree, in general, that they need to improve themselves, but they want to start with someone else. They are used to comparing their work to that done in other companies in Czechoslovakia, and our work has always been good. Now that we are exposed to the West, we see poorer comparative results. The skill levels are high, but there is a lot of complacency.

We have been introducing the International Standards Organization Program for quality improvement that we received from APCI. It involves monthly meetings run by the production unit manager. Before, the meetings were always focused on party politics, but the employees now recognize that the accent has changed. I have asked the personnel manager to add more information on quality to the new-employee training programs. I approached the local technical college to work with them [the college] to change their curriculum—we cannot wait for the Education Ministry.

The union has been flexible and supportive so far, although sometimes it can be unreasonable and want to have influence without responsibility. The union doesn't protect employees who are doing a bad job.

Our progress on quality improvement was reviewed by the chief APCI quality man the last time he was here, and he was not happy with our progress. He lives in quite another world. People who have spent some time here have adjusted better. We were given thousands of pages of English text to process. He says we are too slow; he has doubts about whether we are committed to change.

APCI managers have voiced their dislikes. Our technical procedures are inadequate, our product line is too broad, and we need to focus. But in choosing which products to drop, we cannot make an error because it would involve the loss of many millions of koruny of revenue. APCI itself could be more diversified. There is no reason they cannot sell various equipment as we do. Different products would help them cope with instability in other lines. Not all in APCI have the same opinion. Some see far ahead and want the long-term prosperity of the company.

It's clear that whatever benefits APCI brings to us, it will also take care of itself. There are many completely new situations here. APCI managers have problems knowing who they can trust here. They will face the problem of picking the right people to run Ferox their way, people who have enough energy to turn it around. It will be an enormous amount of work for domestic people. We know that we are all being tested by them. They have been coming here for more than a year and are working around here freely, looking to see if the pace is fast enough. They are evaluating me and the commerce director in particular.

I am convinced that APCI was the right company to make a deal with. We want to enter this marriage without debts and with no liabilities. We want our performance level as close as possible to APCI's even though that is almost impossible. As soon as we achieve that level, it will be easier for us.

We must manage ourselves. But APCI should tell us our goals—so we are moving in the right direction. I'm glad APCI is a U.S. company because I am uncomfortable with the way German businesspeople behave here; the Americans have a milder style. I did not hesitate to support the choice of APCI, because the U.S. market is larger and more dynamic and the United States is the technical leader in many respects.

When APCI management gets control of Ferox, we will learn a lot of things we don't know now. I fully understand that APCI cannot tell us everything freely yet.

Vladislav Petrovka, Personnel Manager

Everything in this department will be affected by APCI's involvement. This is because we have never had a real human resources department in Děčín. Recruitment, performance evaluation, professional development, career planning, civilized ways of handling retirement—all are undeveloped here. I can see hardly any area that will be unaffected.

In this department, we are responsible for all of the support activities—canteens, kindergartens, company flats, company-provided health care—as well as for building maintenance and office supplies. At present, compensation and benefits are in the economics department, but we really feel they should be our business.

My biggest headache is dealing with the serious blow to the personnel department's staff in the aftermath of the November revolution. This department was a stronghold of the Communist party and despised by many. Here were stored the secret files on employees; the employees were not supposed to be able to see them. This department was a refuge for many incompetent workers for whom the party found comfortable positions. Several people were removed in this department after the revolution. It was no tragedy that some of them left, given their attitudes and orientation.

The worst effect has been in the minds of the people: the assumption that we in personnel are dispensable. Many people think we are still doing the same political activities, for example, keeping secret files on people. Our real work—supervising the support activities—is less visible, and they don't see our role in those tasks.

With the exception of the managing director, the supervisors and managers are not interested in using this department effectively. If a supervisor needing a blue-collar worker comes in here, he tells us to get one and "don't you dare deliver one I don't like." But supervisors will not provide any details about their requirements. The delivery system must work, but quality isn't important to them.

It is a difficult task to teach every manager how to be more effective. Some supervisors mistreat their subordinates, so the best people sometimes leave. Some go to other companies, some decide to start their own businesses. Many bosses have no concept that they should take care of their employees' continuous development.

The burden of the past forty years is on our backs. Personnel policy is still something of a dirty word. There would be an uproar if I developed a succession plan—it would be seen as the restitution of the old "cadre reserve system" by which the party controlled positions. In that system, the party looked first for the most loyal people, then within that group, they tried to find the most suitable person for the position. Those in the personnel department were the party's mouth. The stink of the party's dead body is all over us.

Air Products and Chemicals, Inc.

Background

Air Products and Chemicals, Inc. (APCI) is an international gas products corporation of 15,000, headquartered in the United States, in Allentown, Pennsylvania, with $3 billion in annual sales. The APCI acquisition of Ferox was negotiated by a team of U.S., German, and British APCI executives. Initially, Nigel Chandler, a British APCI executive, was appointed as managing director of the new Ferox-Air Products joint venture. In the following interview, Chandler shares his experiences and observations on the challenges Western companies face in acquiring and forming joint ventures in the new Czech and Slovak Republics.

Nigel Chandler,
Joint-Venture Managing Director

I think you can see that Malec really runs Ferox. Last year in APCI there was a great deal of debate about the direction we were moving in forming this relationship with Ferox. You can imagine that it was a difficult decision. I genuinely believe it was the right decision. We will bring several important contributions to Ferox.

First, we bring know-how, which is a lot more than sheer technical knowledge. We bring specific know-how about the gas business. We know how to sell it commercially and where to make changes. We are a large successful gas company. Management skills that we bring are important also, but they're more difficult to define.

Second, we bring financial and accounting skills. Quite clearly, the free market accounting system needs to be adopted—particularly pricing and costing systems, which barely exist now. Everything was done by rules under the old system. We are setting up our accounting systems with the hope that they will be in accordance with the new Czechoslovak tax laws, which are due in January 1993. But at this point we don't even know what kinds of business expenses will be deductible in computing taxes.

Third, regarding the privatization, APCI brings technological skills, as well as marketing skills. Ferox brings local knowledge and a low-cost manufacturing base. It also has an existing customer base. We want to be able to manufacture our products here and also to export our products from this plant to the West. Compared to our other plants, we can make the product more cheaply here.

It is important to us that any acquisitions are made with the full support of local management. We need tremendous mutual cooperation. We think it is a good agreement, but we didn't undertake it lightly. It's not just the money, but the time. Heinz Hoffman, our European vice president, is spending a great deal of his time on this project, and our senior legal people are spending a lot of time on it as well. It is a tremendous investment of our most valuable managerial resources. The senior managers are very involved.

Of course, we have had to sell ourselves to Ferox. Ferox had choices—we're quite aware of that. We want to drive it, but it's important to work together. The engineering staff at Ferox are very good. It was important that we bring our best engineering people out to talk to them.

After privatization we are clearly going to have to bring in a Western accounting person, a manufacturing person, and other staff. Probably they will need to be single, as it would be very difficult to move a Western family to Děčín. There are no English schools here in Děčín.

We will also move key individuals from Ferox into jobs in our Western plants for six months to a year. We will actually place individuals in jobs for which they will be held responsible. We will be interchanging people.

APCI has been in most countries in Western Europe for up to thirty years and has more recently developed businesses in the Pacific Rim. We have experience in starting businesses in developing countries, but we have no experience in a former Communist country. It is very important that a company such as ours understands that this is not a third world country. It is a developed, heavily industrial area that has been dormant for many years but that still has employees with high educational levels and well-qualified engineers. The industry is old, but there is a lot of production capacity.

It appears to be quite difficult to recruit the people we want. There are many good jobs in Prague, and people with the skills we need are unhappy to move to Děčín. It is partly cultural. People in Europe just don't move like Americans, and they value their leisure time more.

It is also important to a large multinational company to understand any extra liabilities that are taken on in the acquisition of a large manufacturing company here. For instance, any liability for previous environmental damage must be fully assessed and minimized by such actions as taking soil samples.

An apparent problem here is the lack of depth in managerial talent. Czech companies are very compartmentalized and are not very good at recognizing young talent; they don't think laterally.

One great concern to any Western company acquiring a Czech manufacturing facility is a general level of overstaffing compared to the West. This is particularly apparent in the administrative areas.

The employment ethic is amazingly harsh here compared to the Western standard. Of course, you know that the remuneration is very much lower and there have been no meaningful pay differentials. A welder may have a higher monthly salary than a salesperson. It is likely that Czechs with commercial and language skills will begin to command higher salaries as they gain experience.

Another example of the harsh personnel practices here is that a supervisor has the authority to cut an employee's bonus pay for what we would consider to be trivial things. At the end of the month he decides the employee didn't do a task he thought should have been done, and he cuts the bonus by 10 percent. Management here is based much more on fear as a motivation. Managers do not know how to motivate without fear. There is no concept at all of carrots, just of sticks. They have the concept of working hard but not the concept of achievement. However, we have built a fantastic commitment on our joint-venture team.

One thing that any Western manager who comes here will have to understand is the cultural differences. I've learned that some aspects of the culture you have to keep.

For one thing, I sign a lot more paper here in Czechoslovakia. This is definitely a holdover from the old Communist system, where all commands were written. It is very difficult to travel here on business; you need written forms and permission to travel. If there is not prior written permission for a trip, the insurance company will not reimburse if there is an accident. Salespeople cannot just get in their cars and call on customers. I have tried to get rid of forms and to just talk to my employees.

The Czech government must first approve the privatization plan, which is expected in the near future. Then, the Ferox and APCI managers will be free to begin to make the changes necessary to meet their strategic objectives, and the process of carrying out the acquisition by APCI will begin.

There are adjustments and changes in store for both companies in the future, but we are sure that Ferox will make a good partner.

Notes

1. The names of all of the individuals in this case have been changed.

■

CHAPTER FIVE

Downsizing of Personnel
at the Slovakia Steel Company

In the fall of 1991, Marian Kavols, top personnel officer at Slovakia Steel,[1] was beginning to believe that his time had finally arrived. As a fifty-year-old business manager in Czechoslovakia, he had been troubled nearly all his life with the thought that he was a man cursed with unfortunate timing. His country had been governed for over forty years by a rigid socialist system and command economy. This presented a manager like himself with unwanted restrictions imposed by tight state control of nearly all business enterprises. With the November 1989 revolution in Czechoslovakia, Kavols thought that perhaps his curse was finally lifting.

Kavols was hardly the stereotype of an Eastern European manager. He dressed in stylish Italian suits, traveled outside Central and Eastern Europe as extensively as he could, and was widely regarded as a gracious host and charming conversationalist. He balanced a self-deprecating sense of humor with a cool command of his staff. He was well educated with a Ph.D. in engineering, formally indoctrinated in Marxism-Leninism, and self-schooled in free market economic principles. Two years after the revolution in Czechoslovakia, he, like many of his management counterparts, faced previously unimaginable opportunities and challenges for both his personal career and his company.

Slovakia Steel

Slovakia Steel is the largest producer of steel plate and sheet products in the former Czechoslovakia. The facility is located in a city of 260,000 residents

Carrie R. Leana is associate professor of organizational behavior and human resources management at the Katz Graduate School of Business, University of Pittsburgh. Her areas of research include participative management structures, authority distribution in work organizations, and responses to plant closings and job loss. She is author of *Coping with Job Loss: How Individuals, Organizations, and Communities Respond to Layoffs* (with D. Feldman).

situated in eastern Slovakia close to the Ukraine border. The enterprise is made up of six divisions (see Figure 5.1); the steel-making division is the largest, employing approximately 15,000. The main products manufactured at Slovakia Steel are steel plates and sheets for commercial and structural use. The facility produces both hot- and cold-rolled steel products and supplies the automobile industry as well as the construction, food-processing, and appliance industries.

The Slovakia Steel facility is a relatively modern one, constructed in the 1960s. The facility is fully integrated, operating a blast furnace as well as steel-making and finishing lines. The Slovakia Steel facility includes all phases of the steel-making process from coke making to product finishing. In 1991, approximately 30% of the steel production at Slovakia Steel was continuously cast, a process now considered essential to quality steel making; the remaining steel production was cast using ingot mold technology, considered to be outdated and inefficient by world industry standards.

In 1991, Slovakia Steel sold its products to a diverse group of customers spanning Eastern and Western Europe as well as Asia and the Middle-East. The company's largest foreign customers in 1991 were Yugoslavia, China, Germany, France, the USSR, Poland, and India. In 1991, approximately 42 percent of Slovakia Steel's products were exported to countries outside of the former Eastern bloc.

The World Steel Industry

The global steel industry has undergone substantial changes since World War II.[2] The most fundamental of these is the growth in raw-steel production, which grew from a little under 200 million tons in 1950 to over 780 million tons in 1989. Since the late 1970s, this growth has been experienced largely by third world countries. Several industrialized countries have reduced capacity and employment during this time period, resulting in overall declines in world capacity. Moreover, the mix of producers within industrialized countries has changed significantly. The United States, traditionally the leader in world production, has now been significantly surpassed by Japan and the combined European Economic Community (EEC) countries (see Table 5.1).

Trade

International trade in steel has also changed markedly. With the entry of many countries into steel producing, trade changed from being essentially an exchange between those countries that produced steel and those that did not to an exchange among steel-producing countries. In 1988, 26 percent of world steel output was traded compared to 10 percent of world output in 1950. These changes in trading and production have resulted in a much more cost-

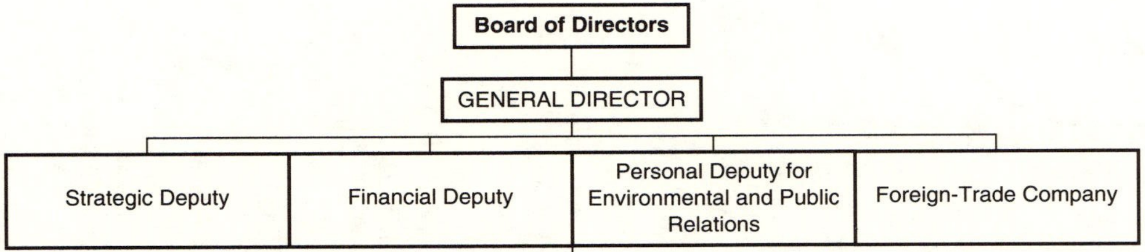

STEEL	MANUFACTURING	CERAMICS	SERVICE	ENGINEERING	INFORMATION SYSTEMS
Furnace	Engineering plant	Limestone quarry	Technical services	Process automation	Projection of automation systems
Technology	Foundry	Lime works	Commercial services	Projecting	Rationalization
Research & Testing	Bridge Plant	Fire-brick plant	House of culture	Realization plant	Technique of automation systems
Sales	Radiator-manufacturing plant	Tar-dolomite plant	Accommodation and recreation	Development	Realization of automation systems
Finishing	Pipe-welding plant	Sand quarry	Storing		
Service center	Electronics	Maintenance	Dwelling service		
15,000 employees	5,000	1,100	2,000	500	2,200

Board of Directors — GENERAL DIRECTOR — Strategic Deputy, Financial Deputy, Personal Deputy for Environmental and Public Relations, Foreign-Trade Company

FIGURE 5.1 Organizational Chart for Slovakia Steel.

TABLE 5.1   Raw Steel Output in the United States, Japan, and the EEC, 1973–1989 (millions of tons)

	United States	Japan	EEC[a]
1973	136.8	119.3	162.0
1974	132.8	117.1	168.1
1975	105.8	102.3	137.8
1976	116.1	107.4	146.1
1977	113.7	102.4	138.4
1978	124.3	102.1	145.3
1979	123.7	111.7	154.0
1980	101.5	111.4	142.0
1981	109.6	101.7	139.9
1982	67.7	99.5	125.1
1983	76.8	97.2	123.2
1984	83.9	105.6	134.4
1985	80.1	105.3	135.7
1986	74.0	98.3	125.9
1987	80.9	98.5	126.5
1988	90.7	105.7	137.7
1989	88.4	107.9	140.0

[a]Includes production of current twelve member countries for all years.
Source: William T. Hogan, *Global Steel in the 1990s: Growth or Decline.* New York: Lexington, 1991, p. 2.

conscious and competitive industry in which continuous technological improvements, capital investment, and labor efficiency are required.

Czechoslovakia in the World Market

In this competitive world market, Czechoslovak producers realized some temporary advantages in labor costs due to low wages and depressed currency, and some severe disadvantages in technology and capital investment. Although Slovakia Steel was considered a modern facility by Eastern European standards, its technology and product quality lagged behind Western countries and many third world producers. Moreover, because the steel industry in Czechoslovakia operated for over forty years in a managed economy where products were allocated rather than marketed, its managers were behind in adapting to the rapid changes inherent in a competitive world industry. In no area was this lag more pronounced than in the management of the labor force.

The Labor Force at Slovakia Steel

In 1991, Slovakia Steel had a total work force of close to 25,000 employees; approximately 15,000 of them were in the steel-making division. The work force at Slovakia Steel was unionized and represented by KOVO, the Metalworkers' Federation in Czechoslovakia, which had a total of over 1.4 million members. In the steel-making division, the work force was relatively young

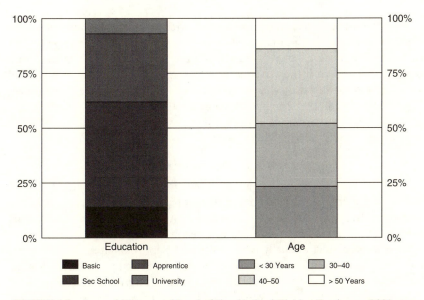

FIGURE 5.2   Age and Educational Level of Slovakia Steel Division Employees, 1991.

and reasonably well educated (see Figure 5.2). Over 50 percent of the blue-collar employees were under forty years of age. College graduates in the company were rare, but nearly half of Slovakia Steel's blue-collar employees had completed apprenticeship programs, and another third had finished secondary school.

A job in the steel division of Slovakia Steel was considered by most residents of the region to be a good one. The job offered relatively high pay for Slovakia—approximately 5,000 koruny per month in 1991. Although this is quite low by U.S. and Western European standards (5,000 koruny = approximately U.S. $166 in 1991), the cost of living was also substantially lower. In addition, the company provided housing and transportation allowances, meals, family recreational facilities, pension payments, and other subsidies not often included in Western compensation packages.

Labor Costs

The low wages relative to Western Europe and the United States provided Slovakia Steel with a potential competitive advantage in world markets. In fact, Slovakia Steel's labor expenses were a smaller percentage of total costs per ton of steel than those in countries such as the United States and Japan, and even in countries with low standards of living such as Brazil and Korea.

Kavols and other managers at Slovakia Steel were concerned, however, that this advantage would not be a long-lasting one. First, with the socialist government no longer in place in Czechoslovakia, the state was beginning to disengage from its role of social provider and price regulator, leaving citizens to manage housing, health care, and sharply rising food costs on their own. This caused a demand for increases in individual wages to cover these escalating costs. Second, even if the state did not disengage from its former roles and spur demand for increased wages, with travel to Western Europe now relaxed, Slovakia Steel and other companies would likely face the loss of their best employees to countries such as Germany, where wages and the standard of living were much higher than in Czechoslovakia.

Labor Force Efficiency

There were other, more pressing, factors fueling Kavols's concern about the ability of the company's work force to compete in world markets over the long term. In particular, he was concerned about the size and efficiency of the work force. In 1991, the steel-making division produced approximately four million tons of steel annually while employing approximately 12,500 blue-collar employees and 2,500 in staff. Although depressed wages kept Slovakia Steel's labor costs per ton low relative to those of international competitors, the company's staffing levels were far higher than those in any other competing country.

In the United States, for example, the integrated steel producers employed 169,000 people while shipping 84,100,000 tons of steel in 1989. This averages to 497.6 tons per employee per year. At Slovakia Steel, 15,000 employees produced four million tons per year or an average of 266.7 annual tons per employee—a little over half of the production per employee in the United States.

With such high employment levels, Slovakia Steel also performed poorly on common measures of productivity such as labor hours required to produce a ton of steel (labor hour per metric ton in Table 5.2). As shown in Table 5.2, integrated producers in the United States, Japan, and Western European countries such as Germany and France averaged between 6.2 and 6.7 worker hours per metric ton. At Slovakia Steel the worker hours to produce a metric ton were nearly double those figures, at 12.4. Using this measure, Slovakia Steel was approximately half as productive as most of its world competitors.

The Need for Work Force Reductions

Kavols was convinced that the only viable way to improve labor efficiency at Slovakia Steel was to drastically reduce the size of the work force. With wages at Slovakia Steel already low and sure to rise as the Czechoslovak government became less willing to subsidize its citizens' standards of living, reducing employees' wages was not a viable option. Slovakia Steel was well below its global competitors in employment costs per hour. The problem for Slovakia Steel was not high labor costs per employee but rather the large number of employ-

TABLE 5.2 Certain Integrated Steel Producers: Comparative Pretax Operating Costs,[a] May 1989

	USA	Japan	West Germany	U.K.	France	Canada	Australia	South Korea	Taiwan	Brazil	USSR[b]
Exchange rate (per $)	$1.00	139	DME1.97	0.62	16.66	C$1.19	A$1.31	W664	NT$25.6	Ncr$1.09	R.62
Operating rate (percent)	95	85	95	95	95	95	95	100	100	100	100
					Dollars per metric ton shipped						
Raw materials											
Iron ore to plant	43	33	35	32	32	41	33	33	34	20	23
Coal to plant	59	67	68	66	66	63	34	67	67	83	65
Scrap[c]	15	-5	-2	6	0	5	—	0	0	0	10
Other	186	195	184	189	184	168	194	192	182	143	202
Materials cost total	303	290	285	293	282	277	261	292	283	246	300
Labor											
Employment cost/hr	26	21	19	15	18	24	18	7	9	4	4
Worker hours/metric ton	6.2	6.6	6.4	6.4	6.4	6.7	7.7	8.4	8.9	14.4	14.5
Labor cost total	158	135	118	96	115	157	136	56	80	52	58
Operating costs	461	425	403	389	397	434	397	348	363	298	358
Depreciation expense	25	75	37	18	28	27	25	85	71	85	44
Interest expense	9	20	14	1	16	16	28	17	11	45	—
Pretax operating costs	495	520	452	408	441	477	450	450	445	428	402

[a]Dollar figures for cold-rolled sheet per metric ton shipped.

[b]The USSR facility is Novollpetsk, which produces 100% continuous-cast steel. This is the best flat rolling plant in the Soviet Union.

[c]Integrated steel mills sometimes generate more scrap than they use.

Source: U.S. International Trade Commission. *Steel Industry Annual Report: On Competitive Conditions in the Steel Industry and Industry Efforts to Adjust and Modernize.* Report to the President on Investigation no. 332–289 under Section 332 of the Tariff Act of 1930; USITC Publication no. 2316. Washington, D.C., 1990, p. 52

ees it was supporting. This was the reason its efficiency measures were so poor. Kavols was convinced that it was only a matter of time before rising wages caused labor costs to become another major obstacle to Slovakia Steel's ability to compete in world markets.

Implementing Work Force Reductions

Although Kavols was sure that work force reductions were necessary, he was less clear about how to implement these personnel cuts. His goal was to slash both blue-collar and staff employees in the steel division by 25 percent—a total of 3,750 employees—within the next two years.

There was no precedent in Czechoslovakia for making decisions regarding which employees would be dismissed and which would remain. Criteria commonly used for implementing work force reductions in Western countries, such as seniority or merit, were never before considered or, in the case of merit, even assessed in most Czechoslovak firms. To help him determine how to best implement these reductions, Kavols solicited advice from a variety of experts both inside and outside the company.

Several months earlier he had contacted Professor John Downey, a leading expert in the United States on the effects of business downsizing and unemployment. Downey had visited Slovakia Steel and consulted with Kavols and his staff on the problems facing the company and its employees. He had subsequently written to Kavols expressing his strong reservations about any reductions in personnel, arguing that the disruptions it would cause far outweighed the benefits Kavols hoped to achieve (see Appendix 5.1).

Kavols had also asked Vladimir Bartwicz, the company's chief psychologist, for assistance in designing a plan to implement the personnel reductions. Bartwicz recommended that the reductions be accomplished through a scientific selection process in which standardized test scores were used to determine which employees would be let go. He summarized his recommendations in a memo (see Appendix 5.2).

Kavols consulted the trade union to assist in his decisionmaking. Predictably, the union was opposed to any reductions in the workforce but agreed that a 5 percent decrease would be tolerable. Union leaders proposed that redundant employees be reassigned to other jobs created through new investments made by the company. If reductions were to occur, the union proposed that those selected for dismissal should be employees best able to find new jobs. This meant retaining some workers who were least efficient while discharging some who were the company's best employees. Kavols received a memo from Ladislav Demko, president of the trade union local, that summarized the union's positions (see Appendix 5.3).

Social and Political Considerations

Regardless of how the work force reductions were carried out, implementing them at all would be a difficult and delicate undertaking. Although unemployment is common in Western Europe and the United States, it was virtually unheard of in Czechoslovakia under the socialist system. Prior to the 1989 Revolution, everyone had the right to a job. In fact, managers were compensated in part on the basis of the number of employees they could attract. At Slovakia Steel this policy was evidenced by the bloated work force, which was systematically built up over the years by its managers. Although many people now agreed, at least in theory, that Czechoslovakia's move from a command to a free market economy would require some painful transitions, most citizens were unprepared for the harsh reality of unemployment.

Kavols was concerned about the effect of the downsizing on the community and the political climate of the region. Slovakia Steel was the largest employer in a region that had little else in its economic base. The city, in fact, grew up around the steel plant, with the population tripling from 1965 to 1990. To accommodate the population growth, additional housing was constructed, health facilities were expanded, transportation systems were built, and educational and cultural services were created. These were all accomplished with the assistance of Slovakia Steel, which now provided not only jobs but also educational, health, and recreational benefits and facilities to a substantial percentage of the city's population.

Kavols was further concerned that those employees dismissed from Slovakia Steel would have great difficulty finding employment elsewhere and would remain on the city's unemployment rolls for the indefinite future. Unemployment in Slovakia was already shaping up as a volatile political issue, fueling the fire of separatism already kindled in the region. The unemployment rate in Slovakia, at approximately 9.5 percent in the fall of 1991, was nearly triple that in the Czech federation, which stood at 3.5 percent. In the city in which Slovakia Steel was located, there were already nearly 10,000 registered unemployed by the fall of 1991.

Kavols's Dilemma

Kavols was scheduled to make a presentation to the board of directors of Slovakia Steel concerning the planned layoffs and their implementation. He was to provide a plan for the board's approval that detailed the timing and nature of the proposed reductions of personnel. Kavols was rather certain of the recommendations he would make concerning the extent and timing of the reductions—15 percent permanent reductions in 1992, followed by a further 10 percent permanent reduction in 1993. But even though he had pondered the issue for months and had information and advice from a variety of sources both inside and outside the company, two weeks before the board meeting Kovals found himself still unsure of the criteria he would recommend to target employees for dismissal.

Kavols knew he must make a decision very soon if he was to have a polished report for the board within the next two weeks. He scheduled a staff meeting for the following afternoon to begin working on the draft. Determined to make up his mind that day, he again began to read through the various memoranda he had solicited to guide his deliberations.

Notes

1. Slovakia Steel is not a real company, and all personal names are fictional. This fictional case is based on the experiences of a state-owned metal-working company in Slovakia.

2. Much of this discussion is based on William T. Hogan, *Global Steel in the 1990s: Growth or Decline* (New York: Lexington Books, 1991).

Appendix 5.1

Mr. Marian Kavols
Managing Director, Personnel
Slovakia Steel

Dear Mr. Kavols:

As you requested, I have enclosed copies of some recent papers and reports I have written which describe my research on the effects of job loss on individuals and their families. Although most of this research was conducted in the United States and Great Britain, our findings should also be generalizable to countries such as Czechoslovakia. Briefly, our studies have convinced us that unemployment has a devastating effect on the individuals who lose their jobs, particularly when there are few opportunities for alternate employment. These effects are so disruptive and long-term that we must counsel against any policy that would increase unemployment in your region.

In our research we have found that individuals experience several types of distress as a result of losing their jobs. In study after study, job loss is associated with diminished psychological well-being. Symptoms range from increases in hostility, depression, and anxiety, to decreases in self-esteem, experienced pleasure, and life satisfaction. Also, more psychophysiological symptoms such as headaches, stomach upsets, sleep problems, and lack of energy are consistently found among the unemployed. More serious, many studies have shown a significantly greater potential for psychiatric illness among the unemployed and suicide rates that are as high as thirty times expected levels. In studies that correlate macroeconomic indicators, a sustained 1 percent rise in unemployment rates has been associated with a 4.1 percent increase in suicides and a 5.7 percent increase in reported homicides in the population.

Unemployment is found to be associated with physiological, as well as psychological, deterioration for the affected individuals. Studies have reported increases in a wide range of ailments evidenced by escalated hospitalization rates, disabilities, cardiovascular dysfunctions, hypertension, ulcers, bronchial disorders, vision problems, and serum cholesterol levels among the unemployed. The macroeconomic studies have reported a 1.7 percent increase in death due to stroke, heart, and kidney disease in the general population for every sustained 1 percent rise in unemployment rates.

Family relations are also likely to be adversely affected by job loss. Numerous studies have reported increased marital friction and stress among married couples when the husband loses his job. Relationships with children also commonly deteriorate. Studies have reported a decline in children's perceptions of their parents' status and parental authority after the parent loses his or her job. The unemployed may also direct more aggression and hostility toward their children. Unemployment, in fact, has been cited as the most common precipitator of child abuse.

As I hope these studies can convince you, unemployment is a serious social problem your country is best to do without. While I realize that improving the efficiency of your workforce is of grave concern to you and other managers at Slovakia Steel, I urge you to refrain from us-

─────────────

This and the next two appendix communications were created by the author for the purpose of discussion.

ing workforce reductions as a solution to this problem until alternate employment opportunities can be created or found for your employees. I believe the human misery and social unrest that will surely accompany the large-scale layoffs you propose far outweigh the short-term advantages you might gain in productivity improvements. If you feel these layoffs must be implemented in Slovakia Steel's steel division, I recommend that the company make corresponding investments to create new jobs in other divisions so that employees may be transferred rather than dismissed.

Please feel free to call on me if I can be of any further assistance.

Sincerely yours,

John P. Downey, Ph.D.
Professor of Organizational Behavior

Appendix 5.2

CONFIDENTIAL MEMORANDUM

TO: Mr. Marian Kavols
     Managing Director, Personnel

FR: Dr. Vladimir Bartwicz
     Director, Psychology Department

RE: Implementing layoffs at Slovakia Steel

Since our meeting last month, I have given a great deal of thought to the issue of how to implement the planned reduction in the size of our workforce at Slovakia Steel. As you recall, at our meeting you had asked me to formulate a recommendation on the criteria that should be used to select employees for dismissal. After much deliberation and consultation with my staff of psychologists and sociologists, I have developed a plan that I feel is the most effective and fair way for the company to proceed with this delicate process.

As you know, my department is in charge of all intelligence, skill, and personality testing of Slovakia Steel employees, along with developing and implementing periodic surveys of employee attitudes and work feelings. As a progressive enterprise, Slovakia Steel has always been committed to this type of testing as the most scientific and advanced way to select and train employees. It is my strong belief that this scientific method of personnel management has contributed greatly to both the harmony in our workplace and the continued success of our enterprise.

I would like to propose that we also base our forthcoming workforce reductions on this scientific method and use the power of scientific testing to guide us in the selection of employees for dismissal. More specifically, I am suggesting that we base our dismissal decisions on the results of previously-administered tests of employee intelligence.

As you are no doubt aware, all employees are required to take the AZQ Intelligence Quotient Test before they are granted employment. Moreover, each employee is administered a new AZQ test every two years to ensure that there is consistency in the employee's intelligence quotient. I propose that we use employees' most recent AZQ Intelligence Quotient Test scores as the basis for dismissal decisions.

My rationale for this proposal is simple yet, I believe, quite compelling. As our enterprise moves to increase its presence in the world market, it will become increasingly crucial to have a well qualified workforce. The fundamental requirement for qualified employees is the capacity to quickly learn new skills and adapt to new methods of work and personnel practices. To learn and adapt, an individual must possess the temperament to do so but also, more importantly, the intelligence. Our AZQ test scores provide us with a precise and scientific method of assessing this intelligence. This is also the most equitable way of making distinctions among employees since the test is based on objective standards rather than subjective assessments.

To summarize, I propose that our dismissals in 1992 be comprised of those employees who score in the bottom 15% of the workforce on the AZQ Intelligence Quotient Test. Our dismissals in 1993 should be comprised of those employees who score in the bottom 10% of the remaining workforce on the AZQ Test. Using this method, at the end of 1993, we should have dismissed the 25% of employees with the lowest intelligence scores. Basing our dismissal decisions on the AZQ scores will ensure not only that we retain employees who are most able to learn and adapt, but also that we conduct the dismissals in the most scientific and therefore fair and equitable manner.

Please contact me at your earliest convenience so that we might further discuss my proposal and begin this delicate process in an orderly and dignified fashion.

Appendix 5.3

MEMORANDUM

TO: Mr. Marian Kavols
      Managing Director, Personnel
      Slovakia Steel

FR: Mr. Ladislav Demko
      President of Trade Union Local

RE: Planned Dismissal of Employees

As you know, it has always been the practice at Slovakia Steel to accomplish any reductions in the workforce through natural attrition–that is, through means such as retirements and voluntary leaves. Our trade union was quite alarmed to learn of your plan to abandon this long-standing practice and instead to now violently pare the workforce through involuntary dismissals. We are *strongly opposed* to your planned action. Although with the recent change in federal labor law management is no longer required to obtain the consent of the trade union to implement employee dismissals, we implore you to take no action without our consultation. If dismissals are not to be avoided, we urge that they be implemented according to the methods I have set forth in this memorandum. Before considering the issue of implementation, however, I would first like to address the more important concern of the level of workforce reductions.

Level of Workforce Reductions   We realize that times have changed. Our trade union supports many of the new goals of our country made possible by the Revolution. We know that with a market-driven economy we will no longer have the right to work by law and the guarantee of 100% employment of our people. Our aim is not to insist upon 100% employment; we realize this is detrimental to productivity and worker motivation. However, our trade union does aim to have the highest level of employment possible. We hope you will join us in our efforts to realize this goal and abandon your current plan of dismissing 25% of the workforce in the steel division within the next two years.

Instead of this level of dismissals, our trade union feels that 5% reductions over two years would be more appropriate. We have several recommendations for how employment in the steel division might be reduced without eliminating more than 5% of the workforce. In general, we believe that current employees can be maintained but transferred to other jobs and divisions. More specifically, we advocate the following steps.

1. Steel division employees who are not needed can be used to perform services such as painting and maintenance that are now contracted to other enterprises.

2. Slovakia Steel is currently considering a plan to open retail outlets for its consumer appliance products. This plan should be pursued and steel division employees transferred to these stores to work as sales clerks, inventory specialists, etc.

3. Slovakia Steel should invest in other businesses that are in high demand in Czechoslovakia (e.g., hotels and other businesses oriented toward tourism). Steel division employees can be transferred to the new jobs created by these new businesses.

4. Steel division employees should be retrained so that they might be more productive and efficient workers. With this retraining, dismissals should not be necessary.

Implementing Workforce Reductions   We as a nation have never before had to face the devastating issue of unemployment. Loss of work is a serious concern to our members and, indeed, to all our citizens. If dismissals are unavoidable in our quest for a market-driven economy, we insist that they be carried out in the most humane manner possible. First and foremost, we must ensure that our less fortunate brothers and sisters are cared for. We cannot abandon them to a competitive marketplace knowing in advance that they will not be able to compete. This would be immoral and detrimental to our society as a whole. We recommend that any unavoidable dismissals be carried out in the following manner:

1. We must protect the older workers. They will not be able to find new employment and cannot be abandoned to the permanent state of unemployment. They have served us the longest and we owe them the most. We therefore recommend that no worker over 50 be dismissed.

2. We must protect the younger workers. The young adults are our future and we must give them an opportunity to develop necessary job skills if they are ever to be successful in a market-driven economy. We therefore recommend that no worker below the age of 25 be dismissed.

3. Our workers who are mentally or physically handicapped are most vulnerable in a market economy. We as a society cannot leave the weak to the cruelties of a competitive marketplace and therefore cannot dismiss any of our small number of handicapped employees.

4. Single mothers must not be dismissed. They are the sole supporters of their children and cannot be left to poverty and unemployment.

5. If any group of workers must be dismissed, we recommend that it be married workers between the ages of 25 and 50, preferably those without children. These workers are most likely to be able to find other employment as they have had the experience to develop job skills, and are not so old as to be unattractive to potential new employers. Moreover, they are the strongest of our citizens and most likely to rebound from a job dismissal.

While I must reiterate that our trade union in no way advocates the dismissal of any employees, if you insist on carrying through with your plan, we must insist that you consider the factors we have outlined and spare the weak among our brothers and sisters. We wish to move to a market-driven economy but we do not want to destroy the good things about our society in the process. We strongly urge you to refrain from these dismissals. However, if we cannot convince you otherwise, we insist that you conduct any dismissals on the basis of our recommendations stated above.

CHAPTER SIX

———————————— ■ ————————————

Ecofluid

By the first of December 1989, Svatopluk and Vladimir Machrle headed an organized group to apply new technologies in the treatment and purification of water. The twin brothers had spent their lives in the study of wastewater purification and other aspects of ecology management. With the fall of the Communist regime in Czechoslovakia on November 17, the last obstacle was removed for the realization of their lifetime dream to create a new venture to commercialize their ideas. The Machrles resigned their positions at the University of Bratislava and began preparations for starting their own company. Forming a new venture in a country that had not known free enterprise for almost half a century would require creativity in organization and finance as well as in technology.

Careers in Science and Technology

The Machrle brothers' father died when they were young. Trained and experienced as a technologist, their father left them a legacy of interest in science. In his last message to the boys, he also left them a challenge: Find solutions to the environmental problems caused by advances in science and industry. This challenge influenced subsequent education and career choices made by the brothers.

Vladimir Machrle earned a doctorate in engineering in Prague. He subsequently received a degree in hydraulic engineering in Grenoble, France,

Frank Hoy is dean of the College of Business Administration at the University of Texas at El Paso. Hoy currently serves as editor of *Entrepreneurship: Theory and Practice,* vice president for special programs of the United States Association for Small Business and Entrepreneurship, and chair of the Central European Small Business Enterprise Development Commission. Miroslav Pivoda is on the management faculty of the Agricultural University of Brno. His current areas of research are strategic management in a market economy and knowledge-based systems. Pivoda chairs the Management from Abroad Group of the Moravian Scientific and Technical Society.

where he continued his education, earning a second doctorate in mathematics. In the meantime, Svatopluk was studying sanitation engineering in Czechoslovakia. He then obtained a doctorate in engineering at the Academy of Sciences in Moscow. The International Atomic Agency in Vienna sent Svatopluk to the Massachusetts Institute of Technology (MIT) in the United States in 1960. While specializing in nuclear engineering at MIT, he paid special attention to procedures for the purification of low-level radioactive waste. At this time, one of his professors led a project on wastewater treatment in Orange County, California. This event made an impression on Svatopluk because it marked the first application of classical water treatment technology that won the approval of environmental hygiene experts.

Also during his days at MIT, Svatopluk attended lectures at the Harvard Business School. He was exposed to various theories of innovation and was particularly impressed by the concept of innovation centers. He began to formulate ideas of how these theories could be applied in the creation and management of innovative organizations.

Upon the completion of their studies, the brothers were employed by the Czech Academy of Sciences. They organized, initiated, and codirected the Institute of Hydrodynamics at Brno. At this time, they developed their theories on wastewater treatment. In the 1960s, many research scientists were developing new technologies for suspension separation by fluidized bed filtration. These technologies had not yet proved feasible for industrial application.

The relaxation of travel restrictions during the Prague Spring in 1968 allowed the brothers to travel to France to apply the technologies based on their ideas for water purification. This opportunity was a watershed event in the lives of the brothers. The Machrles had obtained a number of patents for the chemical treatment of wastewater. Under the Communist government in Czechoslovakia, all patents were owned by the state. The Machrles could not, therefore, create their own company, but under the authority of the Czech Academy of Sciences, they were again permitted to travel to France to put their ideas into practice. Drawing on Vladimir's knowledge of France and contacts in Grenoble, they entered an agreement with SOGREAH. For two years, the brothers developed and commercialized their chemical treatments for industrial applications.

The Grenoble project was aborted following the Warsaw Pact invasion, and the brothers were recalled to Czechoslovakia in 1969. They continued their work in biological purification applications but soon were notified that their jobs in the Academy of Sciences had been abolished.

A Closed Door, an Open Window

The Machrles joined the faculty of sciences at the Agricultural University of Brno. They were unable to continue their work on the chemical treatment of water, but they began experiments on the biological treatment of waste products. Soon, the brothers had patents for a biological approach: fluidized bed purification.

Through a series of informal contacts, the brothers found a firm in Italy interested in applying their concepts. Initially commuting from Brno, they later lived with the Brunelli family, who helped arrange for their expenses to be covered. They were not allowed to accept pay for their efforts. The brothers worked with the Italians for twenty years without official permission from the government of Czechoslovakia. They found Italy to be an ideal testing ground: The Italians exhibited flexible, nonchauvinistic attitudes in dealing with the Czechs, and Northern Italy was home to large corporate farms with thousands of pigs producing liquid manure that required processing.

The Machrles first applied their technologies through NORD Eco S.P.A., a company engaged in water purification. In collaboration with their Italian sponsors, the Machrles proved their technology to be feasible. After constructing plants with NORD Eco S.P.A. for sewage treatment projects, the Machrles worked with Laverda Empienti to purify industrial wastewater and with Orazio Brunelli s.a.c. for the denitrification and dephosphorization of water.

The Machrles' achievements in Italy brought them acclaim. An article of September 13, 1985, titled "In Accordance with 'Magi' from the East and West, Your Waters Will Be Saved" featured a photo of Svatopluk with American professor W. W. Eckenfelder. The Italian newspaper clipping was sent to influential circles. Svatopluk believed the publicity saved his post at the Technical University in Bratislava because Czechoslovak politicians did not want a scandal over their firing a staff member with an international reputation.

The Broad Concept

The lessons the brothers learned implementing their technology in Italy encouraged them to take a broad view of the applications of fluidized bed purification. A study was published in the 1980s by a professor at the Prague University of Economics investigating prospective designs and applications of biological technologies the Machrles had been working on. The professor evaluated ten technological applications of fluidized bed filtration:

1. Packed wastewater purification plants.
2. Modular wastewater purification plants.
3. Monoblock wastewater purification plants.
4. System AGROCLAR—processing of manure of agricultural animals for the production of humus fertilizer.
5. Conception of the reconstruction of the existing communal plants for wastewater purification.
6. Conception of subterranean tunnel plants for wastewater purification.
7. Packed water reclamation plants (for drinking purposes).

8. Modular plants for chemical treatment and purification of water.
9. Monoblock water treatment plants.
10. Systems for the complex purification of communal waters for enrichment of sources of subterranean waters in regions of deficit water sources.

The professor advocated a strategy focusing on one or a small number of these technologies and argued for limiting the extent to which they should be applied. To Svatopluk Machrle, however, the professor's arguments provided a basis for proceeding with a broad strategy. Machrle wrote a paper with counterpoints to each of the professor's arguments, showing the rationale behind a broader concept. Taking the issue a step further, and using one of the models he learned at Harvard, Machrle pointed out the level of innovation associated with each technological application:

Level 7. A new principle of fluidized bed filtration for separation of a flock suspension.
Level 6. New types of integrated reactors for treatment and purification of water. Applications: reactors for chemical treatment and purification; reactors for biological purification of water.
Level 5. New generations of integrated reactors for specific conditions. Applications: packed biological reactors, modular biological reactors, monoblock biological reactors, chemical reactors.
Level 6. Typified performance lines of plants for treatment and purification of water. Applications: packed purification plants, modular purification plants, monoblock purification plants, packed treatment plants, chemical modular treatment and purification plants, monoblock treatment plants.
Level 5. Material variants. Concrete, steel, and laminated versions of variants.

Recognizing that fluidized bed filtration represented the highest level of innovation, the brothers determined that the applications could be implemented only by an innovative organizational structure. In 1989, they published a paper drawing on J.A. Morton's work on innovative organizations. Using the relationship of AT&T, Bell Laboratories, and Western Electric as a guide, the Machrles proposed a design for organizational innovation in Czechoslovakia (see Figure 6.1).

Moment of Decision

By November 1989, the Machrles had proved the feasibility of their technology, had determined to follow a broad concept in its application, and had conceived an approach to organizing for innovation. Svatopluk later admitted that they had not been prepared for the collapse of the government on November 17, nor had they expected it to be bloodless. They were prepared, however, to take advantage of the collapse when it occurred. Within days of

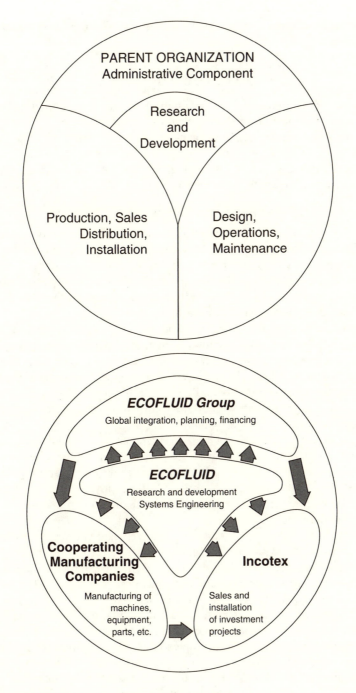

FIGURE 6.1   Structuring for Innovation.

the Velvet Revolution, the brothers resigned their positions at the University of Bratislava.

The Growing Firm

In January 1991, Ecofluid, Ltd. was established, and by autumn it had twenty employees. The firm faced the problem of how to increase its share in both domestic and foreign markets. It was clear that the direction of the firm would be set by the Machrle brothers. They held a majority of shares and were the sources of innovative ideas. The partner firms of Ecofluid believed that they were on the right track for a prosperous future.

Organizing and Financing the Venture

Svatopluk Machrle had never waited, like many other research workers, for somebody else to organize a firm to develop, manufacture, and sell his products. Although his strategy for an organizational form was not traditional (see Figure 6.1), it was very similar to that of AT&T. He had kept this model in mind since his studies in the U.S. Svatopluk was convinced that this structure would serve his innovative firm successfully.

Svatopluk had tried to find a suitable firm to implement his intentions within the previous economic system in Czechoslovakia. In spring 1989, through a network of informal relationships, he came into contact with the director of Incotex in Brno. Incotex was a state-owned enterprise in the textile industry. The director of Incotex, R. Schmidt, was looking for a new business for his firm. "During the first five minutes of our meeting it was clear that we would be partners," said Svatopluk.

Through another network of high-level associates, Svatopluk contacted the director of Agrocons in Bratislava a few weeks before the revolution of November 17, 1989. Agrocons (at that time under a different name) was a state-owned design firm consisting of about 1,200 employees. On November 30, 1991, the Machrle brothers left the Technical University of Bratislava and became employees of Agrocons.

At that time, Incotex and Agrocons were separate entities. Svatopluk was acting between them as "a virus." His aim was to restructure the two firms from within to further the Machrles' goals. Both the external and the internal environments worked in favor of the Machrles' intentions. The changing Czechoslovak economy seriously threatened the firms' survival in their existing businesses. They were attracted to a venture that had great potential.

Svatopluk had to determine whether the two firms would be able to cover all business activities that such complex products as wastewater purification plants represented. He needed to be certain he was not overlooking more effective alternatives. He also had to finance the enterprise, including paying about 1,000 employees. Incotex was able to arrange all the bank financing.

Without the backing of an Incotex or an Agrocons, no bank would have provided money to two professors on such a large project. The two firms also acquired the patents of the Machrle brothers that were owned by the government.

According to Svatopluk, Schmidt, the director of Incotex, played a more inventive role in the start-up phase than did the director of Agrocons, who was willing to accept Schmidt's proposals. The ecological business activities at Incotex made the firm attractive to "insiders"; they did not want the firm to go on the open market via couponing. Schmidt and a few other key managers in Incotex decided to buy the firm in an ordinary privatization process.

Early Achievements

In its promotional brochure, Ecofluid offered its technology for the following applications:

- Purification of municipal and sewage wastewater;
- Purification of food industry wastewater;
- Purification of industrial wastewater; and,
- Processing of farm animal manure.

By Autumn 1991, these applications had been implemented in several places in Czechoslovakia, Italy, France, and Germany.

Due to the modularity of the technology, its applications were cost-effective over a wide range of capacity demands. The biggest economies of scale, however, could be reached in places with high concentrations of people or animals. Ecofluid looked first at these market opportunities. Also, purification plants could be erected in very remote places of the world because reactor vessels were made of steel plates that were easily transportable and cheaper than the traditional concrete tanks.

In 1989, the Machrles added a chemical treatment process to the biological treatment part of their purification plants. This technology made output parameters more attractive to the customers and satisfied even the strictest ecological demands of the most-developed countries. Svatopluk made a prognosis that within the next five years no classical purification plants would be built.

In 1991, the Machrles successfully implemented their humus program, converting ecologically damaging manure and sludge into useful fertilizer. The Machrles had been promoting this program for several years under the name "cyclical compensation loop in the civilization process."

Growth Alternatives

After almost forty years of frustration, the Machrles' ambitions were becoming a reality. They wanted to disseminate their technology throughout the world and to apply it to the most extensive and challenging ecological projects. (One expert's view of global opportunities in the water industry is shown in Appendix 6.1). How could Ecofluid effectively penetrate foreign markets and win bids? How could it penetrate barriers of inertia and what was referred to as the technical mafia in certain countries? How could it persuade decision-makers of vast ecological projects that a firm from the former Communist block was a credible and capable partner? And which countries should have priority in the implementation of the Machrles' global ambitions?

In 1991, Ecofluid established international technical bureaus to develop its processes according to differing national standards and to promote dissemination of the technology. In principle, Ecofluid technology was specialized and economically acceptable for markets in Europe, the United States, and even the delicate Pacific coral islands. Svatopluk knew that there were European countries with serious ecological problems due to high concentration of farm animals. Also, countries such as Holland were importing expensive artificial fertilizers. There were also desert countries that had major needs for humus and drinking water.

The local Czechoslovak market, as well as markets in other former Communist countries, lacked adequate capital for ecology projects. These countries had suitable conditions for exploiting economies of scale, however, especially in Ecofluid's agricultural applications. Financial support from Western countries was directed predominantly at Western firms to support their efforts to export to formerly Communist countries. Programs like PHARE (Poland and Hungary: Assistance for Reconstructing the Economy), although well intended, were operated by administrators and bureaucrats who lacked technical knowledge. Therefore, such programs often provided obsolete technology.

Czechoslovak rivers contributed heavily to the ecological problems in the neighboring states and their seas. The outdated and overloaded wastewater purification plant in Prague was causing serious ecological problems. The city published an international advertisement for proposals to renovate the system.

Strict rules, standards, and bureaucracy in Germany limited the possibility of exporting to Germany to those with impeccable references for ecological technology. Even promising research in biotechnology was difficult to carry out in Germany. Due to their history, the Czech people were very sensitive about being economically dependent on either Germany or Russia.

The Machrles tried to organize a collaboration between European universities and research centers for further development of biotechnology and other supporting basic technologies. Svatopluk knew that if he wanted to enter the U.S. market, he had to be able to show concrete results, not just ideas.

The Czechoslovak firms that implemented Ecofluid technology were on a technically acceptable level and their products were relatively cheap in the

West European market. Svatopluk estimated that if the technology was applied in major ecological projects in Europe, it could employ half of the Czechoslovak economy. In this light, he saw a very bright and not distant future for Czechoslovakia to join the EC countries. The question he faced in the autumn of 1991 was what course of action would enable rapid and healthy growth for Ecofluid.

Appendix 6.1
A Look at the Global Scene

Asked the question, "How do you see 1992 shaping up for the water industry as a whole?" I have to reply on the global rather than on the national situation. Serving for the best of three years up to last May as President of the London, England-based International Water Supply Association (IWSA), which has over 80 member countries, left me with a perception of the enormous challenges that lie ahead in the areas of water supply and wastewater sanitation. Every year we take some important steps forward, and 1992 will be no exception.

On the national scene, the 1986 Safe Drinking Water Act Amendments and the 1987 Water Quality Act called for the implementation of many new water/wastewater initiatives over a number of years. Their rate of implementation has been picking up, and 1992 will be busy for utilities as they put new groundwater and surface water rules into place, become more skillful in how they dispose of sludge, continue to improve pretreatment programs, learn to appreciate the power of electronics and the computer, learn more about the so-called "emerging technologies," play a role in the campaign to prevent pollution rather than cause it, and do all these things with the tight money constraints which persistently characterize our industry.

The international picture is similar in many ways and distinctly different in others. My IWSA travels took me to many parts of the world. Some places (e.g., in Europe and Japan) enjoy water supply and sanitation facilities and systems developed essentially to the same high levels as ours in North America. But the situations in the developing and underdeveloped countries are quite different. There lie the long-range challenges—and a host of opportunities if we want to grasp them—facing the industry in a global sense. Consider what is happening in several areas of the world.

Most people are aware of the dramatic political changes in Eastern Europe. Along with them comes the reality of terrible pollution problems. If the environment is to be improved in Eastern Europe, the newly established democracies must embark on a far-reaching program to respond to the degradation caused by pollution. In the case of Poland, it is said that 70 percent of the country's drinking water is polluted. In addition to the water supply and sanitation problems, there are severe air pollution problems, including the acid-rain effect, estimated to have damaged 100 million trees. Due to contamination both from air and water, leukemia in children may have doubled within the past decade. In East Germany, it is estimated that $2 billion may be required to clean up the rivers and their tributaries. Similar problems were cited in Romania and Hungary. In Czechoslovakia it is estimated that 50 percent of the drinking water is polluted and not safe for consumption by babies. A particular problem has been the excessive use of pesticides and fertilizers which have contaminated ground water supplies. To bring these new emerging democracies up to the standards of the European community will be a significant challenge, requiring great technical, practical, and financial skills.

The African continent is a different story entirely. Most African countries are extremely underdeveloped. Rural areas particularly need help not with the kind of processes and equipment we take for granted, but with simple, easy-to-use-and-understand technology. An example is a hand pump. In an IWSA conference in Abidjan, Ivory Coast, most of the presentations related to the basics of maintaining and operating existing facilities. Papers highlighted current O&M practices, the installation of house services, and the reduction of leaks, water losses, and unaccounted-for water. In the African region, these are significant problems and several authors stated that in rural areas over 50 percent of the hand pumps on wells and bore holes were out of service. In many instances, due to the configuration of villages, it was virtually impossible to provide individual service connections. In some instances, unaccounted-for water in urban and rural systems constituted as much as 60–70 percent of total system supplies.

The Pacific Rim offers another contrasting view of the industry. It is a mixture of rich and poor, well developed and underdeveloped. Water supplies there are needed for roughly 50 percent of the world's population, 2.5 billion people. Within this area, systems with high technology, sophistication, and modern facilities serve the industrialized and newly industrialized countries, such as Japan, Australia, Korea, Taiwan, Hong Kong, and Singapore. Also, vast areas of high population density are emerging including China, Indonesia, Malaysia, Thailand, plus the countries from South Central and West Asia consisting of India, Sri Lanka, Mauritius, and the Seychelles. The need for technology transfer extends from a basic need of finding water and providing a minimum of treatment for drinking purposes to operating large systems for the removal of synthetic organic chemicals.

To sum up, January 1 of 1992 is just another kick-off date. The problems will continue long after December 31—twelve months later—all over the world. But hopefully, we will have solved some of them by that date—and proceed into 1993 to solve some more. Challenges abound, but so too do opportunities for manufacturers, engineering firms, and dedicated professionals in the operating sector. Population growth will be the biggest driving force. Estimates say that world population will double by the year 2050 to 10 billion from the present five billion. Developing countries will account for 87 percent of the increase. And everyone needs and deserves safe drinking water!

William H. Richardson, P.E.
WATER/Engineering and Management, December 1991

CHAPTER SEVEN

■

The Czechoslovak Management Center: Institution Building and Organizational Design

In September 1991, Ted Legof[1] returned to the University of Pittsburgh from his sixth trip to Prague within the year. He had helped found a new institution for management training in Prague, the Czechoslovak Management Center (CMC).

The center was originally created as an independent institution separate from existing ones such as the Prague School of Economics (PSE) and the Czech Technical University. However, some Western funders, CMC board members, the responsible people from the Joseph M. Katz Graduate School of Business at the University of Pittsburgh, and local people questioned this approach due to the difficulty of maintaining a free-standing center.

The CMC board had recently asked Legof to make a recommendation to be presented at the next board meeting. In particular, the board asked Legof to assess the capacity of existing institutions to absorb the new free-market management and economics curricula. Several board members spoke to Legof informally outside the board meetings and urged him to find a way to integrate the center with an existing Czechoslovak institution.

In preparing his recommendations to the board, Legof drew on his experiences with the Czechoslovak Management Center and with the International Management Center—created three years earlier in Budapest, Hungary—and on his general knowledge of Czechoslovak institutions of higher learning.

Daniel S. Fogel, Mona Makhija, both from the University of Pittsburgh, and Karl Žebrakovský, Czechoslovak Management Center, prepared this case with the assistance of Thomas Beretich, MBA student ('92) at the A. B. Freeman School of Business. It was funded by the United States Agency for International Development grant for Management Training and Economics Education and the United States Information Agency grant for Institution Building in Central and Eastern Europe. This case was prepared to facilitate class discussion rather than to illustrate effective or ineffective administrative decisionmaking.

The Czechoslovak Management Center

The political changes that swept through Central and Eastern Europe during 1988–1989 created the impetus for market-oriented economic reforms in most of the countries in this region. These reforms included measures that facilitated privatization of state-owned enterprises and foreign direct investment. Czechoslovakia, like the other Central and East European countries, needed a professional cadre of highly skilled managers who could provide leadership during this period of transition, employ market-oriented techniques in business transactions, and also motivate existing workers.

In order to address these needs, the Ministry of Industry of the Czech Republic and the University of Pittsburgh jointly began the Czechoslovak Management Center in 1990. The CMC was organized as a not-for-profit foundation, the second such organization formed in Czechoslovakia. Appendix 7.1 shows an abstract of the foundation's deed and statutes. The goals of the CMC included the following: (1) to transfer management teaching techniques and information to Czechoslovak professionals; (2) to promote the use of market economy skills to enhance Czechoslovakia's position as an effective and responsive participant in international business; and (3) to strengthen the status of business management as a profession within the country. The University of Pittsburgh had a three-year management contract, containing provisions that the university's Katz Graduate School of Business would help the CMC in several aspects. The most important aspects centered around the development of business courses, particularly an English-language MBA program, and the enhancement of CMC's research capability and output.

The center's curriculum for short-term executive courses emphasized certain themes that responded to the immediate needs of Czechoslovak businesspeople and government officials. The general viewpoint within the country at that time was that every commercial transaction was a zero-sum game. That is, when one individual benefited, the other lost. Thus, CMC faculty needed to address the mutual benefits of economic growth and the moral dilemmas resolved by managers as the economy progressed toward a free market. Another course topic that dealt with the needs of Czechoslovak executives was the forms of ownership and the differences between owners and managers, a somewhat new idea in Czechoslovak business and laws.

An important objective of the center was the training of the professionals who taught the courses. The first year of the CMC's operation included the selection and training of an initial group of Czechoslovak faculty members. Each selected faculty member worked with a Western colleague for three to six months at the colleague's institution. The Western faculty member also returned to the CMC to teach and engage in research activities.

The center's funding came from five main sources—the Czech government, Czechoslovak banks, the U.S. government, foreign private founda-

FIGURE 7.1   Europe in 1993. *Source:* David S. Mason, *Revolution in East-Central Europe: The Rise and Fall of Communism and the Cold War* (Boulder: Westview Press, 1992). Reprinted by permission.

tions, and foreign governments. Additional support was provided by tuition and other revenues. The largest revenue source was hotel and conference fees at the CMC facility. An interesting aspect of the CMC was its immediate relationship with the Czechoslovak government. The training and research carried out by the center faculty was believed to directly influence the reform of the economy and government policy decisions.

The CMC was located approximately twenty-five kilometers east of Prague in a small town called Čelákovice (see Figure 7.1). The activities were held in a 15,000-square-meter building that included, among other resources, 175 sleeping rooms, several seminar rooms, a boardroom, 10 thirty-person class-

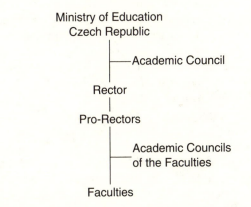

CMC Organization Structure

Board of Trustees
|
Dean
|
Faculty and Staff

PSE and CTU Organization Structures

Ministry of Education
Czech Republic

├──Academic Council

Rector
|
Pro-Rectors

├── Academic Councils
│   of the Faculties

Faculties

FIGURE 7.2   Organization Structure of CMC, PSE, and CTU.

rooms, 2 sixty-person classrooms, office space for over 100 faculty and administrative staff, a 250-seat auditorium, and an in-house TV production facility. The facility had formerly been a Communist party training school for government and industry leaders.

By mid-1992, the CMC had twelve faculty members. The MBA program had twenty-six students, and the faculty trained over 800 executives in short-term courses. Figure 7.2 shows the center's organization structure. The CMC was run by a U.S. dean who had an extensive international background. The research output was mostly cases and research studies on the Czechoslovak economy and its transition. Fund-raising had yielded over $10 million in cash and in-kind contributions.

The International Management Center

The first market-oriented private business school in Central and Eastern Europe was founded in Hungary in 1986. Hungary was chosen for several reasons. As early as 1980, Hungarian managers were active in market-oriented activities similar to those in Western economies. The political changes that took place at the close of the decade provided an ever-widening window through which the Hungarian economy could develop into a more market-oriented system. The early start of the reform process was accompanied by requests for management training by key government leaders of the country as well as by Hungarian managers. Western and Hungarian support was available at this time, as both private and public entities were interested in investing in a quality school.

The International Management Center (IMC) was created by Mark Palmer, then U.S. ambassador to Hungary, and Sandor Demjan, then president of the Hungarian Credit Bank. By October 1987, others joined the project, including George Soros of the Open Society Fund, Adam Szilas of Szenzor Consulting (Hungary), and representatives of the chambers of commerce of Milan and Budapest and of the San Paolo Bank in Torino, Italy. These agencies formed the initial partners of a for-profit joint venture, which was registered in Budapest in November 1988. The IMC was changed to a not-for-profit foundation in 1990.

The partners appointed a Hungarian managing director and a U.S. dean, Ted Legof, who were responsible for running the center. Each partner provided cash, in-kind contributions, and pledges. The money was both in local and foreign convertible currency; the total was over $3.2 million.

Located on a four-and-a-half-acre campus with several buildings, the IMC offered executive courses that lasted two days to two weeks. It also offered a twelve-month, English-language, full-time MBA program known as the graduate management program; two part-time English-language MBA programs; consulting services for in-house training or particular business problems; and an extensive English- and Hungarian-language library. Its goals were similar to those of the CMC.

Despite the fact that it operated in a foreign context, in many respects the IMC looked like a miniature version of a business school in the United States. The faculty consisted of trained educators who also conducted original research. The center's library was dominated by English-language material to support the research activities and the MBA program. The faculty admitted students on the basis of standard tests such as the Graduate Management Admission Test.

Nonetheless, the IMC also had features that distinguished it from Western business schools. One such feature was its affiliation with several universities that provided special support for its varied programs. York University in Toronto, Canada, provided some Canadian funds to support the IMC, linking it to Canadian faculty and businesses. Manchester Business School in England provided access to European managers as well as the opportunity to train the Hungarian faculty in its executive and MBA programs. In addition, the IMC's relationships with the Budapest University of Economics and the Technical

University in Hungary were important for sharing expertise and conducting joint research on the Hungarian economy.

After Legof conducted a comprehensive study, the University of Pittsburgh became IMC's major partner. Because of the university's extensive international ties and programs in Central and Eastern Europe, and the former Soviet Union, as well as an administrative staff willing to commit resources to a new and risky business venture, the two institutions formed an effective partnership. Studies at the time recommended a more international curriculum in business education offered to U.S. college students, and the university responded by looking for ways to internationalize its faculty and create an innovative approach to international linkages. Legof and the Joseph M. Katz Graduate School of Business dean, H. J. Zoffer, easily worked together.

The University of Pittsburgh gave broad support to the center in terms of curriculum and faculty development. It assisted the center's graduate management program (GMP) by providing faculty, specialized courses, and credits toward an MBA degree, as well as scholarships so that IMC students could study at Pittsburgh. In addition, the university provided help in setting up the administrative infrastructure for a degree program and played a major role in faculty development for the Hungarian professors.

In an interesting departure from traditional business schools, the faculty of the IMC worked in teams. Each full-time Hungarian faculty member worked with a foreign colleague in a similar discipline. For example, a Hungarian faculty member in finance worked jointly with a finance faculty member from INSEAD, teaching courses such as finance for nonfinancial managers and valuation of businesses. Faculty also jointly conducted research on the development of capital markets and, in particular, the stock market in Hungary. Other examples of faculty teamwork include the development of an entrepreneurs' club, a consulting project dealing with total quality management for a local manufacturing company, and an additional consulting project with a state-owned firm with regard to its establishment of a joint venture.

A unique aspect of the IMC was its status independent from the government. IMC's managers made the decisions regarding curriculum, investments, students, and so on. This independence was new to Hungarian companies and government policymakers.

Although the IMC was directed primarily toward Hungarians, the executive and GMP programs included Russians, West Europeans, Romanians, and other Central and East Europeans. Of the 1991–1992 GMP students, eight were Hungarian, twenty-two were from other Central and East European countries, and the rest were from Western Europe and North America.

The IMC notes a number of accomplishments to its credit. These include the fact that in its first year, forty-five different executive programs were attended by over 1,000 managers. In addition, faculty completed fifteen case studies on Hungarian companies as they transformed their organizations. The

IMC also published books on consulting and on a comparison of Hungarian and Western accounting practices. Twenty-eight candidates graduated from the first year's GMP class. GMP internships were completed in nine countries in thirty-five different companies. Finally, scholars from over twenty different countries attended eight international conferences held at the IMC.

Despite these accomplishments, the IMC did experience difficulties. The center began as a joint venture in order to take advantage of the favorable hard-currency and tax benefits available through Hungarian joint-venture laws. Because the joint-venture laws in 1988 did not permit the appointment of a foreign managing director, a Hungarian was appointed as the head of the center. Legof's position was subordinate to the managing director.

The managing director appointed by the board to head the center was an entrepreneurial-minded individual, inexperienced in running an academic institution. Specifically, she lacked the administrative skills to create a well-functioning organization. Legof had much experience in this regard. Because of their differential skill levels and Legof's subordinate position, a good deal of tension and conflict resulted. In order to resolve this problem, the board introduced the notion of dual leadership, requiring joint responsibilities and signatures on documents. This failed to resolve the problems and resulted instead in the forced resignation of the managing director and Legof's refusal to apply for a second two-year term.

Despite their previous training, the professors that were originally hired for the center were, for the most part, untested and untrained for the type of programs that the IMC administered. Many long, acrimonious faculty meetings and one-on-one discussions were held during the center's first two years. Nonetheless, as the faculty received more training over time from the IMC and the University of Pittsburgh, they proved to be more competent and successful in meeting the center's needs.

Maintenance of the IMC's independence was a high priority for all the founding parties. This priority translated into excluding the Hungarian government from any direct involvement in the development of the center. Thus, the center was ineligible for most government-to-government aid programs because it was viewed as a private business. Although the IMC's independence excluded it from this network of people and information, this was offset by the pride expressed and intangible support offered by individual ministers and government officials. In addition, the IMC received direct aid from several foreign governments, including those of the United States, Canada, the Netherlands, Italy, and the United Kingdom.

Czechoslovak Institutions of Higher Learning

Czechoslovakia's history of higher education parallels much of the country's economic and political history. In many respects, higher education was rigidly centralized and politically controlled in terms of access, curriculum, staffing, and resources.

Czechoslovakia's system was originally developed on several models. The most influential were the Austrian, German, and Soviet traditions of higher education. The Austrian and German traditions had a pervasive influence on Czechoslovakia beginning in the mid-fourteenth century. One feature borrowed from the Austrians and Germans was the chaired professor as the center of academic activity. The chair system included a distinguished scholar as the department head, usually a full professor tenured for life, and other scholars and professors engaged in research and teaching. By tradition, each university had only one chair in each discipline or field. Appointment of the chaired professor was based on academic and political criteria. Thus, the chair was both a scholar and an agent of the state.

In the Russian tradition, government-run academies conducted mostly research; universities were limited to instruction. Both institutions were under strict government control. This control included restrictions on what could be taught, to whom, and how instruction would be delivered. Access to universities was related to the economic needs of the country, especially in training Communist citizens for jobs prescribed by the Central Plan. Universities were also the main source of ideological training for citizens who pursued a higher education.

The structure of the Czechoslovak higher education system was at the time of this study a product of these two traditions. Czechoslovakia had thirty-six universities (twenty-three in the Czech Republic and thirteen in Slovakia), few of which did any research. Prior to admittance to a university, students attended one of three types of secondary schools: technical schools, vocational schools, or the gymnasiums. Most university students came from the gymnasiums.

Czechoslovakia had somewhat low participation rates in universities compared to its European neighbors. In 1991, approximately 1,100 students of 100,000 attended universities. This figure compares with an average of 2,400 for the European Community universities at this time.

On May 4, 1990, the Act on Czechoslovak Higher Education Institutions abolished all previous legislation related to higher education, particularly the requirement to teach Marxist dogma. The new act guaranteed academic rights free from governmental control, prohibited political parties from organizing on university premises, renewed university self-governing bodies, and established new countrywide governing bodies.

Higher education in Czechoslovakia underwent rapid change in other ways as well. Four major themes ran through all reform proposals as well as through the new law. These themes were developed from a combination of market forces or perceived outcomes of market forces, historical traditions, the reformers' attitudes, and advice from abroad.

The first fundamental structural change was that institutions became autonomous from the state. Reformers perceived this autonomy as indispensable to creating new curricula, hiring the best-trained faculty, and educating a new wave of students. The restructuring also forced a reallocation of resources.

The second reform supported the value of democracy within institutions. This change influenced the ways in which universities made decisions regarding faculty members, the governance of the institutions, and the means by which educators introduced new curricula.

The third reform allowed institutions to create linkages within and outside the region. These linkages influenced the acquisition of new resources, developed a new community of scholarship, and increased the credibility of the universities.

The final reform made necessary new financing methods to supplement the state's budget for higher education. Prevalent were financing proposals advocating a tuition system. Universities planned to charge higher tuition for continuing education than for undergraduate and postgraduate degree programs. The funds generated from these courses would be used to support other university activities.

The Czech Technical University (CTU) and the Prague School of Economics (PSE) are two examples of institutions that underwent rapid change in accordance with these themes. Legof believed that both were potential institutions for housing the CMC.

Czech Technical University

The origins of the Czech Technical University, also known as the Czech Institute of Technology, can be traced back to the sixteenth century, when it was established as a school for the technical education of noblemen. It was considered to be the most respectable technical university in Czechoslovakia, and in recent times was known for quality education and research and consultation activities in the areas of engineering and nuclear science.

CTU was composed of a number of schools, known as faculties in Czechoslovakia, including Mechanical Engineering, Electrical Engineering, Civil Engineering, Nuclear Sciences and Physical Engineering, and Architecture, and the Masaryk Institute of Advanced Studies. Each faculty was headed by a dean and had a number of departments, laboratories, and a library.

Prior to November 1989, the coursework for the engineering degree, which was equivalent to the U.S. master of science degree, took approximately five years and required passing comprehensive state examinations and defending a thesis. In addition to the engineering coursework, foreign languages (Russian and one of the Western European languages) were a compulsory part of the curricula for all students. Compulsory for all students whether undergraduate, postgraduate, or doctoral was the study of the history of the Communist party of Czechoslovakia, Marxist philosophy, political economy, and Marxist sociology. Within each of the schools pertaining to the different engineering disciplines, courses were taught that related to Marxist political theory and management. These courses were the responsibility of the departments of economics and management. They had marginal relevance to the free market economic principles that were implemented in Czechoslovakia in the period after 1989.

The political and economic changes in Czechoslovakia after 1989 resulted in proposals for several radical changes in curricula structure and organization within CTU, which were gradually implemented. Although each school proceeded to develop different versions of curricula in line with their traditional independence, the new curricula were structured similarly to those found in U.S. universities. The first two to three years culminated with the first state examination and the attainment of a bachelor's degree. The next three to four years culminated with a comprehensive state examination and the attainment of a master's degree. A credit system—every course was assigned credits—was also being adopted, but the credit system was not uniform, varying between schools. It was expected that a common system for all the schools would eventually be adopted to provide greater flexibility to the students.

In addition, certain market-related courses in management, human resources management, financial management, and economics and entrepreneurship were assigned a great deal of importance. Some of these courses were compulsory; others were optional. The quality of these courses was continually upgraded through intensive contacts with academics in West European countries and the United States. This was in contrast to the past, when cooperation with foreign academic institutions was limited by the available financial resources and political restrictions.

Most students at CTU were Czechoslovaks, but there was a small percentage of students from other Central and East European nations, and from some of the Middle Eastern countries and developing countries. As all lectures were in Czech or Slovak languages, these students had to demonstrate proficiency in these languages. It was planned that as changes continued to occur, some lectures would be delivered in English and the number of these would increase over time.

There were some fundamental challenges for the academic community at CTU. These included the need to adjust the form and content of the engineering curricula to the international standards of quality and to incorporate the study of management and economics into these curricula. In Czechoslovakia, the top executives of firms were usually engineers by profession who had never had exposure to management and economics courses. Many thousands of such executives existed within the country at the time of this study.

Prague School of Economics

PSE was established in 1953. It focused on providing education for business-people, tradespeople, teachers of economics, and scholars. During its first forty years, the PSE served the official ideological requirements of the government. However, like CTU, after the Velvet Revolution in November 1989, fundamental changes took place.

After the revolution, PSE was composed of five schools, or faculties: Finance and Accounting; International Relations; Business Administration; Informatics and Statistics; and General Economics. For all students, either at the bachelor's or master's level, a common core curriculum defined and guaranteed a basic knowledge of economics. At the bachelor's level, after completing the core courses, a student was required to pass the bachelor's degree examinations; at the master's level, state examinations and a master's degree thesis were required.

Four departments provided language courses: the English Department, German Department, Department of Romance languages (French, Italian, and Spanish), and the Russian Department. Language training included the basic language itself, business language, and advanced courses for state language examinations. A student was required to pass the final language examinations in at least two foreign languages.

The changes at PSE were based on four principles:

1. The PSE should develop an internal structure that will enhance the academic strengths of the school as well as facilitate the developments of the various disciplines.
2. A three-tier approach to education will be incorporated to allow for greater flexibility of the curricula. These three levels include the bachelor's, the master's, and the doctoral levels of study.
3. A credit system will be instituted in which the student obtains the necessary credits to apply for relevant examinations. This system replaces the previous year-based approach. The credit system is believed to give the students and teachers greater flexibility in selecting and finishing coursework and in offering new and exploratory courses.
4. Finally, accreditation will be the guiding principle toward controlling the educational quality. The accreditation committees will be appointed internally by the PSE rector or the dean of the appropriate faculty, depending on the nature of the issue.

The Issues

The involvement of Western experts in the training of managers and educators required institutionalizing the methods and information brought to Central and Eastern European countries. The question was whether to start a new institution or to work through an existing institution. Legof believed he needed to take into account structural issues, the content of the curriculum, and management issues in determining the most suitable organizational design for the CMC.

Structural Issues

The institutions of higher learning in Czechoslovakia incorporated a nomenclature and a faculty that reflected forty or more years of Communist party rule. In many respects such an orientation was completely at odds with that of free market–oriented management education.

The creation of an entirely new organization involved a large investment and a substantial commitment to develop an organizational structure that facilitated the educational goals. Sponsorship of local governments and extensive foreign institutional support were critical to the credibility and financial viability of such organizations.

Legof knew that funding was always a problem in free-standing institutes, and the availability of large government grants was diminishing. The revenues from tuition in such centers were very small, and competition from free, high-quality programs was growing. Many existing institutions of higher learning received substantial foreign government grants to support programs run by foreign faculty with excellent credentials. TEMPUS (Trans European Mobility Plan for Universities and Students) and the British government's Know-How Fund contributed substantially to management education and training in state-run institutions to educate as many local managers as possible.

The need for networking, or the ability to gain consistent access to information and people, also plays a role in determining the appropriate structure. Aside from professional organizations, a number of networks were set up. The Citizens Democracy Corps supported voluntary initiatives of U.S. citizens who wanted to help emerging democratic institutions and market economies in Central and Eastern Europe and the former Soviet Union. In addition, the European Foundation for Management Development coordinated management development endeavors and information throughout Europe. The existing higher education institutions received the most consistent contact with these and other similar networks.

The Curriculum Content

The curriculum that needed to be taught through such programs was not straightforward or easily developed. Designing curriculum raised a number of questions: Should the center present strictly market-oriented material that came from Western business schools? Should the center use case materials developed in U.S. and West European advanced management programs, as one program in Poland attempted to do? That is, could finance be taught with standard textbooks used in the United States? Despite the free-market orientation of the management education provided at the center, educators could not ignore the existing institutions of the country within which business transactions needed to take place, or issues related to the transition of the economy over time.

Central and East European educational systems had different methods, perspectives, and infrastructure. These were not in place in Western countries and needed to be taken into account when considering curricula changes. The use of a systematic curriculum with external accreditation was important to Western educators. The students and host institutions from Central and Eastern Europe had expectations of a curriculum more adaptable and flexible than would have been offered in a Western degree-based program.

An important issue related to the center's success was the composition of the student body. Legof believed that CMC students should come from abroad as well as from within the host country. Such a broadening of the student base would quickly internationalize the curriculum and student body and require the faculty to address issues faced by the other countries from which the students came. The interactions between students would be invaluable for mutual understanding and would reveal new perspectives on world business. From the first, foreign students would be invited to participate in all center programs. In contrast, in Czechoslovakia, considerable nationalism contributed to the perception that national institutions served only the national interest.

There was a unique need in Czechoslovakia for training existing and potential managers of small- and medium-sized enterprises. The significance of this target group stemmed from the historical lack of such organizations within the culture, the important role played by small- and medium-sized organizations in economic development, and the unprecedented opportunities these businesses presented for managers to act like owners.

Finally, Legof believed that language training was imperative for meaningful education in a business training center. The first few years of operation should include English-language training. Some of the programs also could include Western business practices, but the focus needed to be on language. PSE and CTU established language departments, and CMC contracted the language courses from Bell Education Trust, a British-language school.

Management Issues

An important aspect of a management program such as the CMC is the nature of its own management. Such a center serves as an example of what can be done in terms of efficiency and quality products and standards. The programs and staff need to be of the highest quality without compromise of standards due to political pressure or expediency.

In particular, a high priority needs to be placed on training the educators who deliver the programs. In this regard, interaction between the home- and host-country faculty needs to be facilitated (i.e., residence within Western institutions) in order to develop course materials, teaching methods, and to understand more fully the nature and culture of an academic institution and the role it plays in educating its managers.

In considering all the previous issues, Legof believed, with Vaclav Havel, that universal solutions did not apply, that imagination and creativity were needed to find unique solutions to the region's problems. He believed that Western business schools could interact with Czechoslovak colleagues to find new and long-lasting solutions to the introduction and stabilization of free market economies in the region. In so doing, they would not simply be setting up business programs or business schools but creating a postmodern arena for human individuality and peaceful coexistence.

Notes

1. Ted Legof is a fictional name.

Appendix 7.1

ABSTRACT OF CMC DEED AND STATUTES

The following are *excerpts* from the CMC Deed and Statutes:

*Deed of Foundation of the Czechoslovak Management Center
Foundation, Prague*

According to the resolution of the Government of the Czech republic dated 10th May 1990/No. 139, it has been adopted to set up the Czechoslovak Management Center and a Foundation to support its activities in cooperation with the University of Pittsburgh, Pittsburgh, Pennsylvania, USA, with the intention to "extend the spiritual values of Czechoslovakian citizens."

The objective, organization, aims and uses of the Foundation are governed by the Statute of Foundation published by the partners in cooperation. Registration of the Statute by the Local National Committee, Prague 1, is also necessary for its validity.

Details of the process for capital operating and special contributions are governed by the Statute of Foundation. The Foundation capital will consist of contributions from the Ministry of Industry and any other individuals or corporate entities. Resources may also be given to the Foundation to support operating expenses or special programs.

Statute: Czechoslovak Management Center Foundation

Purpose and Objectives: Notwithstanding any other provisions of this Statute of Foundation, the objectives and purposes of the Foundation shall be exclusively non-profit, charitable, and educational.

1. The objectives and purposes of the Foundation shall include, but not be limited to:

   - advancing business education and management training for junior, middle and senior level managers and executives in both large and small entities and government agencies;

   - organizing consulting services for economic enterprises in such areas as strategic planning, marketing, and development of new products;

   - arranging conferences and other professional meetings to promote the exchange of information about comparative management practices;

   - promoting English language business communication and skills development;

   - promoting research on management issues relevant to the Czechoslovak environment.

2. As a means of accomplishing these objectives and purposes outlined in section III, the Foundation shall have the power to:

   - raise, accept, hold, and administer funds exclusively for its objectives and purposes and to that end, to receive, by purchase, grant, gift or bequest, or as beneficiary of any trust, any property, wheresoever situated;

- make donations in furtherance of such purposes;
- invest the funds and other property of the Foundation;
- collect and receive the income, if any, from any investment of such funds or property;
- apply the income, and if the Foundation decides, the principal of such property as the Foundation may from time to time possess, to the purposes of the Foundation. The Foundation is authorized to receive foreign currency and the foreign currency accounts may be maintained in the currency deposited. The Foundation is also authorized to designate institutions in countries other than CSFR to receive and distribute funds in the currency of that country as authorized and regulated by the operating rules of the Foundation and Foundation Statutes.

3. It is the intention of the Foundation to be exempt from income and VAT taxes under applicable Czechoslovak law.

Disposition of Proceeds The Foundation shall not be conducted or operated for profit, and no part of the net earnings of the Foundation shall inure to the benefit of any partner in cooperation, trustees, officer, or person connected with the Foundation; provided, however, that this shall not prevent the payment to any such person of reasonable compensation for services rendered to or for the Foundation in effecting any of its purposes.

Board of Trustees

The affairs of the Foundation shall be managed and all delegations of power in the Foundation shall be exercised by a Board of Trustees (the "Board"). The partners in cooperation [the University of Pittsburgh and the Czech Ministry of Industry], those persons whose names and addresses are set forth in the Deed of Foundation, will act as trustees until new trustees are appointed as provided in the Deed. Each partner in cooperation will appoint half of the number of trustees. The number of trustees shall not be less than six (6) nor more than fourteen (14), as may be fixed from time to time by the Board, provided that no decrease shall shorten the term of any incumbent trustee. Thereafter, the Trustees shall be elected by a vote of two-thirds of the Board of Trustees at the Annual Meeting of the Board or at any adjournment thereof, and shall serve until the election and qualification of their successors, unless he or she shall sooner die, resign or be removed. A Trustee has no obligation to provide financial contributions to the Foundation or assume any liability for past actions of the Foundation.

Directors

Dean The Board shall elect a Dean who shall serve at the pleasure of the Board. The Dean shall be chief executive officer of the CMC. The Dean shall manage and supervise the educational activities of the Foundation, including, but not limited to, the development and design of academic content of the Czechoslovak Management Center (CMC) and the selection of faculty. The Dean shall perform such other duties from time to time as may be assigned by the Board, the Chairman of the Board or the Chairman of the Executive Committee. The Dean shall report to the Chairman of the Executive Committee, and shall be an *ex officio* member of the Board.

PART THREE

■

Privatization and Meeting Market Demands

CHAPTER EIGHT

■

Ex-Émigré Entrepreneur
Viktor Kožený
and the Harvard Group

The collapse of communism in Eastern Europe in the late 1980s closed the doors on thousands of state-run enterprises and opened the door for an even greater number of new, entrepreneurial ventures. Nowhere in the former iron curtain countries was this more true than in Czechoslovakia (the Czechoslovak Federal Republic, or CSFR). And nowhere in Czechoslovakia was this more true than with a fledgling company originally called Harvard Capital and Consulting (HC&C), which now goes by the name the Harvard Group, with HC&C as one of its units. No native-born entrepreneur gained more fame and notoriety after the demise of communism in Czechoslovakia in November 1989 than the founder of HC&C, Viktor Kožený. Kožený, at the beginning of his rapid rise to prominence in the renewed "Prague Spring" of April of 1990, was twenty-seven years old and had recently completed an undergraduate degree in economics from Harvard University. He had barely nine months of prior full-time work experience in the world of business. With brashness and agility, he set out to take advantage of the new climate in Prague that allowed for true individual initiative for the first time since World War II. In the process, he played an important role in getting more than eight million citizens to participate in the privatization process that was economically and socially transforming the country.

John McIntyre, a doctoral candidate of the Graduate School of Management at the University of California, Irvine, teaches in the MBA program at the Czechoslovak Management Center in Prague. Lyman Porter is a professor of management and special assistant for academic affairs to the executive vice chancellor at the University of California, Irvine. Petrá Wendelová is vice president of the Harvard Group. Before joining Harvard Capital and Consulting at the end of 1990, she taught statistics at the Prague School of Economics.

What follows is the story of the company Viktor Kožen created and the impact he and it had throughout the country in little more than two years. It is a story of East going to the West and bringing the West to the East. It begins with a summary look at the entrepreneur himself, his management team, and the eleven units that made up the Harvard Group as of June 1992, and it concludes with a review of the critical management issues facing the group.

Viktor Koženÿ and
His Management Team

Viktor Koženÿ was born in Prague in 1963. His father, a mathematics professor at Prague Polytechnic University, died in 1969, and Viktor was reared primarily by his mother, a medical doctor. From his early years Viktor began to appear unusually talented in sports, math, and physics. At fourteen, he won a national competition in physics and was permitted to attend university lectures in math and physics. After emigrating to Germany in 1980 at the age of seventeen, Koženÿ, who never graduated from secondary school, entered Ludwig Maxmilian University in Munich in order to study physics. In 1982 he left Germany to go to the United States, where he spent a year doing research in applied physics and improving his English at the University of New Mexico. The following year, he entered Harvard University where he studied physics for about six months before trying to transfer to law, business, or finance. Though asked to meet the general requirements of Harvard College, he somehow found ways to enroll in finance, economics, and law courses in Harvard Business School, Harvard Law School, and MIT. His efforts to take whatever courses he pleased delayed the completion of his undergraduate degree in economics until 1989. He dismissed the fact that he spent over six years at Harvard by saying that he went there to get an education, not a degree.

After leaving Harvard, Koženÿ worked for a short time in London for Robert Fleming in privatization projects. He reported that while with Fleming he helped launch some investment funds. Given the astounding changes that were sweeping through Eastern Europe and the resulting business opportunities, as well as Kožen's desire to apply the knowledge that he had gained as a student at Harvard and his penchant for doing things his way, it is not surprising that he turned his attention toward the country of his birth and sensed great potential.

In April 1990 Koženÿ returned to Czechoslovakia to participate in the economic reconstruction of the country. He reportedly had $1,000 at the time and lived temporarily with his grandfather. Using his grandfather's old Russian automobile, he began traveling throughout the country in order to visit companies and offer advice and consulting services. He considered this a period of testing the market and reported that he was generally received by managers with courtesy, as well as with surprise and curiosity. As he put it,

> I was treated like a very interesting, but exotic, animal and often, while being shown around the factories, many employees would come to see this strange young man with his fancy Harvard education, Czech mixed with many English terms, who talked about things they had never thought of before. At this time, business or financial consulting services to firms were absolutely unknown in the CSFR and most of the state enterprises' directors never thought they might need to hire an advisor of that kind. Still, my trips generally left a positive impression and some of these companies later became clients of HC&C.

Feeling that his education and experience in the West gave him unique insights into where changes to a market economy would lead Czechoslovakia, Koženy began to use as many contacts as possible to attempt to meet other individuals who might join him in exploiting the business opportunities that were beginning to emerge in the new political and business environment. He sought a mix of individuals that would include not only analytical young professionals and economists from the Prague School of Economics who were not associated officially with the Communist ruling apparatus but also others who had extensive contacts or unusual access to information because of their wide-ranging activities as officials in the previous regime. Due partly to his family's good name and reputation, as well as to his own strong drive and forceful personality, the young entrepreneur succeeded in meeting accomplished and experienced people who were willing to join him and help him evaluate and apply his abilities and zeal. His ambition, determination, persuasiveness, knowledge, and clear concept of where his country was heading captured the attention of many capable individuals. A number of them decided to cast their lots with this young, convincing Harvard-trained businessman who was becoming recognized as one of the expatriate experts who had returned to the CSFR with skills and an educational background that could be put to good use. Six of the most influential members of this newly formed management group were Václav Varcop, Pavel Sauer, Miroslav Zarecký, Lemura Kanoková, Miloš Krivka, and Tomas Klaus.[1]

Václav Varcop met Viktor Koženy in July 1990 and started working for him two months later. In addition to having a Ph.D. in organic chemistry, Varcop brought some twenty years of managerial experience to the Koženy group. He had served as manager of the Technical Directorate of the Federal Ministry of Interior, where he was in charge of 1,000 employees engaged in research and development. He was also in charge of the production of equipment and techniques used by the ministry. As one might expect of a prominent official in the Interior Ministry, over the years Varcop had also developed widespread contacts throughout the government and business community. Thus, by September 1990, when he joined Koženy, it was clear that his managerial experience, knowledge, and contacts marked him as a valuable addition to Koženy's emerging management group. He served for a time as director of consulting and also helped organize National Security Printing (see further on), where he played an important role in recruiting many of his friends from the state printing company. Though he was not completely accepted by some of the managers more skilled in financial analysis, his contacts and ability to help bring in new business led Kožený to see him as an especially valuable colleague and to promote him to be his top deputy. Kožený described him as a "rain maker who is really instrumental in the success of our company." At the time of this study, Varcop was the executive vice president of the Harvard Group and director of Credit Control Services.[2]

After completing a degree in economics from the Technical University of Kosice in Bratislava, Pavel Sauer joined the Foreign Ministry and served at the Czechoslovak embassy in the United States for two years, where he gained a measure of knowledge of Western economic institutions and practices. When he returned to Czechoslovakia, he lived in Prague and became a neighbor of Václav Varcop, who subsequently introduced him to Viktor Kožený. Kožený was impressed by Sauer's blend of familiarity with Slovak conditions and insights into Western economic practices, as well as by his political savvy and leadership skills. Kožený indicated the degree of his confidence in him by suggesting that Sauer "makes basically *no* strategic political mistakes." He further described him as "really a great man, a natural leader who gets respect and knows what he wants." In January 1991, a few months after returning from the United States, Pavel Sauer decided to cast his lot with Kožený and joined HC&C. The following June he opened an office in the Slovak capital, Bratislava, and at the time of this study oversaw the office's three companies (HC&C-Slovakia, Credit Control Services–Slovakia, and Victoria Auditing), as well as its two investment funds. He reported directly to Kožený but made many of the major decisions for the Slovak region. Though Kožený visited him in Bratislava only once, he met with him every couple of weeks or so in Prague and they communicated by telephone every few days. Also, Sauer usually accompanied Kožený on monthly business trips to the United States.

Miraslav Zarecký was another of Kožený's close associates. He graduated from the Prague School of Economics in 1973 and then joined the Ministry of Foreign Trade. After two years in Prague, he was sent by the ministry to the United States for a four-year stint as commercial attaché. After returning to Czechoslovakia, he was assigned to the Ministry of Foreign Affairs, where he dealt with many economic concerns as adviser to the first deputy minister. In 1985 he was sent to the Czech embassy in Ottawa, where he served as deputy chief of mission for four years, including a one-year period as chargé d'affaires. In 1989 he was appointed director of the minister's cabinet for foreign affairs, and in 1990 he became director of the Secretariat-General, responsible for coordinating the activities of the Ministry of Foreign Affairs with the other state bodies. Thus, by the time Zarecký decided to join Kožený's HC&C joint-venture section in September 1991, he had gained considerable experience as an economist, diplomat, manager, and government official and had many contacts throughout the government. In January 1992 he was made managing director of HC&C and was responsible for its consulting activities.

Lemura Kanoková graduated in econometrics from the Prague School of Economics in 1984, after which she accepted a position doing research and teaching courses in the Department of Statistics at the Prague School. In 1989 she completed her Ph.D. and was sent to participate in a U.S. Information Agency conference dealing with management in Eastern Europe at Harvard University. Asked by the Harvard Club to help locate possible members in Prague, she eventually met Viktor Kožený in the summer of 1990. She joined HC&C the following November and quickly established herself as one of the firm's most capable financial analysts and number crunchers. She served for a time as managing director of HC&C and at the time of this study was on the board of directors of six of the Harvard Group companies. She was later appointed managing director of Investors' Stock Brokerage (ISB, see further on).

After completing his law degree at Charles University, Miloš Krivká served for five years as a civil judge. Then he spent eleven years as an attorney for the Office of the President of the Republic, as well as three years dealing with legislation for the president's office. From the spring of 1990, he served as an external attorney to Kožený, and in February 1991 he left the president's office in order to join Kožený. Krivká became the managing director of the legal branch of Kožený's group, International Legal Consulting (see below). Because of his legal experience and expertise, as well as the contacts that he made during his career with the president's office, he was considered by Kožený to be a valued and astute adviser.

Tomas Klaus earned a Ph.D. in chemistry in 1984. From 1972 he was with the Research Institute in Organic Chemistry in Prague, where he served as head of a research group in general projects, including production, company development, and strategy for the chemical industry. From 1987 until 1991, he was with the Czech Ministry of Industry, where he served as deputy director of strategy and development for the Department of Chemistry. One of the leading representatives of the Civic Forum at the ministry during the Velvet Revolution period, he began cooperating with Kožený during the summer of 1990. He helped HC&C make contacts and get several clients from the chemical industry sector while still working at the ministry. Finally in 1991, he left the Ministry of Industry and joined HC&C, where he was seen as a valuable adviser and source of knowledge on the country's important chemical industry. He later became senior vice president of the Harvard Group.

From Harvard Capital and Consulting
to the Harvard Group

Shortly after his return to Czechoslovakia in April of 1990, Kožený realized that because of the changing economic environment and the government's plans to privatize the economy, there were many exciting business opportunities. First he turned his attention to what he saw as an enormous potential market in the area of business and financial consulting. There were only a few foreign consulting firms beginning to set up operations in the CSFR, and as Kožený saw it at the time, these firms had to contend with several problems. They faced a language barrier; a shortage of clients who were able to pay for services received; the special conditions of the Czechoslovak economic environment, where many of the usual Western approaches to financial analysis might not be appropriate; and their own traditional orientation and organizational structures. Believing that a great opportunity existed for a Czechoslovak consulting service that could offer its clients knowledge of local conditions, international experience and know-how, a multilingual staff, and competitively low prices, Kožený set about attempting to apply what he had learned in the West.

Harvard Capital and Consulting

In October 1990 Kožený officially founded Harvard Capital and Consulting. Because he had spent nearly seven years at Harvard—almost all of his adult life up to that point in time, he decided to name his company after his famous alma mater. Though he would later be criticized for attempting to mislead the public into thinking that his company had an official relationship with Harvard University, Kožený had been keenly influenced by his years at the famous U.S. academic institution and was proud of his accomplishments there. Returning to his home country with the intention of applying the knowledge that he had gained at Harvard, he did not feel that it was inappropriate, unethical, or illegal to choose this name. He never declared any formal association with the university and, in the beginning, did not think that officials at Harvard would ever hear of his company anyway.

HC&C became an official adviser on privatization in the CSFR and was one of some twenty firms (many of them foreign) authorized during November and December 1990 by the Czech Ministry of Industry to carry out business-consulting services for state-owned enterprises. Most of these enterprises needed business valuations, and some of them retained HC&C to help them find joint-venture partners. The government paid approximately 50 percent of the fees for the services rendered by HC&C and the other firms to the state-owned enterprises. HC&C gained many clients during this period and began to generate high profits, as well as to gain much knowledge about many of the state-owned enterprises that were to be privatized. During 1991, a sister company, HC&C-Slovakia, was established in Slovakia in order to perform similar activities in the territories of the Slovak Republic. Viktor Kožen became increasingly well known and in December 1990 was appointed to the federal government's Legislative Board, a body of experts charged with advising the government on proposed legislation that was to be presented to parliament.

VH Publishing

Because of the prosperity of HC&C and the resulting inflows of capital, as well as the realization that for all practical purposes privatization consulting would be a one-shot affair, Kožen began to look for new ventures. Noticing the enormous lack of quality professional economic and business literature available in the Czech language and drawing upon his brief experience with the Galaxie Publishing Company, he decided to open a publishing house that would help remedy this situation. In January 1991, he officially founded VH Publishing (VHP). The company bought copyrights, hired qualified translators, and designed an ambitious plan for translating and publishing—mainly U.S. university texts on finance, marketing, management, and other business-related subjects. The first book appeared on the market in February 1992 and was sold primarily by subscription. Though the price for the *Dictionary of Finance and Investment Terms* was high (more than 800 koruny, or about 25 percent of the average monthly salary for a Czech worker), the book sold well because of the lack of a local substitute. As of June 1992, four books were out, and company officials stated that others would follow at shorter and shorter intervals.

Corporate Security Products

In February 1991, Kožen founded Corporate Security Products (CSP) because he expected a large demand in the security products industry in the CSFR and wanted to invest some capital in production. He also hired a group of well-qualified experts for the project of designing, producing, and selling security products such as safety bars, locks, and safe deposit boxes. Largely because of the high costs involved in using independent contractors to produce some of the components, this company was not as successful as Kožen had expected. In spite of this lack of early success, Kožen did not disband CSP. Rather, he chose to cut back on production in order to reduce expenses and to keep the core of the highly qualified staff for placement in positions in his other business activities. Karel Junek, a Corporate Security Products employee, was later appointed to the important position of technical director of

Kožený's Investors' Stock Brokerage, which was incorporated in March 1992.

National Security Printing

Incorporated in March 1991, National Security Printing (NSP) was the first private securities-printing company to be licensed in Czechoslovakia. Kožený believed that there would be an enormous market for securities printing in the country in connection with the privatization process. He felt that most of the companies would go public and that they would want to have their securities publicly visible and available.

Kožený found that the only experts in this highly specialized field worked for the government's State Bank Note Company, and he was able to persuade a number of them that their career prospects would improve if they joined him. For example, the technical vice-director of the State Bank Note Company joined NSP as director. Other experts in printing machines and printing technology also left the government agency in order to work for Kožený. In terms of its work force and printing equipment, NSP was probably the best-equipped printing company in the country that could provide complete services in connection with printing securities of the quality required for trade in middle-rank European stock exchanges. It provided the customers with shares and other securities that were equipped with the ISIN coding system, which was required for quoting abroad. Company officials suggested that even the State Bank Note Company was not able to guarantee such a high quality of print. NSP became a well-established company, and due to the strict regulations relating to securities printing and other practical concerns, it became completely independent from the rest of Kožený's enterprises. Kožený, however, continued to hold the major ownership of NSP.

Advance Investment Fund and Asset Management

Both of these companies were incorporated in July 1991 for future strategic reasons. The plans for launching a classic investment fund were postponed due to the fact that most of the top staff became very busy with the privatization funds business during the last part of 1991. Advance Investment Fund (AIF), however, planned a large initial public offering (IPO) campaign by the end of 1992 to sell shares in a closed mutual fund. Asset Management (AM) functioned as a center responsible for the administration of the voucher funds, such as mailing information to agents and shareholders and maintaining data bases on all of the employees associated with the voucher funds.

Credit Control Services

The credit management business began in early 1991, but in the beginning it worked under HC&C. For practical reasons and also to avoid possible conflict of interest, Credit Control Services (CCS) became independently incorporated in September 1991. The idea of becoming involved in the credit management business occurred to Kožený when he kept hearing that a chain-like insolvency crisis existed in Czechoslovakia. Kožený estimated that approximately Kčs 300 billion (around $10 billion) of debt existed in Czechoslovakia, and most companies did not have the cash to meet their obligations. Companies may have had high reported revenues and large accounts receivable balances, but frequently those who owed them money did not have the cash to pay. Consequently, these companies with high revenues and large accounts receivable did not have enough cash to apply to their own payables.

Using what he called the theory of big numbers, and an approach involving a very small outlay of cash, Kožený sensed that this market could be lucrative. He drew up a contract with an offer to assume collection responsibility for a firm's accounts receivable in exchange for a fee of 5 percent of the amount collected, plus—in some cases—a small retainer fee (.2 percent of accounts receivable, not to exceed Kčs 50,000). Investing only around $15,000 in start-up costs and a large mail campaign, Kožený was able to elicit the business of many firms. He reported that within the first two months his company was managing approximately $3.3 million in accounts receivable and had projected a cash flow from these accounts with a net present value of around $150,000. Also by the end of the first two months, the firm had received collection fees totaling over $30,000. Kožený estimated that as of June 1992, CCS managed around $200 million of accounts receivable. He further estimated that CCS at that time had from 75 percent to 80 percent of the market share and speculated that this market share would eventually stabilize at around 70 percent. He felt that CCS had an experienced staff and controlled "probably the best and largest database on companies' credit/debt relationships in Czechoslovakia."

Credit Evaluation Services

Credit Evaluation Services (CES) was incorporated in September 1991 but is not yet an active company. Kožený expected to activate this company, however, by 1993. Using the very large data base of financial and strategic information on CSFR companies, CES's mission was to provide rating services similar to Dun and Bradstreet based on official, publicly available information on CSFR companies. Kožený felt that there would be a high demand for such a service company because of the solvency problem and the general lack of reliable information at the time. Potential investors would need information about the credit history of potential business partners, for example. The ratings and related credit information would be based on Western methods of financial analysis. In the beginning, according to plans, CES would provide publicly available information to any company that requested it. Later it would provide special services to the clients that entered the company's scheme. Company officials did not rule out the possibility of some type of cooperation with one of the major world firms in the area, such as Dun and Bradstreet.

International Legal Consulting

INLECO, incorporated in September 1991, was created by separating the legal services department of HC&C from the parent company. It mainly was involved in advising privatization projects and specialized in medical services privatization and agricultural privatization. In addition to this, INLECO helped various clients in legal issues and cooperated with HC&C in such activities as supporting joint-venture projects. It also provided all necessary legal support for HC&C and the other companies that Kožený and his associates had founded.

Investors' Stock Brokerage

Kožený incorporated Investors' Stock Brokerage (ISB) in March 1992. It received a license from the Central Bank of the CSFR for carrying out security trading services for itself or others' accounts and for providing all major related services, including underwriting. With the developments in the privatization process and the creation of a capital market, ISB planned to open the futures-forwards trading market in Czechoslovakia. Kožený was working on a method to create ISB's own network of brokers. ISB also applied for membership in the Prague Stock Exchange, which was operational by the end of 1992, and was one of the few private stockbrokers granted membership there. Also, ISB signed an agreement with Reuters to list the shares it would trade through the Reuters Equities 2000 listing and, according to company officials, it was the only firm in the country to sign such an agreement. An ISB spokesperson suggested that this would help international investors become involved in the emerging Czechoslovak market.

The Voucher Scheme and HC&C's Involvement in It

A major feature of the economic reforms envisaged by the new leaders of the CSFR was the privatization of the economy. In October 1990 the federal parliament passed the "little privatization" law, which sought to open the way for free enterprise in the sagging, overly bureaucratic service sector and to encourage private ownership of small businesses. The act called for the privatization of approximately 120,000 small shops and restaurants by means of public auctions. In February 1991 the government passed another privatization law that called for the transfer of much of the remainder of state-owned enterprises to the private sector. The cornerstone of this larger privatization plan became known as voucher privatization. Through it, the government intended to transfer ownership of approximately 40 percent of the economy—around 3,000 medium- to large-scale companies with an estimated value of around $8 billion—to its citizenry. All citizens of Czechoslovakia over the age of eighteen could participate by paying a nominal fee of approximately $35, which was equal to about a week's salary, to purchase and register a voucher booklet. The government hoped that roughly four million citizens would participate. The sale and registration of voucher booklets began in October and November of 1991, respectively.

The Czechoslovak government introduced the idea of using investment funds (mutual funds) in the privatization process to manage the citizens' voucher allocations. Early proposals called for permitting banks and private companies to create twenty to thirty such funds. By the time the voucher scheme got under way, however, approximately 450 funds had been set up; among them were eight investment funds belonging to Harvard Capital and Consulting.

In the beginning, people were slow to participate in the voucher scheme. In spite of the government's hope that nearly one-fourth of the country's sixteen million citizens would participate, by the end of 1991 only around half a million had registered their vouchers. During Christmas, however, HC&C began a massive television and newspaper advertising campaign. The company promised a tenfold return on the investment after "a year and a day" (the traditional formula for Czech fairy tales) for anyone signing over their vouchers to HC&C. Soon HC&C became the biggest and best known of the funds, and other investment funds began to make similar or even more extravagant promises. Koženy and his aides succeeded in quickly recruiting over 20,000 agents to help educate the people about the privatization process, as well as to convince investors to sign their vouchers over to the investment fund.

Many observers, including government officials, noted that HC&C electrified interest in the voucher privatization process and was responsible for the buying frenzy that began in January 1992. An HC&C-commissioned opinion poll conducted by an independent public opinion institute during early January revealed that approximately half of those planning to use the various investment funds planned to choose Harvard Capital and Consulting. This success alarmed many government officials, who feared seeing so much economic power concentrated in the hands of one individual. Koženy felt that the government, under the prompting of the minister of privatization, Tomas Jezek, began a systematically organized campaign to discredit his company. Ministry officials openly stated their concerns about the social and economic repercussions of one man gaining so much influence in the country's economy. Koženy reported that he made an informal agreement with the federal finance minister, Václav Klaus, to cut back his advertising campaign and to limit his share to 20 percent of those using the investment funds. Nevertheless, the parliament passed a law at the end of April 1992 that placed several limitations on the activities of the investment funds. For example, it limited the share of any voucher fund to 10 percent of the investment market, limited any fund from owning more than 20 percent of any one company, and required each fund to have at least ten different investments, with no more than 10 percent of its assets invested in any one company.

By the end of May 1992, it was clear that HC&C had done well in the privatization process. Privatization funds claimed almost three-fourths of all privatization vouchers. Of the more than eight million participants in voucher privatization, approximately 814,000 investors chose to let HC&C handle either all or part of their voucher points. (Each investor had 1,000 voucher points.) HC&C ended up with around 638 million voucher points, which was second best in the country and number one among the noninstitutional fund managers. HC&C's managing director, Miraslav Zarecký, saw these voucher points as representing assets worth approximately $800 million.

The Harvard Group

HC&C was Koženy's first company; the others were offshoots. He began to see the necessity of organizing his companies into a more orderly structure in order to avoid possible accusations relating to insider trading and conflict of interest, as well as to deal with practical concerns such as accounting issues and occasional quarrels between companies about the allocation of resources. Koženy created the Harvard Group as a holding company for all of the other companies, including HC&C. The Harvard Group was a private joint-stock company owned by Koženy and his family. The group owned either all or a major stake in all of the individual companies. (See Figure 8.1.)

Issues

Establishing, maintaining, and expanding a capitalist-type, financially based holding company with multiple operating enterprises in a formerly Communist country was obviously fraught with potential obstacles and challenges. Some of the more important issues faced by Koženy and the Harvard Group are discussed here.

Financial Stability of HC&C

One obvious contextual problem faced by the HC&C unit of the Harvard Group especially, and potentially affecting all of the operating units, was the future course of the Czech economy. This was clearly beyond the control of Koženy and his colleagues, but it would impact in a major way the ability of the company to meet all of its financial obligations and guarantees. As one of the principals in the firm stated, "The future success of HC&C depends directly on the future political and economic developments in Czechoslovakia."

Perhaps the most critical specific concern regarding the financial stability of HC&C was its ability to meet on demand the 10:1 payout guarantee for redeemed vouchers. This was an issue mentioned both by those in the company,

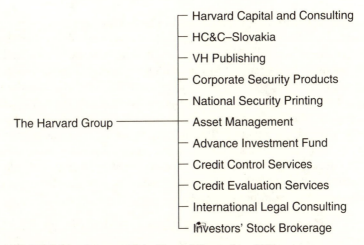

FIGURE 8.1   Structure of the Harvard Group, June 1992.

who were optimistic in this regard, and by those external, who were mildly to strongly skeptical. Company officials believed (and hoped) that potential joint ventures or partnerships with major foreign financial conglomerates would provide adequate backstop liquidity in a worst-case scenario. Outside observers believed that Kožen would have considerable financial difficulties in the future unless he could keep the number of his investors who wanted to cash in to below 20 percent; otherwise, they believed that the drain on his resources would be severe. This problem, as one such observer noted, would be especially exacerbated if the trading of shares was delayed, after shares were distributed, by a year or so due to Czech government policies relating to the establishment of official trading procedures.

Finally, the future level of financial stability of HC&C and other companies in the Harvard Group would likely be affected by the development of competition for providing some or all of its services. This competition, which would come particularly from large Western multinational financial services firms (e.g., Price Waterhouse), but also from other Czech companies, was already affecting the consulting activities of HC&C at the time. As a result of such competition, HC&C was forced to lower its fees.

Kožen's Role

There was no doubt in anyone's mind in the Harvard Group that this was an organization dominated by the ideas, energy, and determination of one man: Viktor Kožen. Exactly what his role was, however, and, especially, what it *should be*, was a frequently discussed topic among the company's core managerial employees. One of them, for example, believed Kožen's primary role should be to find specialists to work for the firm, and his secondary role should be to find good clients to engage the firm in projects that would make money for the company so that it could get increased credit from the banks for continued expansion. Another thought that Viktor's greatest strength was his creativity. "Viktor keeps thinking up ideas and activities faster than the authorities can keep up with him," this manager said. Kožený himself said that "my role is more as a strategist in the holding company. I try not to get involved in the day-to-day details, yet my aim is to stay 'very close' to the market. It is very important to stay close to the market." There was a general consensus among Kožený's top management group, as well as elsewhere in the company, that Viktor retained the final say-so on all important decisions. "However," as one top-echelon executive said, "someone must tell him about the decisions that need to be made and explain to him *why*." As this implies, there were questions being raised within the firm about the degree to which Kožený did or did not delegate.

Management Structure of the Harvard Group

As in any new enterprise that is growing and expanding its products and services, the management structure of the Harvard Group evolved over time. In fact, it seldom, so far in its short history, has had a stable structure. This was in large part due to Kožený's explicit belief that the structure should be kept extremely fluid. As he stated, "I purposely decided to create a very unstable structure. Even today the aim is to make a nearly horizontal corporate structure." However, he did expect that there would be greater overall systematization of the structure, but the degree of structural stability would vary from company to company due to the necessity of meeting government-imposed regulatory constraints. "The nature of the business [of each company in the group] will determine the structure," he said. "The structure will depend on which tasks can be standardized, and which cannot."

At the time of this study, the management structure of the Harvard Group involved a brain trust of eight or nine key individuals. Included, in addition to Kožený, were Varcop, Sauer, Zarecký, Kanoková, Krivká, and Klaus, as well as a few other managing directors of the key operating companies. It is only since spring 1992 that this group has even started holding regular meetings every two weeks, a move that several of Kožený's lieutenants had urged him to do for some time. But, Kožený emphasized, this top group of executives was "*not* a collective decision-making body—as in the West." A reasonable inference is that Kožený listened at these meetings but reserved the right to make the ultimate decisions on any issues he considered sufficiently crucial. One of the Harvard Group's more-experienced directors suggested that one of his primary functions was not so much to make decisions independently but to act as a balancing force on Kožený's theoretical or creative impulses and to help him channel his fantasies into real-world projects.

Under this top management group were the directors of each of the operating companies. As noted previously, some of these company directors also formed part of the top management team. The later reorganization of the overall enterprise into the Harvard Group (HG), with a top management brain trust and a set of operating companies reporting to it, also had the effect of creating additional management positions and therefore more opportunities for those who wanted to assume greater responsibilities. Some of these sets of responsibilities appeared to be clear for some managers but somewhat vague and diffuse for others. This state of affairs was not seen as a disadvantage by Koženy, but some others in the HG expressed concern about the lack of well-defined boundaries for their authority.

Recruitment of Key Managerial Personnel

Given the circumstances that surrounded the building of a miniconglomerate of the nature of the Harvard Group in a country that had only recently shifted abruptly after forty years from communism to capitalism, Koženy and his top aides were finding it difficult to recruit well-qualified middle-management personnel. As Varcop put it, "It is very hard to find good *managers* in this country for our type of company." The Harvard Group relied on its contacts in the government ministries, in banking circles, and the like. The ideal new managerial hire was someone with two to six years experience in the West (in embassies, etc.), good analytical skills, and who had access to information in the government and elsewhere. The difficulties of finding this type of employee were especially acute in the Slovak companies of the HG, where the sought-after combination of technical and English-language skills was an even scarcer commodity than in the Czech part of the country. "In the future," said Varcop, "our ability to obtain good employees will depend on our success."

Monitoring Companies in Which the Harvard Group Invested

A problem foreseen by Koženy and others such as Varcop was the need for the Harvard Group to have its own representatives on the boards of directors of the companies in which HC&C invested, so that assistance could be provided to those companies in developing their strategic plans and also so that the progress—or lack of progress—of the companies could be monitored closely. The need, as put succinctly by Varcop, was to have the managers in those companies "cooperate with us."

Compensation of Key Personnel and Managers

As noted in the section on the management structure of the Harvard Group, Koženy made it an item of faith to attempt to keep the structure as nearly horizontal and as amorphous as possible. Consequently, there was very little differentiation in compensation between those at the top and those at the bottom of the holding company until the middle of 1992. This situation in turn caused a degree of discomfort for some senior managers who felt that they did not have sufficient discretion to offer monetary incentives for superior performance by those who reported to them. This apparently became an acute enough problem that Kožený felt obliged to intervene and raise the salaries of the topmost executives and to give the managing directors of most of the individual companies more authority for making salary decisions for their subordinates. It was too early to tell whether this change had solved the problem or only dampened it for a while.

Relations with the Government

The Harvard Group's relations with the government, beginning when there was only one operating company (HC&C), continued to be characterized by wariness on both sides. As previously noted, the minister of privatization criticized HC&C because of a concern it was obtaining too high a percentage of citizens' vouchers in the privatization process. Also, the minister was critical of HC&C's promotional activities in attempting to obtain the vouchers—its "promises," its use of the Harvard name, and the aggressive tactics of its sales agents (who were not HC&C employees). These criticisms, in the early months of 1991, "did some damage," according to an HC&C official, but "the damage was limited." At the time of this study there had not been any recent direct confrontation between the government and the Harvard Group, and indeed Kožený and his aides worked hard to maintain favorable contacts within the relevant ministries.

The Public's Image of HC&C

Since the early days of the founding of the initial company of the Harvard Group, HC&C, and its active promotion of the voucher plan, the public was very aware of Victor Kožený and his financial enterprise. As one mid-level government official stated: "Viktor Kožený has a 'special position' in this country. Without his activity the majority of people [in Czechoslovakia] would have no interest in the coupon [voucher] business. This interest is all due to his 10:1 offer." When pressed further, this official summarized his view of the public's perception of HC&C as "a product of the market economy ... and, so far, the people are satisfied with the company's activities." This public image was also apparently helped by the fact that at the end of 1991 and the first part of 1992, Kožený's company sponsored the translation of twenty-nine episodes of the "Dallas" TV series and, thereby, was able to get the firm mentioned in advertisements accompanying the series. It appeared that the average citizen was aware of HC&C and its activities, had a generally positive image, and was waiting to see whether the company would in fact follow through on its payoff promises when the time came to sell the vouchers.

The Future of the Harvard Group

From the perspective of Viktor Koženy, the Harvard Group was in a "hypergrowth stage." Eventually, Koženy planned to separate the financial operating companies from the nonfinancial companies, some of which might eventually be merged with Western firms. Koženy did not anticipate this latter happening until those (nonfinancial) companies were of sufficient size and had enough managerial depth. When this was done, however, the plan was for the Harvard Group to continue to have a minority equity position in this set of companies. The financially based companies, in Koženy's vision, would be "doing a lot of leverage deals" such as moving into forward contracts on privatized vouchers. Also, Koženy's goals for the future included launching such financial enterprises as a bank and a security brokerage firm. "If we are successful," said Viktor, "we can overhaul the whole financial sector of this country overnight."

These would have been ambitious plans for an entrepreneurial company of this type in a well-developed Western country with a fundamentally sound economy. For a two-year-old firm in a country just emerging from forty years of a state-controlled socialist economy, the challenges appeared especially daunting.

Notes

1. Fictitious names are used for the members of Koženy's management team. The short biographical sketches are based on interviews with the managers.

2. Except for Harvard Capital and Consulting, fictitious names are used for the individual companies making up the Harvard Group.

∎

CHAPTER NINE

Czechoslovak Airlines:
Pricing in a Market Environment

In March 1992, Luděk Hladiš, the young, newly appointed manager of tariffs for Czechoslovak Airlines (ČSA), faced the challenging task of developing passenger fares that would make his state-owned enterprise more profitable and an attractive candidate for privatization. Hladiš and his small professional staff of six were responsible for developing passenger fares and cargo rates for both domestic and international flights. He and his staff were also expected to negotiate the fares and rates with their respective foreign partners.

Domestic fares were a major problem for Hladiš and his staff. In 1991, fares were raised nearly 100 percent in three steps so that they might cover direct costs. However, costs also rose in 1991, so fares were still not high enough to cover them. ČSA's top management asked Hladiš and his staff to come up with a proposal for new increases in domestic fares. Hladiš promised to make a recommendation regarding domestic fares to senior management within a month.

Overview of Czechoslovak Airlines

Founded in 1923, Czechoslovak Airlines has a long history.[1] Like many airlines around the world, it was a government-owned enterprise from its creation. By the end of 1930 ČSA inaugurated international flights within Europe and joined the international fare-making body, the International Air

This case was prepared by Josephine E. Olson of the University of Pittsburgh and by Jana Matesová of the Czechoslovak Management Center. The authors wish to thank Ing. Luděk Hladiš (engineer) and the many people at Czechoslovak Airlines who generously lent their time and expertise in the preparation of this case, particularly Dr. Miroslav Bělovský, Ing. Tomáš Kaufman, Ing. Martin Kovář, Ing. Roman Lokaj, Ing. František Slabý, Dr. Alena Vaňhová, and Ing. Matouš Sedliský.

Traffic Association (IATA). The airline grew rapidly and before World War II it averaged sixty-three takeoffs and 15,000 kilometers a day. By 1947 it had reestablished its old routes, interrupted by World War II, and it added routes to the Middle East.

The Communist takeover of Czechoslovakia in 1948 had a considerable effect on the operation of the airline. Financial goals became less important. The airline was managed by a plan that set physical, rather than financial, targets for routes, passenger miles, and the like. Differential pricing was introduced for citizens of Communist and non-Communist countries.

In 1957 ČSA became one of the pioneers of the jet age with its introduction of the Russian-made TU-104A jet aircraft. In 1960, the airline added the Russian IL-18 turboprops, which carried more than 100 passengers, and inaugurated its longest route, from Prague to Jakarta, Indonesia. The 1960s saw the growing importance of ČSA's international routes and renewal of its aircraft fleet with second-generation Russian planes, and in the 1970s and 1980s, it continued to modernize its fleet. In 1989 the airline again considered introducing new planes and ordered two Airbus A310-300s to replace its Russian planes in long-distance routes. Four ATR-72s and five Boeing 737s were ordered in 1991 and were to be delivered in mid-1992. ČSA's business strategy was to introduce new European lines, for which it needed these new, economical, and comfortable planes. It also planned to replace some of its smallest planes on domestic routes with these new planes.

Beginning around 1980, financial considerations once again became important to the airline. As seen in Table 9.1, ČSA experienced losses in all but one year between 1975 and 1982. A 100 percent increase in the price of fuel in 1980 and a cut in the plan allocation of fuel to ČSA in 1981 led to a decision to eliminate many domestic flights, resulting in a reduction in domestic passengers carried (see Figure 9.1). Cuts in domestic routes continued in 1982 when ČSA operations were limited to eight domestic airports.

As seen in Table 9.1, even after these changes, domestic routes still had large but decreasing losses. The domestic losses, however, were now more than offset by profits on international and charter flights, so by 1983 the airline was profitable overall. In the language of economists, it appeared that after 1982 the domestic routes were "cross-subsidized" by international routes.

The end of the Communist government in November 1989 led to further changes in the airline's business strategy. ČSA eliminated some of its international routes to Communist countries such as Cuba and Vietnam because business contacts with these countries became much less important. It maintained only chartered flights to these countries, which always were profitable. In 1990, the airline also made organizational changes to facilitate its future privatization. These included dividing the company into three separate entities—the airline and an airport administration in each of the two republics.

TABLE 9.1 ČSA Profits and Expenses (in millions of koruny)

	1975	1976	1977	1978	1979	1980	1981	1982	1983
Total profits/losses	-66.3	3.9	-100.8	-248.0	-251.2	-247.9	-284.3	-91.3	367.9
Operating profits/losses	na	na	na	na	na	na	-180.4	-43.6	298.7
Scheduled International	na	na	na	na	na	na	-96.8	-4.8	298.6
Charter	na	na	na	na	na	na	56.0	42.1	56.8
Domestic	na	na	na	na	na	na	-134.6	-80.1	-56.7
Total Expenses	1,478.7	1,351.5	1,318.4	1,508.7	1,678.2	1,703.2	1,743.7	1,661.4	1,586.6

	1984	1985	1986	1987	1988	1989	1990	1991
Total profits/losses	172.8	237.7	291.1	326.3	432.1	499.8	435.0	202.3
Operating profits/losses	169.7	251.0	269.2	369.3	547.8	514.8	261.5	170.9
Scheduled International	204.8	300.8	291.1	382.8	532.6	440.1	278.3	146.4
Charter	46.1	51.8	70.3	70.3	76.8	120.2	37.2	108.5
Domestic	-80.5	-101.6	-92.2	-83.8	-61.6	-45.5	-54.0	-84.0
Total Expenses	1,816.6	2,006.8	1,933.9	2,068.5	2,163.4	2,113.3	3,141.7	5,969.3

Source: Presentation of ČSA: Czechoslovak Airlines, Prague, March 1991, and letters from František Slabý, February 24, 1992, and April 10, 1992.

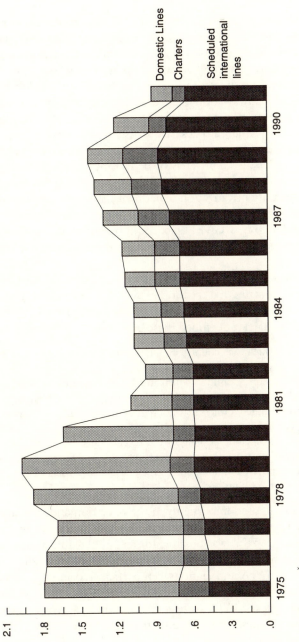

FIGURE 9.1   ČSA Passengers Carried (in millions).
Source: Presentation of ČSA: Czechoslvak Airlines. Prague, March 1991, and letter from František Slabý of February 24, 1992.

The International Market

Airlines, including ČSA, were under quite different constraints in setting international and domestic passenger fares.[2] In addition, almost all major international airlines with the exception of those from the United States and a few other countries were government-owned enterprises whose missions might be other than profit maximization. According to Barrett, "[b]elow-cost selling is a feature of many aviation markets as governments use national airlines to earn scarce foreign exchange, promote tourism, or simply 'carry the flag' to more destinations."[3] Many airlines used cross-subsidization to cover their unprofitable routes, and some governments also provided direct subsidies to their national carriers. Even privately owned airlines tended to be heavily regulated by their governments. This situation was beginning to change by early 1992, with increasing privatization of national airlines, a push toward greater competition in the European Community, and the possibility that air service might be included in new GATT (General Agreement on Tariffs and Trade) rules,[4] but the international market in passenger travel was still highly controlled.

International air passenger traffic was governed by bilateral aviation agreements between countries. Except for the United States and the United Kingdom, these agreements usually provided for one carrier from each country on their joint routes. Barrett described these bilaterials:

> The sovereignty which each country exercises gives it the right to refuse permission for the aircraft of any other country to use its air space. These rights are exchanged in bilateral agreements. Countries which attach a high priority to their own airlines' interests usually aim to secure the right of those airlines to a half-share in the traffic on the routes exchanged. Others may not require actual equality of market share but seek instead 'fair and equal opportunity' for their carriers. The more restrictive bilateral air agreements include pooling of the revenues earned by all carriers on the route, regulation of capacity offered, agreement on the fares to be charged by airlines of both countries, and limitation of the number of carriers from each country to be allowed on the routes.[5]

The IATA also figured importantly in the operation and pricing decisions of international airlines. The organization also acted as a trade association for airlines, and after 1978 it was possible for an airline to be a member of the trade association without also agreeing to the tariffs. As of 1990, 200 airlines were members of IATA and eighty-seven participated in its tariff coordination.[6] Although the U.S. Department of Justice and the Department of Transportation attacked IATA's fare-setting activities as a constraint on trade, as of 1992 most airlines, including ones from the United States, still participated in its fare-setting activities.

Events in Czechoslovakia in 1989 had little effect on how ČSA set its international passenger fares except for the elimination of special lower fares for citizens of Communist countries. In addition, the government was less likely to order low fares for special groups.

ČSA had long participated in the fare-setting activities of IATA and continued to do so. Like most international airlines, ČSA had several types of fares; the most general and the highest were IATA fares. The ČSA, like other international airlines, determined the IATA fares and rates on its routes through bilateral and multilateral talks and agreements. Most carriers operating on European routes attended IATA conferences that were held once or twice a year. At the first stage, fares for each route were discussed by partners on a route; they negotiated and came to an agreement. In the final vote, all airlines had to agree on all fares as a package.[7] IATA fares were valid for all carriers on a route, thus interlining (establishing a single fare over two or more airlines) was possible, and these fares could be used on some indirect routes. Because tickets applied to any airline that agreed to IATA fares, passengers with IATA fare tickets could travel on any airline and change the airline as they wished, although this was subject to any restrictions when purchasing the ticket. IATA fares could be and frequently were changed between conferences as long as there was agreement between the two national airlines on the route and as long as other airlines did not protest the new fares or rates.

In addition to IATA fares, there might be bilateral fares between two national airlines. These "bilaterals" should not be confused with the more general bilateral aviation agreements between countries described earlier. However, bilateral fares, which were lower than the IATA fares, were valid only for the two national carriers, and they could not be introduced unless both airlines and their governments approved them. In Czechoslovakia, the relevant government agency was the Civil Aviation Authority of the Ministry of Transport.

Both IATA and bilateral fares could be for first, business (Class C), and normal-economy classes, though ČSA did not offer first-class service. In addition, there could be both IATA and bilateral unrestricted full fares and restricted promotional fares such as excursion, APEX, PEX, Super-APEX, Super-PEX, weekend, youth, and other fares designed to attract leisure and off-peak travelers while excluding business travelers. The restrictions on promotional fares usually included one or more of the following conditions: minimum stay (e.g., over a weekend), maximum stay, advanced booking and payment, return and stopover limitations, named groups (e.g., youth or senior citizens), and wholesale fares (for tour packages).[8] Despite this range of fare possibilities, most bilateral fares were aimed at the leisure market. ČSA had the same range of promotional fares offered by most international airlines.

Determination of International Fares

Like most airlines trying to determine a reasonable fare or fares on a given international route, the ČSA Tariff Department started with an analysis of costs for the flight or route supplied by the Economics Department. Airline costs could be somewhat arbitrarily divided into four categories: passenger-related costs, flight-related costs, route-related costs, and airline-related costs.[9] As long as the flight was operated in any event, the costs relating to the number of passengers on the flight were quite small; they might include the costs of meals and drinks, passenger insurance, and extra fuel costs related to extra weight. More important were the costs related to a given flight; these included fuel, airport landing and navigation fees, a major portion of the crew costs, and use-related maintenance and depreciation costs. These in turn depended to a great extent on the type of aircraft and distance flown. Costs related to adding or dropping a particular route were also substantial. A new route might require additional aircraft and crews. Additional maintenance facilities might be needed as well as investment in ground facilities. Finally there were the general overhead expenses of operating an airline, which had to be covered if the airline was to be profitable. Some of these were costs of general administration, the reservation system, and advertising.

When ČSA negotiated fares on an existing route, it examined load factors (actual passengers as a percentage of total passenger seats) by flight, time of week and type of fare, and any trends in these bookings. Airlines could set the mix of fares on particular flights, thus setting quantitative limits on cheap fares. For example, if an early-morning flight was in heavy demand by business travelers, few cheap fares could be assigned to this flight. When trying to determine the optimal fare, Hladiš's staff also had to consider competition such as fares on flights from neighboring countries to the same destinations.

For new routes ČSA investigated the market to determine what kind of traffic by passenger categories there were likely to be. The staff calculated the cost, decided on some potential fares by category, and then determined whether these fares would cover costs. If not, they changed the fare assumptions again.

Despite ČSA's sophisticated pricing strategy for international fares, Hladiš felt his airline was at a disadvantage compared to some of its Western competitors. Although he had considerable passenger information on ČSA's international flights, he did not have much contact with other airlines and he lacked market information from computerized data bases used by travel agents and airlines in other countries.

The Domestic Market

Compared to international fares, domestic airline pricing faced different constraints. Most countries, including Czechoslovakia, restricted domestic routes to their own carriers. (These are known as "cabotage" restrictions.) ČSA had had no airline competition on its domestic routes for many years and had only recently faced airline competition on a few routes from a couple of small, for-

TABLE 9.2   Costs of Alternative Means of Transportation in Czechoslovakia, March 1992

Route	Distance (kms)	Time Required	Accommodations	Cost (Kčs)
Train				
Praha-Bratislava	398	5–6 hrs	1st class	183
			2nd class	122
			sleeping coach	212–343
Praha-Sliač	613	9–10 hrs	1st class	225
			2nd class	150
			sleeping coach	255–385
Praha-Košice	708	9hrs15'–10hrs15'	1st class	252
			2nd class	162
			sleeping coach	282–412
Praha-Ostrava	658	4hrs15'–5hrs	1st class	183
			2nd class	122
			sleeping coach	212–343
Praha-Tatry	607	8–10hrs	1st class	225
			2nd class	150
			sleeping coach	200–385
Bus				
Praha-Bratislava	336	4hrs40'		118
Praha-Sliač	479	7hrs10'		182
Praha-Košice	729	13hrs10'		274
Praha-Ostrava	399	5hrs25'–6hrs		118–150
Praha-Tatry	560	8hrs40'h		238
Car				
Praha-Bratislava	330	3hrs30'–4hrs30'		660
Praha-Sliač	525	6hrs30'		1,050
Praha-Košice	657–720	9–10hrs		1,300–1,450
Praha-Ostrava	342–380	5 hrs		680–760
Praha-Tatry	542	7–8hrs		1,080

Source: Czechoslovak State Railroad Company (CSD) Time Table and Price List, Czechoslovak State Bus Transportation (CSAD) Time Table and Price List, Čebus Bus Travel Company Time Table and Price List, Road Map of Czechoslovakia, and own calculations.

merly charter airlines such as Tatra Air, Slovair, and Air Vitkovice. However, Czechoslovakia was a relatively small country (its total area was 127,876 square kilometers), and many of its routes were fairly short. Thus competition for ČSA might include not only other domestic airlines but trains, buses, and automobiles. Table 9.2 shows distances, fares, and trip times for these modes of ground transportation for various ČSA routes. It was anticipated that rail and bus fares would increase in the near future.

Except when a domestic flight was a segment of an international flight, domestic fares did not involve IATA. Many airlines offered fewer classes on their domestic flights, and because of its relatively small planes, ČSA offered only economy class.

Determination of Domestic Fares

With preparations for eventual privatization, domestic air fares again came under consideration. These fares, which had not been increased since 1980, were raised three times in 1991 in an attempt to ensure that the fares at least covered direct operating costs. However, costs also increased; at the beginning of 1992 domestic fares were still not covering the variable (direct) costs.

Distance was the principal factor on which ČSA set its domestic fares.[10] Each route was assigned a scale based on distance; the scales remained constant, but the fares assigned to the scales can be changed. ČSA's fares did not increase proportionally with distance, perhaps reflecting the fact that a significant portion of the cost of a flight, regardless of distance, was the cost of taking off and landing. Table 9.3 shows ČSA's domestic fares as of November 1, 1991, for tickets purchased within and outside the country.

ČSA was moving to a ticketing procedure and promotional fare structure for domestic fares similar to what it used for international fares, but in early 1992 there were still some differences in the types of promotional fares it offered. In addition to offering normal economy fares, ČSA had several domestic promotional fares aimed at encouraging leisure travel by Czechs and Slovaks. These included lower fares on Saturday and Sunday; a special "spa fare," or excursion fare, with return trip restricted to between seven and thirty days; and a weekend fare good only for departure on Friday morning with the return trip on Saturday or Sunday. It also offered a 20 percent discount on round-trips for its normal economy fare. As can be observed from Table 9.3, these promotional fares were also related to distance, so they did not manifest the apparent inequity of a cheaper fare on a longer distance, a phenomenon frequently found in international fares (including ČSA's) and fares within the United States. A comparison of rail rates in Table 9.2 with ČSA's fares shows the two sets of rates have a similar structure with respect to distance, but ČSA's excursion fare was about four times the equivalent first-class rail rate.

ČSA not only based its domestic fares primarily on distance but tended to use across-the-board percentage increases when it raised fares. For example, the fare increases that went into effect on November 1, 1992, were approximately 30 percent on normal economy tickets and 60 percent on promotional fares.

Several other complications existed with respect to ČSA's domestic passenger fares. Domestic tickets sold outside of Czechoslovakia cost more than tickets purchased within the country (see Table 9.3). In addition, a domestic flight on ČSA might be included as part of an international ticket sold by another airline. For example, a passenger wishing to go from Frankfurt to Bratislava could buy a ticket from Lufthansa for a flight from Frankfurt to Prague on Lufthansa and then a flight to Bratislava on ČSA. In this case Lufthansa reimbursed ČSA for the domestic portion of the trip. ČSA generally had spe-

TABLE 9.3   ČSA Domestic Fares as of November 1, 1991 (in koruny)

Route	Tariff Distance One Way	Normal Economy Fares				Spa/ Excursion Fare	Friday AM Departure Fare	Foreign Sales One Way
		Monday to Friday		Saturday to Sunday				
		One Way	Round Trip	One Way	Round Trip			
Praha-Bratislava	188	940	1,510	640	1,280	1,410	1,160	1,450
Praha-Košice	326	1,250	2,000	850	1,700	1,880	1,540	1,920
Praha-Ostrava	176	890	1,430	610	1,220	1,340	1,090	1,370
Praha-Piešťany	191	940	1,510	640	1,280	1,410	1,160	1,450
Praha-Sliač	243	1,040	1,670	710	1,420	1,560	1,280	1,610
Praha-Tatry	280	1,200	1,920	820	1,640	1,800	1,480	1,860
Bratislava-Košice	188	840	1,350	580	1,160	1,260	1,030	1,280
Bratislava-Tatry	155	760	1,220	520	1,040	1,140	930	1,160
Bratislava-Piešťany	na	320	520	230	460	480	390	520

Source: ČSA Tariff Department.

TABLE 9.4   Basic Macroeconomic Statistics, Czechoslovakia, 1988–1991

A. Gross Domestic Product and Gross Material Product (billion Kčs)

	1988	1989	1990	1991
Gross domestic product in current prices	740.0	759.4	819.9	977.8
Gross material product created in constant prices	662.7	669.3	669.4	561.8
Gross material product utilized	648.5	668.9	702.4	511.2

Sources: *Statistická ročenka CSFR* (Statistical Yearbook of CSFR). Prague: SNTL, 1992; *Quarterly Statistical Bulletin*. Prague: Federal Bureau of Statistics, March 1992.

B. Percentage of Annual Change in Employment, Consumer Prices, and Wages

	1988	1989	1990	1991
Employment	+0.5	−0.1	−3.5	−13.1
Consumer prices	+0.2	+1.4	+10.0	+57.9
Foodstuffs	−0.3	+0.1	+11.1	+45.3
Nominal average monthly wage (excluding farming coops)	+2.3	+2.3	+3.7	+16.4
Real average monthly wage (excluding farming coops)	+2.0	−0.8	−5.8	−24.3

Source: *Quarterly Statistical Bulletin*. Prague: Federal Bureau of Statistics, March 1992.

cific fares, called "provisas," that were charged to the other airline. If no provisa existed, the fare was based on prorated factors related to distance.

Hladiš and his staff faced a variety of problems in making domestic pricing decisions. One of the most important was that they had much less information on domestic demand than they had on international demand. Except for some limited aggregate information, data were not available on the structure of passengers (domestic vs. foreign, normal fares vs. promotional fares). Despite the existence of a variety of promotional fares for domestic flights, Hladiš had the impression that few passengers used them, perhaps because most passengers were either foreigners or domestic residents traveling on business.

Although Hladiš and his staff had few specific data on domestic demand, they knew that the economic conditions in Czechoslovakia were not favorable to domestic air passenger travel, at least by CSFR citizens. The transition to a market economy along with the complete collapse of the CMEA trade arrangements had caused a significant drop in real income and increasing unemployment. Prices of most goods and services were liberalized at the beginning of 1991, but wages were not. Although there is some question as to how reliable the government's national statistics were given the dynamic changes the economy was undergoing, most Czechs and Slovaks experienced a significant drop in their real income after 1991 (see Table 9.4). Air travel tended to be quite income elastic, and leisure travel also tended to be price elastic.

Therefore, Hladiš worried that any price increase at that time might be self-defeating because of a drop in travel.

Another serious problem facing the Tariff Department was the condition of ČSA's fleet. Aside from the two Airbus A310-300s that were used on its longer international flights, ČSA had twenty-six Russian planes of four different types (see Table 9.5 for their characteristics). Of these four, the largest, the IL-62(M), was used exclusively for international flights in 1991, and the next largest, the TU-154M, was used primarily on international flights. This left the TU-134A and the small, very energy-inefficient JAK-40K for domestic flights.

Moreover, the situation worsened considerably after early 1991 because several of the larger planes were out of service due to the inability to obtain parts. As a result, some of the TU-134As were diverted to international flights, leaving most domestic routes to be serviced by the fuel-hungry JAK-40Ks. These structural and equipment changes dramatically increased costs, making domestic pricing decisions even more difficult. One of the few exceptions to this diversion of equipment was the Prague-Bratislava-Tatry route, which still used the TU-134A.

ČSA expected the fleet situation to be eased somewhat by the arrival of four 66-passenger ATR-72s in mid-1992 and by the additional orders of planes under consideration. In the meantime, however, its JAK-40K aircraft made its domestic routes very expensive, and no one had a clear idea of what the operating costs of the ATR-72s would be.

As mentioned earlier, ČSA raised its domestic fares three times in 1991 (on February 15, July 1, and November 1) for a total increase of 100 percent in an attempt to ensure that the fares at least covered direct operating costs. In addition, the number of flights were decreased on some routes and other routes were completely eliminated, partly as a result of changes in the types of aircrafts used by the airline. Nevertheless, costs continued to rise. As a result of the division of ČSA into an airline and two airport administrations, the airline paid landing fees to the airports. Navigation fees were expected to increase again in 1992. In addition, reconstruction of the landing strip at the Košice airport greatly increased costs on what was one of ČSA's best routes because ČSA's larger planes could not land at Košice. As a result ČSA flew a TU-134A to Bratislava on the Prague-Bratislava-Košice route. Those passengers continuing on to Košice were loaded onto two small JAK-40Ks for the remainder of the trip. The reverse was done on the return trip. Needless to say, this more than doubled the costs on the Bratislava-Košice segment of that route. Table 9.6 shows actual average revenue and cost figures and average load factors for domestic flights for 1990, 1991, and the first quarter of 1992.

As a result of the cost increases, Hladiš estimated that the new domestic fares would only cover 75 percent of the direct costs in 1992.

TABLE 9.5   ČSA Airplane Types, 1992

	A-310-300	IL-62(M)	TU-154M	TU-134A	JAK-40K	ATR-72
Number of planes	2	8	7	5	6	4
Number of crew	2	5	3–4	3	2	2
Number of seats	214	174	136	76	32	66
Maximum take-off weight (MTOW) in tons	157	167	100	49	13.7	21.5
Maximum payload in tons	33	23	18	8.2	2.7	7.3
Year of delivery	1991	1969–84	1988–90	1971–77	1974–77	1992[a]
Producer	Airbus	USSR	USSR	USSR	USSR	ATR
Fuel consumption per one gross hour of flight (kg)	4,190	6,420	4,520	2,710	1,060	600
Maximum distance with max number of passengers	8,800	7,000	3,640	2,060	510	1,950
Fuel consumption in grams per passenger (km)	26.6	53.7	52.6	64.6	121.7	22

[a]Planes were planned to be delivered before the end of May 1992.
Source: Letter from František Slabý, February 24, 1992.

TABLE 9.6 ČSA Revenue and Cost Data for Prague-Bratislava-Tatry and All Domestic Routes, 1990, 1991, and First Quarter 1992

Year and Aircraft	No. of Flights	Revenue per Flight	Total Cost per Flight	Direct Variable Cost per Flight	Direct Cost per Flight	Avg. Load Factor	Ratios of Revenue to Total Cost	Ratios of Revenue to Direct Cost
All Domestic Flights								
1990	3,405.5	37,089kčs	52,951kčs	28,298kčs	31,909kčs	63.45	70.0%	116.2%
1991								
TU134	999.0	93,116	132,496	100,190	103,943	58.97	70.3	89.6
JAK40	1,563.5	28,067	51,773	35,121	37,469	81.83	54.2	74.9
Other	181.5	30,904	72,777	50,584	55,234	70.52	42.5	56.0
All	2,744.0	51,937[a]	82,551	59,833	62,845	63.75	62.9	82.6
1992[b]								
TU134	179.0	87,034	145,101	93,682	95,469	47.72	60.0	91.2
JAK40	481.5	39,670	65,551	40,467	41,990	78.70	60.5	94.5
Other	76.0	43,066	133,395	83,566	90,487	38.76	32.3	47.6
All	736.5	51,532	91,886	57,848	59,992	60.64	56.1	85.9
Prague-Bratislava-Tatry (OK126/127 route)								
1990	307.5	62,312	76,543	44,852	49,948	64.29	81.4	124.8
1991								
TU134	298.0	101,621	152,970	117,812	122,047	58.18	66.4	83.3
JAK40	15.5	28,065	74,452	52,064	55,355	78.29	32.7	23.0
Other	6.0	132,667	246,500	169,833	198,833	45.22	53.8	66.7
All	319.5	98,635[c]	150,917	115,599	120,254	58.36	70.8	98.5
1992[b]								
TU134	67.0	127,164	179,836	127,119	129,612	48.43	70.7	98.1
JAK40	3.5	58,571	79,714	52,571	54,857	78.87	73.5	106.8
Other	5.0	153,800	215,200	129,200	152,400	49.13	71.5	100.9
All	75.5	125,748	177,536	123,801	127,656	48.88	70.8	98.5

[a] About 28 percent of this revenue was from foreign sales.
[b] Figures for 1992 are for first quarter.
[c] About 34 percent of this revenue was from foreign sales.
Source: ČSA Economics Department.

TABLE 9.7   Average Number of Passengers per Flight Segment, Prague-Bratislava-Tatry Flight

Segment	*November 1990 to January 1991*	*November 1991 to January 1992*
Prague to Bratislava	34	30
Bratislava to Prague	22	21
Prague to Tatry	28	22
Tatry to Prague	25	17
Bratislava to Tatry	31	14
Tatry to Bratislava	24	13

Source: Luděk Hladiš's calculations made from raw data.

TABLE 9.8   Planned Cost for Prague-Bratislava-Tatry Flight as of February 25, 1992

Tariff Distance in km	1,380		Type of Aircraft TU-134-A	
Length of Flight in hrs	2.45			
Number of Passengers	45			
Total Passenger kms	62,100			
Volume of Tank in kgs	8,250			
				Kčs
Fuel				
Prague	29%	2,392.5kg	7.7Kčs/kg	18,422
Bratislava	50	4,125.0	9.133	37,674
Tatry	21	1,732.5	9.133	15,823
Total Fuel				71,919
Oil/Hour	1.8	4.41	33.67	148
Filling costs			0.41	2
Catering				8,208
Direct wages				
Pilots (3)			0.5616Kčs/km	775
Stewards (3)			0.16704	231
Maintenance			7864Kčs/hr	19,267
Fees				
Handling	1		3,800Kčs	3,800
Grnd navig.	4		1,078	4,312
Landing-PRG	1		5,411	5,411
Landing-BTS	2		2,891	5,782
Landing-TAT	1		5,411	5,411
Bus	1	640	640	
Navigation				3,289
Insurance			0.0085783Kčs/pas-km	527
Total dependent cost				129,721
Direct wages				
Pilots (3)			682Kčs/hr	1,671
Stewards (3)			73	179
Depreciation			0Kčs/hr	0
Other direct costs				
Social Security—20% of wages				571
Aircraft Insurance			36Kčs/hr	88
Total hourly and other direct costs				2,509
Total direct cost				132,230

Source: ČSA Economics Department.

The Prague-Bratislava-Tatry Route

Although the practice had been to raise fares by the same percentage across all routes, Hladiš and his staff were paying particular attention to passengers and cost data for the Prague-Bratislava-Tatry route in trying to decide what to do about domestic fares. (Average revenue and cost figures for this route are also shown in Table 9.6.) This was the only route that had not had a change in equipment or in the number of flights since the new fares had been put into place. Tatry is near popular mountain resorts, and Hladiš thought many of the passengers were foreigners, and perhaps some CSFR citizens traveling there on skiing or camping vacations.

As mentioned, there was little reliable information on domestic passenger trips by route. However, Hladiš was able manually to extract data on the average number of passengers on each segment of this route for the three-month periods of November 1990 to January 1991 and November 1991 to January 1992. These figures, shown in Table 9.7, represent equivalent time periods just before and after the three-stage fare increase of 1991. However, normal economy tickets could be used for six months after their purchase, and some people might still have been flying on the lower fare. The somewhat lower number of passengers in the more recent period may suggest the negative effects of the higher fares and lower real incomes on passenger travel. Unfortunately, Hladiš had no way of telling whether the passengers were citizens or foreigners or whether they were on regular or excursion fares. He did know that about 30 percent of his revenues came from foreign purchases, but many knowledgeable foreigners were buying their tickets in Czechoslovakia to take advantage of the lower prices.

From the Economics Department, Hladiš also received detailed estimates of the 1992 costs of aircraft for each of ČSA's domestic routes. The direct costs for a round-trip on a TU-134A on the Prague-Bratislava-Tatry route are shown in Table 9.8.

Notes

1. Most of this information on ČSA comes from two documents prepared as disclosure for potential foreign investors entitled "Presentation of ČSA: Czechoslovak Airlines," April 15, 1990, and March 1991. Additional information was provided by František Slabý, head of the Planning Department, in a letter dated February 24, 1992.

2. Much of this information comes from L. Hladiš and his assistant, Tomáš Kaufman, and from Sean D. Barrett, *Flying High: Airline Prices and European Regulation* (Aldershot, UK: Avebury, 1988).

3. Barrett, *Flying High,* 10.

4. See for example, Mark Maremont, "'The Carnival is Over': Can Europe's Airlines Weather Deregulation and Tough New Rivals?" *Business Week* (December 9, 1991): 16–20; and IATA, *Annual Report 1990* (Geneva): 15–16.

5. Barrett, *Flying High,* 7.

6. IATA, *Annual Report 1990,* 3, 42–44.

6. IATA, *Annual Report 1990*, 3, 42–44.

7. Technically only a majority need to agree, but in fact the decisions are made unanimously.

8. Information from Hladiš and from Stephen Shaw, *Airline Marketing and Management* (London: Pitman, 1985), 214–217.

9. This discussion is largely based on the cost discussion in Shaw, *Airline Marketing*, 221–223.

10. This is in contrast to international fares, at least the bilateral promotional fares, which tend to be set route-by-route and are not closely correlated with distance.

CHAPTER TEN

———————— ■ ————————

Glavunion:
The Privatization Option

One fact occupied Štěpán Popovič's thoughts as he drove home one night in March 1990 from a seminar on foreign investment in Czechoslovakia organized by the Washington-based consulting and investment firm PlanEcon: Foreign investors ranked the glass industry second among industries in which they were willing to invest.

Popovič was general manager of Sklo Union State Company (SU), a producer of flat and container glass and glass fibers, located in Teplice, North Bohemia. Even before this seminar, SU was among the first enterprises to initiate a search for potential foreign partners to form a joint venture. No foreign investor, however, was interested in entering such a venture given the current structure of the company.

Štěpán Popovič, age forty-five, had assumed the responsibility of general manager on September 15, 1989. In the twenty-one years that Štěpán Popovič had been with Sklo Union he had held various managerial positions. He had worked as the manager of three different plants; for three years he had served as the production director of Sklo Union.

Štěpán Popovič was conscious of the opportunities that had been created by the dramatic political, legal, and economic changes that had transpired since the Velvet Revolution of November 1989. Clearly this was a time of great challenge and opportunity. The challenge was to transform the company into an entity capable of competing in international markets. To meet

This case was prepared by Jana Matesová of the Czechoslovak Management Center and Michael H. Spiro of the University of Pittsburgh. The authors wish to thank Štěpán Popovič, general manager of Glavunion, Karel Zdvíhal, secretary of the board of Glavunion, and numerous other people of Glavunion; Rudolf Hanus, deputy minister of the Czech Ministry of Industry; and Stan Rudcenko, vice president, Bankers Trust International Limited London, who generously lent their time and expertise in the preparation of the case.

this challenge, Štěpán Popovič believed that the company required more decentralization of the decisionmaking process and needed greater managerial skills and expertise.

Štěpán Popovič was aware of four facts. First, SU required new capital in order to modernize facilities. Second, budget constraints imposed on state enterprises made it unlikely that the state would provide such capital. Third, foreign firms were the only likely source of capital and the needed technical and managerial knowledge. Finally, such a venture would also advance the privatization process.

Quick action was needed to initiate the reorganization process and to develop an evaluation and selection procedure for a foreign investor.

Historical Overview of Sklo Union and the Czechoslovak Glass Industry

The glass industry in North Bohemia dates to the early medieval period. Since the eighteenth century, table glass had been the primary product produced in most glass companies. The North Bohemian flat glass companies were established in the nineteenth and early twentieth centuries, and they enjoy a reputation for high-quality products. They are among the technological leaders, exploiting the most advanced manufacturing methods, including those developed by Belgian, U.S., and, most recently, British companies.

SU was formed in 1965 as a state-owned company merging two major Bohemian producers of flat and container glass. Each was established from numerous small producers when the glass industry in Czechoslovakia was fully nationalized after World War II. In 1965 SU had plants spread mostly over Western and Northern Bohemia. Sheet and container glass and also machinery for container glass production were the major products. Expansion occurred in 1979 when nine plants producing various products such as technical and laboratory glass, glass fibers, optical glass, lighting glass, and TV screens and tubes were added to SU. Other plants joined the company in the 1980s, adding new product lines such as fireproof fibers and optical fibers. In 1988, SU employed 27,000 workers.

The substantial changes in the legal environment in Czechoslovakia that took place in 1988 and 1989 supported decentralization of management at the enterprise level. All state-owned enterprises were supposed to change their legal status. The new policy encouraged the managers of formerly independent plants, and the branches and divisions of Czechoslovak enterprises, to apply for separation from their headquarters. As the political and economic climate for doing so was favorable and the responsible government agencies were supportive of these initiatives, many, if not most, of Czechoslovak enterprises split at that time. Many of SU's plants became independent. Flat glass

FIGURE 10.1   Location of SU's Plants, 1991.

production remained nearly untouched, but the firm lost two-thirds of its container glass production, and most other product lines.

Fifteen plants remained part of SU at the end of this restructuring. Management considered this situation temporary and implemented a very simple organizational structure for the remaining units, making each a cost center until an optimal organizational structure was found. The fifteen plants were all located within 150 kilometers of the SU's headquarters in Teplice (see Figure 10.1).

Of the 9,500 workers in the plants and at headquarters, nearly 6,000 were in flat glass production, 2,600 were in container glass production, and 400 were in glass fibers production. The company was completely unionized.

Additional state initiatives after 1989 provided the company with greater independence in decisionmaking. A board of supervisors was formed consisting of government officials, enterprise management, and outside experts from the glass production field. Under Czechoslovak law the workers were invited to elect the CEO of the Sklo Union State Company. Štěpán Popovič was their choice.

Overview of the Glass Industry in Europe

At the time of this study the export market for SU's products was segmented into two main product lines, flat and container glass. The European market for flat glass, in which Sklo Union had primary interest, could be characterized as an oligopolistic market structure dominated by the following major companies:

- Pilkington of the UK, the world's largest producer of flat glass and the second largest European producer of glass.
- Saint Gobain of France, the leading European glass manufacturer and a major producer of flat glass.
- Glaverbel, the Belgian subsidiary of the Japanese firm Asahi and the third largest producer of flat glass in Europe.
- SIV of Italy.

Three U.S.-based companies with European subsidiaries were also active in the market.

- Ford Motor Company, the second largest automobile and truck producer, and the largest automotive glass producer in North America.
- Guardian Industries, primarily oriented toward markets for automotive and architectural glass.
- PPG, one of the major producers of flat glass in the world.

Flat glass accounted for approximately 23 percent of total glass production by the European Economic Community countries in 1990. Seventy percent of these products served the automobile and construction industries. Additions to capacity of flat glass were made almost exclusively with the float glass process. In 1990 there were approximately forty float glass lines operating throughout Europe, including the two lines at SU. Several additional lines were under construction by other manufacturers.

The industry structure was relatively stable. During the 1980s, acquisition activity was quite low. Major producers preferred joint ventures to mergers and acquisitions. The market typically was highly cyclical, but it experienced stable, strong growth during the second half of the 1980s. Output declined in the early 1990s because of the recession, but large growth potential may be associated with the expected restructuring of the Eastern European economies and the resulting increase in demand for both housing and cars. For domestic and export sales of flat glass see Tables 10.1 and 10.2.

The container glass market was much more stable than the flat glass market because it supplied such noncyclic industries as food, beverages, and pharmaceuticals (Tables 10.3 and 10.4). Growth prospects were good because recycling makes glass products environmentally friendly, consumers associate glass containers with high-quality products, and such containers are increasingly popular. Container glass accounted for some 65 percent of total EEC glass production in 1990. It was dominated by the following producers:

- Saint Gobain of France, the largest European container glass producer.
- BSN of France, the largest European producer of food and beverages with its own packaging division and the second largest container glass producer in Europe.

TABLE 10.1   Flat Glass Division: Sales (Kčs million)

Product Line	Domestic Sales		Export Sales	
	1989	1990	1989	1990
Float	60	102	337	414
Sheet	145	184	70	77
Wired	57	61	11	10
Patterned	40	37	26	23
Laminated	140	149	57	69
Double Glazed	104	98	18	22
Tempered	161	180	28	37
Processed	273	185	30	0
Total	984	996	583	652

Source: SU's records, information provided by Štěpán Popovič.

TABLE 10.2   Domestic Markets Served by the Flat Glass Division

Customer	Domestic Sales (Kčs m)	% of Total Sales
Building industry	550	56
Automobile industry	301	30
Furniture	135	14
Total	986	100

Source: SU's records, information provided by Štěpán Popovič.

TABLE 10.3   Container Glass Division Sales (Kčs million)

Product Line	Domestic Markets		Export Markets	
	1989	1990	1989	1990
Container	449	362	71	na
Pressed	84	95	22	na

Source: SU's records, information provided by Štěpán Popovič.

TABLE 10.4   Domestic Markets Served by the Container Division, 1990

Customer	Domestic Sales 1990 (Kčs m)	% of Total Sales
Breweries/Distilleries	292	58
Pharmaceuticals	26	5
Producers of canned food	43	10
Cosmetics	22	4
Wholesale	95	19
Miscellaneous	22	4
Total	500	100

Source: SU's records, information provided by Štěpán Popovič.

- Rockware, the UK packaging company.
- Gerresheimer, a German packaging company.
- PLM of Sweden, a major European packaging group producing glass, plastic, and metal containers.
- United Glass of the United States.
- Vetropack of Switzerland, which focused on glass and plastic containers production, foil production, and recycling.

Sklo Union enjoyed a dominant position in the domestic markets for most product lines. After 1989 the container glass division had several strong domestic competitors. SU had no serious competitors in the market for flat glass; its share of that domestic market ranged from 85 to 100 percent.

The Privatization of Sklo Union

Major Goals

In early 1990, soon after the Velvet Revolution of November 1989 and before the first free parliamentary election after many years, privatization began to be stressed as one of major elements of the economic transition from the highly centralized, state-planned economy to a market economy. It was a part of the economic programs of all political movements and parties except for the extreme left. At the time, it was conceived primarily as a political move designed to transfer property nationalized by the previous Communist regime to private ownership. Some of the parties recognized private property as an incentive for the preservation, proper utilization, and accumulation of capital and the implications for economic efficiency and growth. These issues, however, were not central to the debate. The mechanism by which state-owned property would be transferred into private hands was not known at the time.[1]

The goals that Sklo Union's management sought to achieve through privatization were clear. It hoped to rid itself of the bureaucratic influences and control of the state ministries and gain greater freedom in the making and implementation of decisions. SU also hoped to attract foreign investors that would provide the company with additional capital and management and technical expertise. Sklo Union knew Western markets because the company was a large exporter of its highest-quality products to these markets while at the same time marketing its standard-quality products to domestic and Eastern European markets. The management, however, foresaw that demand for standard-quality products in these markets would decline after Eastern European markets were opened to Western competition. "There is a lot of fear of foreign investors, but we are not afraid of them. Even in a large country such as Germany, the float glass production is not fully in the hands of Germans," Štěpán Popovič stated.

In pursuing a foreign partner, Sklo Union had to protect its dominant position in the domestic market while it established itself as a force within the wider Western European market and former Eastern bloc markets. Furthermore, it had as its goal the modernization of the whole company. Thus, foreign investors had to be willing to invest in divisions that were technologically backward, such as sheet glass, and assist in identifying new markets for SU's products.

Štěpán Popovič knew that he needed large investments. He viewed the completion of a new float line as essential. SU's plant in Sokolov (West Bohemia), which produced flat sheet glass, required total reconstruction. The plant would have to be shut down if the new line was not built, resulting in a reduction in output and employment and in a loss of market share. Public opinion was strongly opposed to laying off workers. Thus, his primary short-term objective at the time was to maintain employment. The float glass process is a prerequisite for high-quality glass production such as windshields, side-lights, furniture glass, and mirrors. There appeared to be no problem in obtaining credit from a foreign bank for this kind of restructuring. However, such credit would not provide the company with the needed technical and managerial know-how. "We are ready to learn by doing the business together with foreign managers," the Sklo Union general manager said.

The Search for Potential Foreign Partners

In order to finance the growth of high-volume and high-margin production, maintain or increase the company's market share, and share managerial skills, Sklo Union's management decided to search for a foreign partner or partners. It formulated the following criteria for the search:

- Partners are expected to help develop Sklo Union's operations rather than to acquire the firm's market share.
- SU wishes to maintain majority control over flat and container glass divisions.
- Mutual agreement on the strategic plans of the divisions and willingness to cooperate in their execution and a commitment to finance required investments and provide access to new markets are important factors.
- Partners should be ready to share technical and managerial skills with Sklo Union, especially in management and marketing, and to cooperate in developing an in-company training program.
- Partners' valuations of Sklo Union's business is a significant criterion.

Within a short period of time, early in 1990, five major glass producers who were interested in some form of future partnership approached Sklo Union. These were Ford (U.S.), Guardian (U.S.), Pilkington (GB), PPG (U.S.), and Saint Gobain (France).

The major interests of these companies centered on flat and container glass. Each company required a clear division of businesses, high independence of production units, and a focused business. The specific feature common to all of these companies was that none seemed willing to invest in all of SU's product lines. None of the companies were willing to enter the firm as long as it maintained its organizational structure and legal status as a state company.

The reasons seemed obvious: The legal form of the enterprise was not transparent enough for foreign companies; the organizational structure was perceived as complicated and inefficient and did not enable a clear delegation of rights and responsibilities.

Restructuring Begins—Changes in Organization

Štěpán Popovič and the management of SU decided quickly that the first step to restructuring and privatization had to be a change of the legal status of the enterprise, and a change of its organizational structure.

Contrary to the situation during the previous Communist regime, the more open legal environment in Czechoslovakia in 1990 made it possible for state-owned companies to transform themselves into joint-stock companies and form joint ventures with foreign partners. Both changes still required the approval of the government.

SU's management hired Leadtime, a small Pittsburgh-based consulting firm, to advise it regarding the optimal organizational structure. The management had several major goals in mind.

The first goal was to simplify and rationalize the administrative and communication structure while increasing SU's quality and performance. SU's production comprised several product lines with different technologies and different markets; Leadtime advised SU to design a divisional structure appropriate for this product line mix.

The second goal was that the organizational design had to provide for appropriate specification of the scope and roles of the functional areas, production management, marketing, finance, and human resources.[2] SU's management placed great emphasis on the essential role of high-quality marketing, sales, services, and logistics. This emphasis increased after SU took over foreign marketing and sales from a specialized foreign trade company that it had employed previously. Specialized activities such as legal services, a computer center, and engineering had to also be included in the organizational structure of the company. Many supporting activities such as cleaning, packaging, maintenance, and security could be contracted to independent firms.

The organizational structure had also to take into account old liabilities on the balance sheet of the enterprise, many of which had resulted from decisions made by the government, not by the enterprise itself. Potential future liabilities resulting from previous activity of the enterprise such as environmental damage should not burden the newly created business units.

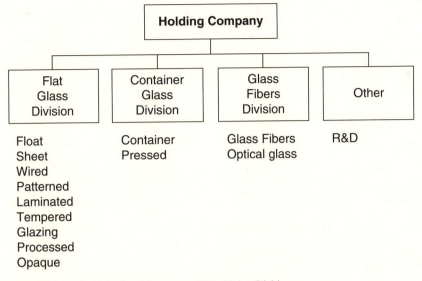

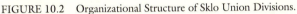

FIGURE 10.2   Organizational Structure of Sklo Union Divisions.

In accordance with the recommendations of the consultants, SU's management decided to reorganize the company into a holding company with three major divisions based on product lines, flat glass, container glass, and glass fibers and glass specialties such as optical glass. This organizational structure placed various functional departments such as marketing and human resources within each division (see Figure 10.2).

Furthermore, the decision was made to transform the company into a joint-stock company wholly owned by the state. This form seemed particularly advantageous because it set relatively clear rules for the structure of corporate governance, financial structure, and relationships with the state. Furthermore, it was quite compatible with Western standards and experience.

Attracting Foreign Partners

In early spring 1990 Sklo Union's management began negotiations with Guardian Industries on its own. At the same time, Štěpán Popovič and his people met businessman Michael Cicak of the United States, a producer of equipment for the glass industry. "It makes little sense to negotiate without an intermediary. The best consultants are the Americans, but they won't understand our way of doing business. Try hiring a U.S. consulting firm with a European branch office," was Cicak's advice. Sklo Union hired the Bankers Trust Company of New York as a strategic contractor, switching soon after to Bankers Trust International Limited, London.

In anticipation of negotiations, Bankers Trust retained a consultant to conduct a study valuing SU.[3] Štěpán Popovič first asked the consultant to review

TABLE 10.5   Principal Flat Glass Manufacturers

Company	Location of Headquarters	Number of Employees	Total Sales[a] (US$ m)[b]
Asahi Glass	Japan	na	15,128
AFG Industries	US[c]	5,567	648
Ford Motor Company	US	367,000	96,146
Glaverbel	Belgium[c]	6,111	1,336
Guardian	US	na[d]	na
Nippon Sheet Glass	Japan	na	3,599
PPG	US	35,500	5,734
Pilkington	United Kingdom	60,300	4,751
SIV	Italy	5,871	1,076[e]
Saint Gobain	France	87,816	19,785

[a]Financial year 1989.
[b]Exchange rates used: pound sterling/US $1.63; 138 yen/US$; 39.4 Belgian franc/US$; 1,302 Italian lira/US$; 6.38 French franc/US$.
[c]The ultimate control is by a Japanese company.
[d]A private company; no detailed information publicly available since 1986.
[e]Adjusted for equity accounting; 1988 figure.
Source: Calculations based on Bankers Trust internal information for SU.

TABLE 10.6   Principal Container Glass Manufacturers

Company	Location of Headquarters	Number of Employees	Total Sales[a] (US$ m)[b]
BSN	France	46,693	14,570
Gerresheimer	Germany	5,056	1,004
Owens Illinois	US	na	3,605
PLM	Sweden	7,958	1,821
Rockware	UK	5,291	412
Saint Gobain	France	87,816	19,785
Vetropack	Switzerland	1,392	375

[a]Financial year 1989.
[b]Exchange rates used: 6.38 French franc/US$; 1.88 German mark/US$; 6.45 Swedish krona/US$; 1.63 $/Pound Sterling; 1.64 Swiss franc/US$.
Source: Calculations based on Bankers Trust internal information for SU.

the principal business strategies of Sklo Union's potential foreign partners. Even before key negotiations with foreign firms began, these reviews served as guidelines for the managers of Sklo Union and the Czech government to determine the compatibility of Sklo Union's strategy with the strategies of its potential partners. Summary statistics of these reviews are contained in Tables 10.5 and 10.6. The relevant highlights of these reviews follow:

Ford Motor Company   With more than 360,000 employees throughout the world, sales in 1989 in excess of $96 billion, and a net yearly income of approximately $4 billion, Ford Motor Company was one of the world's largest manufacturing corporations and the second largest automobile and truck producer in the United States. Its own glass division was the largest automotive glass manufacturer in North America and supplied Ford's own automobile assembly plants and a number of outside clients. Ford was trying to expand in Europe. Ford's glass division was following a similar strategy of geographical diversification.

Glaverbel   Glaverbel was the third largest flat glass producer in Europe, with more than 6,000 employees and sales over $1,336 million in 1989. Besides a wide product line of flat glass, Glaverbel produced some specialty glass goods such as liquid crystals and was also involved in ceramic welding. The company was controlled by Asahi Glass of Japan, which owned 75 percent of Glaverbel's stock. The company's strategy was primarily oriented toward flat glass, emphasizing diversification of products and an increasing share of high-quality and high-value products. The company intended to increase its capital in order to expand internationally and to substantially increase its market share in the Western European flat glass market. Its strategy of expansion emphasized acquisitions and the creation of joint ventures.

Guardian Industries   Guardian was a private U.S. nonlisted glass-producing company. In 1985 it was acquired by its president and CEO. The primary focus of the company in recent years had been on high-volume production of a narrow range of glass products. Guardian was particularly interested in flat glass production for the automobile market and glass fiber production for construction. The company owned several float lines throughout the United States and Europe. Guardian had recently formed a joint venture in Hungary with Hunguard Float Glass. Forty-nine percent of Hunguard's initial capital was owned by Guardian, and 51 percent was owned by the Hungarian government. Its strategy consisted of maintaining a very focused, narrow product line and aggressive geographical expansion, based frequently on setting up joint ventures in regions where it lacked expertise.

Pilkington   With more than 60,000 employees and sales of $4,751 million in 1989, Pilkington was the world's largest producer of flat glass, the second largest glass producer in Europe, and the fourth largest capital goods supplier in Europe. Its core business was flat and safety glass. In addition, Pilkington produced optoelectronics, vision-care tools such as lenses, and insulation. While Pilkington was diversifying its production in some of its high-growth and high-margin product lines, it was also eliminating production of some of its optoelectronics and its vision-care product line. Its strategy consisted of a strong international expansion, often based on forming joint ventures. Pilkington did not hesitate to close plants that faced financial or marketing difficulties. Local management in Pilkington's overseas divisions and plants were, however, given significant autonomy.

PPG   PPG was a large U.S.-based corporation with approximately 35,000 employees throughout the United States, Europe, and the Far East. Its principal businesses were glass—generating more than 40 percent of sales and profits—chemicals, and coatings. PPG was a major flat glass and glass fibers producer. Its flat glass capacities were mostly located in the United States and Europe. PPG had four float lines and had intentions of building or acquiring another. PPG had already gained experience in trading with Eastern Europe through its Italian subsidiary.

PPG's strategy of expansion stressed internationalization of its markets. It endeavored to expand particularly in the European market in order to protect itself from the cyclical fluctuations of the U.S. economy. Its flat glass capacities fulfilled their cash-generating role; some other products such as glass fibers had a particularly high growth potential.

Saint Gobain   Saint Gobain was Europe's leading producer of both flat and container glass. In addition to carrying these product lines this French company produced glass fibers, insulations, building materials, pipes, and industrial ceramics. It also manufactured wood and paper products. In 1989 Saint Gobain employed approximately 87,000 employees in Europe and North and South America.

The strength of the company was in its technologies. Its acquisition activity was very high and was followed by extending its own technology to the acquired firms. The acquisitions policy was designed in part to protect Saint Gobain's leading position and dominant market share in the high-growth flat glass market and in the container glass market. Eastern Europe seemed, therefore, a natural area for its expansion.

Sklo Union's Decision

In the summer of 1990, some three months after Štěpán Popovič's first meeting on foreign investment, he believed he was ready for negotiations. He considered the potential suitors that best fit SU and his plans for privatization.

Notes

1. In 1991, all the state-owned companies and cooperatives that accounted for more than 90 percent of the Czechoslovak market were required to prepare their strategies for privatization, called privatization plans. The process of privatization of large state-owned enterprises was regulated by the law on large-scale privatization approved for parliament. The law listed nine different ways for privatizing a state-owned enterprise. They included restructuring the state-owned enterprises into joint-stock companies and selling shares of their stocks to domestic or foreign investors; selling shares of companies' stocks to citizens through a voucher scheme; offering competitive tenders with more than one selection criterion; holding auctions in which price was the one and only criterion; providing for foreign direct investment and direct sales to domestic investors on a noncompetitive basis; or allowing former owners whose property was nationalized after February 1948 or their heirs to reac-

quire their lost property rights. At the time when SU was making its decision, in spring and summer 1990, these rules were not yet clear.

2. Under the state planning system, SU's management, similar to the management of most other companies, was production-oriented because the distribution of goods and other functional areas of management were based on a plan implemented by state agencies. In market economies, however, functional areas such as marketing, finance, and human resources are the responsibility of the company.

3. Given the total absence of a stock market and the great uncertainty in the business environment, valuation of businesses was based on Czechoslovakia's rough approximations employing the standard valuation methods. These included estimations of the present value of future cash flows, price to earning ratios of comparable Western companies, and the replacement value of assets. The results of these valuations were regarded as proprietary.

CHAPTER ELEVEN

■

Lusico: In Search of Market Opportunities

Copy Shop

In July 1990 Lubomír Šilhavý established a small firm called Copy Shop. This firm offered copying services to the general public in space rented from the department store Maj, located in the middle of Prague. The copying services were well received, and many potential entrepreneurs were interested in buying copy machines directly from Šilhavý to start their own businesses.

Copy Service

When Šilhavý realized there was sufficient potential demand for copy machines in Czechoslovakia, he turned to the Swiss representative of Gestetner, from which he initially had purchased his own copy machines. During the negotiation process, Šilhavý met with Gestetner's representatives in their headquarters in Denmark, where he signed an exclusive agreement to sell Gestetner's copy machines in Czechoslovakia. Prior to this agreement, Gestetner was not directly represented in Czechoslovakia.

By November 1990, Šilhavý's new business, Copy Service, was strategically located in Prague and Brno. The original location in Prague sold to and serviced a competitive but well-established market. The second location in Brno sold to and serviced clients in the middle of the country. At this point Copy Service specialized in selling and servicing copy machines and in providing re-

This case was prepared by Marie Přibová, a member of the faculty at the Czechoslovak Management Center in Čelakovice, Czechoslovakia, and Professor George Tesar of the University of Wisconsin–Whitewater as a basis for class discussion rather than as an illustration of the effectiveness or ineffectiveness of Lusico's management. At the time this case was written Professor Tesar was visiting at the Umeå Business School, Umeå, Sweden.

lated supplies to the general public. From November 1990 to the end of January 1991, Copy Service's sales volume exceeded DM 1 million.[1] During this period the firm had twenty-five employees. The firm was ready to handle the diversity of a transitionary market where copy services were a relatively new phenomenon among business managers, academic institutions, and individual customers.

Gestetner's participation in the operations of Copy Service consisted of providing training and sales and service know-how and lending its reputation as a reliable manufacturer of quality copy machines in Europe. Gestetner had approximately 10 percent of the copy machine market in Europe. It was a partner in NRG holding company, which also owned Rex Rotary, a brand of copy machines better known than Gestetner in the Czechoslovak market. For the past twenty-five years, Rex Rotary had been sold and serviced by Kancelářské stroje.[2]

While Copy Service was successfully and profitably marketing Gestetner copy machines, demand for Rex Rotary machines decreased. Copy Service submitted a proposal to Rex Rotary to take over its representation in Czechoslovakia. Copy Service's proposal was documented with a comprehensive marketing study and accompanied by a formal business plan.

The proposal was accepted by Rex Rotary, and Copy Service expanded its product lines by including Rex Rotary copy machines, fax machines, answering machines, and high-speed offset printing equipment.

The rapid and aggressive growth of Copy Service was attributed to the excellent management capabilities of Šilhavý, the owner-manager. His goal was to guarantee customer satisfaction with the sale and installation and also guarantee fast professional service after purchase and installation.

By mid-1991 Copy Service was well established in the Czechoslovak market for copy machines, duplicating machines, and telecommunication equipment. The firm needed additional capital and managerial know-how to continue to grow. Two additional investors were brought into the firm, and the name changed from Copy Service to Lusico in late 1991.

Lusico

With the name change, more working capital, and additional managerial skills, the company was faced with a new era in its relatively short and successful existence. It was confronted with two challenges: finding new opportunities in a dynamic and unstable transitionary market and clearly defining a new mission.

The Market

The Czechoslovak market for copy machines and related duplicating and printing machines was relatively new and complex.[3] A variety of customers were beginning to enter the market. They included, among others, private and public firms; government offices; private and public organizations, associations, and interest groups; political parties; schools and universities; and libraries. These groups differed principally with respect to their needs for speed and volume.

Customers who required fewer copies were generally satisfied with copy machines producing fewer than thirty-two copies per minute. These light to medium users were designated as market segment 1. Based on marketing research studies, this segment accounted for about 60 percent of the total Czechoslovak market for copy machines.

Most of the remaining customers required larger copy machines capable of generating over thirty-two copies per minute. This second segment accounted for approximately 40 percent of the total market for copy machines in Czechoslovakia.

It was estimated that 35,000 to 40,000 small- and medium-sized copy machines were then being used in Czechoslovakia and that in 1991 the market for these types of copy machines would grow by 20 to 25 percent, representing an additional 8,500 to 10,000 copy machines. The average price of a copy machine in segment 1 was DM 4,000. Thus the market in Czechoslovakia for 1991 was projected to be approximately DM 34–40 million.

Lusico managers decided to focus on the Czechoslovak market for small- and medium-sized copy machines. They perceived that this market segment would grow much faster than segment 2. These perceptions were based on two fundamental considerations:

1. The formation of new businesses in Czechoslovakia stimulated the need for copy machines. Most of the businesses being formed were small and thus need small- and medium-sized copy machines.
2. Even large businesses and enterprises had a tendency to decentralize copying services. Smaller machines were more desirable because they could be placed in locations easily accessible to individuals who needed copy services.

The Competition

The market for copy machines in Czechoslovakia was becoming highly competitive. Before the establishment of Lusico in 1991, Minolta dominated the market with about 25 percent of market share (see Table 11.1). In 1991 other competitors entered the market—most notably Toshiba and, of course, Lusico, representing both Gestetner and Rex Rotary—changing the competitive makeup of the market significantly (see Table 11.2).

The leading competitor was Minolta, which had its own manufacturing facilities in Czechoslovakia. Minolta had developed an aggressive marketing strategy. It was heavily investing in television, magazine, and outdoor advertising. One of Lusico's top managers suggested that Minolta's costs for a

TABLE 11.1   Market Share of Firms Selling Small- and Medium-Sized Copy Machines in Czechoslovakia in 1990

Firm	Estimated Market Share (%)
Minolta	25
Rank Xerox	15[a]
Oce	15[a]
Utax	15
Rex Rotary	10
Agfa	5
Canon	5
Others	5
Total	100

[a]Also sold large copy machines.
Source: Lubomír Šilhavý's estimates.

TABLE 11.2   Market Share of Firms Selling Small- and Medium-Sized Copy Machines in Czechoslovakia in 1991

Firm	Estimated Market Share (%)
Minolta	25
Utax	15
Canon	10
Rank Xerox	10
Lusico	10
Oce	8
Toshiba	7
Agfa	5
Other	10
Total	100

Source: Lubomír Šilhavý's estimates.

broad introductory promotional campaign were so high that it would take several years for Minolta to fully recover costs.

Minolta's sales and service facilities were strategically located throughout the Czechoslovak market. Its products were highly competitive and its strategy seemed to focus on a broad product line and fast service. Minolta could deliver its products within three working days.

Utax held 15 percent of the market in 1991 and aggressively sold low-priced copy machines. Its strong position was based on prompt deliveries and service.

Canon copy machines had been sold in the Czechoslovak market for several years by an organization called Druzstvo mechaniku. Canon established its own representation in 1991 and rapidly developed a network of its own sales and service outlets. Canon's products had a high reputation for quality and service in the market and were sold at very low prices (its, and Toshiba's, prices tended to be the lowest). Canon was successful in closing large orders with a variety of public and private offices.

TABLE 11.3 Lusico's Estimated Sales Volume in Units for 1992–1996

	1992	1993	1994	1995	1996
Sales volume	1,500	1,650	1,850	2,100	2,300
Rex Rotary's share	800	900	1,000	1,100	1,250
Gestetner's share	700	750	850	1,000	1,050

The oldest competitor was Rank Xerox. Rank Xerox had a representative office in Prague staffed only with foreign managers. It did not maintain its own sales and service outlets but instead marketed its products through a network of local dealers. Lusico's management thought that Rank Xerox's recent loss of market share could be explained by its inability to adjust to recent changes in the Czechoslovak market for copy machines.

Lusico marketed its products at average prices with slightly higher price levels than its competition for some models. Lusico's fast delivery, installation, and service were competitive. Management strove to establish stable prices that were slightly lower than those of its principal competitors.

Lusico's Goals and Objectives

Lusico set its short-term goal for the second half of 1991 at 900 units. Lubomír Šilhavý's estimates of future growth are presented in Table 11.3. Its main objective was to maintain its market share for small and medium-sized copy machines, and also to develop a strong market position for fax machines and telecommunication technology. These goals and objectives could be achieved only through implementation of an aggressive marketing strategy. A summary of the fundamental elements of the marketing strategy follow:

1. Fast delivery (delivery within three working days from existing inventory directly from its warehouse; even faster deliveries at the expense of the customer).
2. Immediate service.
3. Sales of supplies (developer, toners, and other supplies) at lower than competitor's prices.
4. A comprehensive leasing program.
5. Stable prices slightly lower than the prices of its principal competitors.
6. A growing network of dealers in the market.
7. Systematic advertising and promotional effort.
8. Creation of Lusico's stable market image as a partner for all potential customers for small- and medium-sized copy machines.
9. Broadening of its product lines to include products such as fax machines, duplicating offset type machines, and "copy-printers" most of which represented major innovations in the market.
10. Service and repurchase responsibility for previous customers of Rex Rotary copy machines.

Personnel and Management Issues

In the first half of 1991 Lusico (then still known as Copy Service) employed fifty-five individuals; thirty-five were technicians who installed and serviced the copy machines. Lusico strongly emphasized sales and service in all of this locations. Regional sales and service offices were opened in Brno, Ceske Budejovice, Hradec Kralove, Kosice, Ostrava, Plzen, Prague, Teplice, Usti nad Labem, and Zlin. Each regional office employed one marketing specialist. Lusico maintained a network of thirty additional dealers who supplemented the activities of the regional sales and service offices. It was expected that the network would be expanded in 1992 to include additional dealers; exclusive sales and service territories would be developed for each dealer.

The service component was an extremely important part of Lusico's aggressive marketing strategy. Lusico's top management believes that high-quality service helps support the product in the market and helps generate satisfied customers for new products and product maintenance in a rapidly changing competitive market.

A promotional effort was being implemented according to a plan developed for Lusico by DDB Needham Worldwide, a foreign advertising agency. The promotional strategy encompassed television, newspaper, and outdoor advertising that included advertising on automobiles used by the firm. Small promotional items displayed Lusico's logo. Lusico also actively participated in all trade fairs and exhibitions in Czechoslovakia.

During the first half of 1991 Lusico (then still Copy Service) generated an average monthly sales volume of 6–7 million Kčs, which suggested that the goal for 1991 would be realized. Given Lusico's performance and its organizational changes, top management began to look for additional market opportunities and perhaps a new direction for growth and diversification. Top management was confident that its market segment was well defined and secured. The next key issue was how to maintain and increase growth in a rapidly changing market with aggressive domestic and foreign competition.

Notes

1. German marks were used for more effective international comparison and forecasting. The Czechoslovak koruna had not been sufficiently stabilized to be used for these comparisons.

2. Kancelářské stroje was a government-owned enterprise that had an exclusive right to market and service office equipment in Czechoslovakia. Copy machines were not freely available for sale to private companies and individuals prior to November 1989 due to the political conditions that existed in Czechoslovakia at that time.

3. Most of the duplication services found in most markets around the world were virtually nonexistent in Czechoslovakia before November 1989. A market had existed for some time but consisted of government-owned enterprises that had special permission to purchase this type of equipment. Consequently, the market was still in its infancy.

CHAPTER TWELVE

■

Electro-Products Limited

Josef Novák,[1] an engineer formerly in charge of product design and development at Electro-Products Limited (EPL) and recently appointed manager of marketing and marketing analysis at Electro-Products Limited, was faced with a dilemma. A number of marketing issues important to his firm had surfaced suddenly. Some of these issues related directly to the role marketing needed to play in the future operations of the firm; others related to the strategic question of survival in a rapidly changing economy. The most troublesome issue was EPL's relationship with a large European client.

EPL, located in a semi-rural area of Czechoslovakia, manufactured small home appliances. A significant portion of EPL's production was being exported under an exclusive agreement with a large European-based international electronics manufacturing and marketing firm (LIEM). Under this agreement, EPL was responsible for manufacturing handheld vacuum cleaners for LIEM. LIEM marketed these products under its own brand name in Western Europe; EPL retained exclusive rights to market the products domestically under its own brand name, ZETA.

The Czechoslovak economy was going through a major transition: Privatization, foreign ownership, and new consumer demands have contributed to an emerging competitive market. Domestic and foreign competitors were entering the market. Both EPL and LIEM realized that the Czechoslovak market needed to be systematically reexamined.

Prior to the changes in Czechoslovakia that began in late 1989, LIEM had had no interest in the Czechoslovak market. After the changes, however, LIEM actively sought market opportunities under its own brand name in

This case was prepared by Professor George Tesar of the University of Wisconsin–Whitewater and Marie Přibová, a member of the faculty at the Czechoslovak Management Center in Čelakovice, Czechoslovakia, as a basis for class discussion rather than as an illustration of the effectiveness or ineffectiveness of the management of Electro-Products Limited. At the time this case was written Professor Tesar was visiting at the Umeå Business School, Umeå Sweden.

EPL's domestic market. EPL's small marketing group faced several issues that might potentially evolve into major confrontations with LIEM.

EPL realized that its agreement with LIEM helped EPL understand product development efforts in the context of a large firm. It also helped EPL engineers comprehend the dynamics and quality-control requirements of Western markets. And, to a certain degree, the agreement assured EPL of future revenue. However, LIEM was a large international firm that viewed EPL as a captive supplier of a product whose attributes were set by LIEM's marketing personnel.

Novák wanted to develop a cooperative relationship with LIEM, to work closely with LIEM's marketing personnel so that he and his staff could learn more about marketing practices in Western Europe. He was particularly curious about LIEM's entire product development process. LIEM's management had ignored overtures from EPL.

EPL had organized a small marketing group in late 1990. Until recently, this group had not played a significant role because it was positioned too low in the organization to significantly influence top management's decisions. Under Novák's leadership, marketing concepts were slowly being recognized and accepted in the strategic development and growth of the firm. Novák and the marketing group began to develop promotion, retail, and distribution strategies for generating new opportunities.

Electro-Products Historical Overview

The Product Line

EPL had been manufacturing and exporting a wide range of small home appliances and heating elements since 1943. After the general nationalization in the late 1940s, it became the sole producer of small home appliances in Czechoslovakia. Before late 1989, approximately 43 percent of its total production was vacuum cleaners and 13 percent was steam and dry irons.

EPL exported about one-quarter of its products to European markets. Western European markets demanded higher quality and better-designed products. Quality was not an issue in Eastern Europe due to general shortages of consumer products. Vacuum cleaners accounted for 68 percent of exports and dry irons, 24 percent (see Table 12.1).

EPL's latest catalog listed numerous products available for domestic and export sales:

Blenders
Coffee grinders
Coffee makers
Dry irons
Electric cooking pots

TABLE 12.1　Production of Small Home Appliances and Sales Before 1989 (%)

		Sales		
Product line	*Production*	*Domestic*	*Foreign*	*Total*
Vacuum cleaners	43	32	68	100
Steam and dry irons	13	76	24	100
Other	44	92	8	100

Note: The percentages are estimates only. Actual production figures were not available.

Electric countertop units
Electric frying pans
Food mixers
Food processors
Handheld food mixers
Heating elements (domestic use)
Heating elements (industrial use)
Plastic welding units
Portable electric plates
Portable grills
Portable space heaters
Roasting ovens
Steam irons
Vacuum cleaners
Ventilators

According to the marketing group, handheld vacuum cleaners represented the most lucrative and the most advanced product in EPL's product line. They believed that these vacuum cleaners exemplified the level of quality demanded by the Western consumer.

Working with a Trading Company

Before 1990, EPL was represented exclusively by Alfa, a state-owned export trading company located in Prague. Alfa controlled all of EPL's exporting activities, including initiation of contacts, negotiations of sales agreements, and delivery of finished products. The individuals responsible for product development and sales had no direct contact with customers. Alfa also controlled all communications between EPL and its customers abroad.

This arrangement was not unusual prior to late 1989. State-owned export trading companies represented abroad all Czechoslovak manufacturing firms and state-owned enterprises. Management of firms and enterprises had no direct contact with foreign customers or consumers. It was only in early 1990 that Czechoslovak enterprises were free to conduct business abroad without the state-owned export trading companies. But even after these changes were made, these trading companies withheld important information about foreign contacts, customers, and consumers from the firms they had represented.

In some cases, these enterprises were completely dependent on individuals within the export trading companies and could not operate without them. This dependency resulted from the inability to communicate with the outside world, lack of foreign-language competency, and even the inability to travel to foreign markets.[2]

Consequently, EPL's top management and the entire engineering, manufacturing, and purchasing staffs had little or no direct contact with clients such as LIEM. They did not understand LIEM's customers. Alfa served as a filter for all marketing and competitive information.

The Agreement with LIEM

An agreement between EPL and LIEM to produce a new handheld vacuum cleaner was negotiated by Alfa during 1987. Before the November 1989 political changes in Czechoslovakia, LIEM insisted that the agreement be kept secret. The agreement clearly defined the roles and responsibilities of each party. LIEM was responsible for developing product specifications based on marketing information. The overall product specifications can be classified into several categories:

- Dimensions and technical parameters.
- Physical design and color specifications.
- Number and type of models (economy, standard, and deluxe).
- Purchase price of each model.
- Annual purchase schedule of each model for the next four years.

These product specifications not only represented engineering specifications but also provided clear cost guidelines. In other words, under this contract EPL became a captive fabricator and supplier of handheld vacuum cleaners to LIEM.

It was also agreed that during the engineering process, testing would be conducted by both parties separately. This included inspection, verification, and documentation of tooling, dies, and fixtures. The prototypes and sample products from pilot production runs were also subject to testing by both parties.

EPL calculated the cost of engineering and manufacturing at the end of pilot production of all models specified under the contract. It became apparent that EPL could not deliver any of the three models at the price specified by LIEM. After a series of negotiations, LIEM agreed to a price increase of 18 percent. At the same time, the projected mix of models based on the original set of specifications was also changed, as indicated in Table 12.2.

A crucial factor in the arrangement between the two firms was the way in which their representatives met to discuss important points during the engineering of the handheld vacuum cleaner. Five meetings, all scheduled by Alfa,

TABLE 12.2   The Original Purchase Schedule by LIEM Compared to the Final Purchase Schedule for 1991

	Model (%)		
Purchase schedule	Economy	Standard	Deluxe
Original	25	55	20
Final	35	45	20

TABLE 12.3   Initial Negotiations to First Shipment of Handheld Vacuum Cleaner

Early 1987	Negotiations between EPL and LIEM begin.
Event ended by:	
January 21, 1988	Product developed by LIEM.
March 15, 1988 (Meeting)	Product design and engineering specifications completed by LIEM.
May 1, 1988 (Meeting)	Mutual agreement between EPL and LIEM on the final product design, engineering specifications, and cost structure.
August 1, 1988	Production of the first functional prototype by EPL.
November 1, 1988	Production of the final prototype by EPL.
December 1, 1988 (Meeting)	Testing and verification of the final prototype by LIEM.
February 1, 1989 (Meeting)	Product changes and modifications by EPL resulting from final prototype testing by LIEM.
February 1, 1990	Technical development and manufacturing engineering for mass production of the final product by EPL.
March 1, 1990	Delivery of manufactured products by EPL to LIEM for final testing and verifications. End of pilot production run for EPL.
May 1, 1990 (Meeting)	Testing completed by LIEM. Calculation of final costs by EPL completed.
July 1, 1990	Final product modifications completed by EPL.
October 1, 1990	LIEM's purchasing process begins.
December 1, 1990	Mass production begins by EPL.
January 15, 1991	First shipment leaves EPL's production facility.

were held during the product engineering process, as shown in Table 12.3. Notes were taken during each meeting, the main points on which both sides agreed were recorded, new deadlines were set, and managers responsible for specific tasks were appointed.

EPL's representatives included the chief design engineer, the engineer directly responsible for the product, and the manager responsible for the pricing and delivery of the product. LIEM's product manager, product designer, technical specialist, quality-control specialist, and sales manager attended the meetings. Top management of EPL did not routinely meet with the product manager from LIEM but held only informal discussions during trade fairs or industrial exhibitions.

Once the engineering process had been completed for the handheld vacuum cleaner, all the decisions regarding the production machinery, sources of raw material and components, and sources of packaging material were EPL's responsibility. The agreement did not allow product modifications during manufacturing. Only minor production changes, or changes that did not alter the cosmetic or functional characteristics of the product, could be made without LIEM's approval.

Modifications were incorporated into the engineering process as necessary. Color specifications changed four times during the engineering process. LIEM completed final performance and quality testing before commercialization. The final product was shown at two major exhibitions. Two months after the presentation of the product, the product was available for sale in retail outlets.

From Novák's perspective, the agreement between EPL and LIEM had several problems: EPL was not part of the marketing process managed by LIEM; LIEM ignored requests by EPL for one or more of its managers to visit LIEM's operations; and, most important, EPL could not communicate directly with LIEM due to the language barrier. Representatives from Alfa sat in on all meetings, including meetings that were strictly technical in nature, and served as translators and interpreters. In September 1991 LIEM offered to work directly with EPL without involving Alfa, but EPL did not have marketing personnel with the language skills needed to conduct negotiations.

New Developments and Strategies

The latest plans proposed by the marketing group had three important objectives: (1) developing an effective and efficient domestic distribution and sales networks for its products, (2) broadening its cooperation with foreign firms in areas of product development and cross-marketing arrangements, and (3) improving the overall image of its brand name ZETA in Western European markets.

According to Novák, these were realistic and strategically implementable objectives under normally operating market conditions. However, given the nature of the transitionary economy in Czechoslovakia, these objectives presented a complex combination of challenges not only to the small marketing group but also to the entire firm.

EPL's relationship with Alfa changed significantly after late 1989. Alfa's management established a new unit concerned only with the export of EPL's products, and Novák saw strong potential for cooperation with this unit. With Alfa's assistance, EPL also began to export some of its vacuum cleaners to Western Europe under brand names owned by various retail store chains.

As mentioned, EPL management offered to cooperate with LIEM as part of the new marketing perspective, and LIEM appeared uninterested. When EPL offered to represent LIEM in the Czechoslovak market, LIEM declined the offer and opened offices for all its products in Prague and Bratislava. In

September 1991, LIEM's unit dealing with small home appliances offered EPL the possibility to negotiate representation in the future.

At the time of this study, EPL was at a crossroad. It needed to upgrade its manufacturing and marketing and become better known in its own domestic market. Management also realized that EPL needed to enter foreign markets to generate capital for its operations. The agreement with LIEM was an annoyance to EPL's marketing group. And, most significantly, EPL's business climate and the domestic market were progressing through rapid changes.

Notes

1. All names of individuals and firms, domestic or foreign, have been changed.

2. Many of these situations were created by direct government policies. Individual manufacturing firms had no input into the creation or implementation of such policies.

CHAPTER THIRTEEN

■

Total Quality Management in Czechoslovakia

In early 1990 Czechoslovak companies faced a whirlwind of abrupt change in the required quality levels of their products. A new postrevolution competitive manufacturing environment forced companies to transform a prerevolution environment insulated by bureaucratic centralization employing coercive planning that hindered quality management. Changing from a closed market system to a free market system would be difficult for even the most resilient companies; abrupt changes in the new free market environment further complicated that transition. For example, the conversion of the European countries into a Common Market created an extremely dynamic and competitive environment. All of these changes increased the need for Czechoslovak companies to adopt new quality-management techniques quickly and effectively.

The following study reviews, analyzes, and prescribes changes in the state of quality management in Czechoslovakia prior to and after the revolution. The analysis compares the 1992 state of quality management in Czechoslovakia with the internationally dominant philosophies of Japanese and U.S. compa-

Pandu R. Tadikamalla is professor of business administration at the Katz Graduate School of Business. He teaches courses in operations/production management, simulation, statistical techniques for management, and total quality management. He has consulted for several corporations including Westinghouse Electric Corporation, PPG Industries, Weirton Steel Corporation, Roadway Services, and II-VI, Inc. Dagmar Glückaufová is professor of operations research and director of the MBA program at the Czechoslovak Management Center. Dr. Glückaufová taught at Charles University, and also at the University of Birmingham, England, during the 1970s. She also carried out research at the Czechoslovak Academy of Sciences' Econometric Laboratory and has lectured throughout Europe on multiple-criteria decisionmaking. Stephen L. Starling is currently working toward a Ph.D. in operations management at the University of Pittsburgh. He received a B.S. degree in operations management from Arizona State University in 1988, and an M.B.A. from Northern Arizona University in 1990.

nies. In conclusion, a general prescription for transforming Czechoslovak quality management from its current noncompetitive positioning to a competitive and dynamic positioning is discussed.

Review

A quality management situation in Czechoslovakia was greatly influenced by the political changes that occurred after the revolution. However, the ability to compete internationally was still hampered by past negligence and by the lingering perceptions of potential customers resulting from this negligence.

Postrevolution industries were burdened with low technology levels, a limited variety of products, and shortages of raw materials, creating inflexibility and preventing the industries from meeting delivery due dates, proper service levels, and other needs of customers. Czechoslovaks were quick to point out that these problems developed under the prerevolution government and were being resolved, but the complacency toward quality improvement remained.

The most obvious reason for this complacency was the noncompetitive environment prior to the revolution. The prerevolution market was a seller's market, where demand almost always exceeded supply and producers had domestic monopolies. Trade within the Soviet bloc nations was carried out on a barter basis. The combination of the barter system and little internal competition limited the need for and ability of companies to make advances in research, development, and technology. In addition, producers had little incentive to improve productivity or quality.

The Prerevolution Period

Prior to the revolution, very few Czechoslovak products were internationally competitive. Products that were exportable consisted primarily of commodity products such as lumber and steel. The main exceptions were military products such as tanks and guns. Commodity products did not require high-technology levels and came out of labor-intensive industries, allowing Czechoslovakia to compete due to its inexpensive labor base and government-controlled pricing practices.

Realizing that quality levels were too low to compete internationally, the government established a state office for standardization to look into quality matters. The state office tried to improve quality by imposing regulations and rules; however, the regulations and rules were largely ignored. Because producers had domestic monopolies, there was no incentive for improving quality. Some of the regulations required the development of quality-control departments; however, these departments were viewed as an administrative encumbrance and were not effective.

The lack of success in competing internationally shifted the focus back to the domestic market. In 1968, the government introduced production evalu-

TABLE 13.1   Categories of Evaluated Products (%)

	1980	1981	1982	1983	1984	1985	1986	1987
Category 1	26.3	26.2	27.4	29.7	34.2	36.7	37.3	37.2
Category 2	72.8	73.5	72.4	69.9	64.8	63.0	62.2	61.3
Category 3	.9	.3	.2	.4	1.0	.3	.5	1.5

Source: Vaclav Martinovsky, "Kvalita rizeni" (Controlling Product Quality). Institute of Economics, Academy of Sciences working paper no. 218. Prague, 1989.

ations that produced positive results. The main goal of the production evaluations was to improve the relative quality of products for both foreign and domestic markets.

The success of production evaluations led to technical improvements in complex production in the early 1970s as part of an effort to match products produced by foreign competitors in more-developed countries. Czechoslovak companies could therefore improve their products by using foreign products as a benchmark without the threat of direct foreign competition.

This approach improved the quality of products, but three major drawbacks limited its success. First, access to foreign competitors' product documentation was limited. Second, it was inappropriate to compare products in the development stage with those that were already being mass-produced. Third, using the benchmarking strategy, Czechoslovak companies continually lagged behind foreign competition in areas of productivity and quality.

Although some technological delay existed, the evaluation and comparison of foreign products provided some incentive to produce quality products that was not provided solely by the existing market disequilibrium. Recognizing this, the government established technical test centers. The goal of the test centers was to maximize the range of evaluated products. Despite the test centers, about 40 percent of the products were not evaluated. The evaluated products were placed into one of three categories depending upon their technical specifications. Products placed in Category 1 had the highest technical specifications; products placed in Category 3 had the lowest. Table 13.1 shows the percentage of evaluated products in each of the three categories for the years 1980 through 1987.

From Table 13.1 we can see that in 1987, 37.2 percent of the products were categorized as having high technical specifications. Only 61.3 percent were placed in Category 2 and the balance of 1.5 percent in Category 3. The increase from 1980 to 1987 in the percentage of Category 1 products was accompanied by an increase in the evolution of new products (see Table 13.2).

In Table 13.3, we can see statistics on the evolution of exports and imports to and from capitalist and socialist countries. Exports do not exhibit strong growth; however, we can see a small increase in the export of products to capitalist countries for the years 1982 to 1987. More interesting is the approximately 9 percent increase in imports of products from capitalist countries.

TABLE 13.2   Evolution of New Products Relative to Whole Production (%)

	1976	1980	1981	1982	1983	1984	1985	1986	1987
New products	8.1	10.6	13.4	13.5	15.3	18.4	20.9	17.7	16.2

Source: Vaclav Martinovsky, "Kvalita rizeni" (Controlling Product Quality). Institute of Economics, Academy of Sciences working paper no. 218. Prague, 1989.

TABLE 13.3   Evolution of Exports and Imports to and from Socialist and Capitalist Countries of Advanced Products (% of all advanced products)

	Exports						
	1981	1982	1983	1984	1985	1986	1987
To socialist countries	21.2	21.8	21.4	21.9	21.6	21.2	20.8
To capitalist countries	7.5	5.8	5.3	5.1	5.4	6.7	6.9
	Imports						
From socialist countries	13.0	13.0	13.9	13.2	13.4	13.1	12.8
From capitalist countries	18.4	19.2	20.4	23.2	24.2	26.5	27.3

Source: Vaclav Martinovsky, "Kvalita rizeni" (Controlling Product Quality). Institute of Economics, Academy of Sciences working paper no. 218. Prague, 1989.

Combining the two observations, we can see that an inevitable increase in the trade deficit is the result.

Greater than one-third of the products were in Category 1, but low-technology products were the only ones that were competitive internationally. And products in Category 1 were selling internationally at only average or below-average prices. The problem lay in the bias and complacency of the test centers. The test centers were controlled by respective ministries that benefited from higher evaluations of some products, and other products were arbitrarily evaluated and categorized.

The Postrevolution Period

After the revolution, Czechoslovak manufacturers began to be aware of the challenge to produce better-quality products and to commit themselves to becoming internationally competitive. The outlook was good: The work force was well-educated and trained, possessing strong engineering and manufacturing skills, and basic quality-control systems were already in place in many companies.

For example, many companies had already made substantial efforts to create manuals on quality and quality-management systems. The use of statistical quality control (SQC) and total quality management (TQM) within these manuals and systems highlighted the fact that progress was being made. SQC refers to the application of statistical techniques (such as control charts and measures of central tendency and dispersion) through inspection by sampling.[1] The companies who implemented quality-management techniques had successes that provided models for other companies.

Spolana Case Study

One such company that can serve as a model for other companies is Spolana Neratovice, a Czechoslovak petrochemicals producer that had success exporting products to highly developed countries such as Germany, England, and Japan.

Spolana was under the control of the government as a part of the state enterprise Chemopetrol Prague until July 29, 1990. At that time, Spolana was established as an independent state enterprise. The founder and superior body of Spolana was the Ministry of the Chemical Industry of the Czech Republic.[2]

Spolana had produced plastics in its petrochemicals plant since 1975. Three of its major products at the time of this study were VCM, suspension PVC, and granulated PVC. VCM was primarily used in the production of PVC at Spolana, but some was exported to Germany and Belgium. To meet PVC production goals, VCM was produced in-house and purchased from other suppliers. The production levels for VCM and PVC products remained stable over 1985–1990. PVC was exported to Germany, Australia, Switzerland, the Netherlands, Italy, France, Finland, Denmark, Sweden, Greece, England, and Japan. The succes of these PVC products encouraged the development of new ones.

Since 1947 Spolana had also been producing rayon staple. Customers for the rayon staple were domestic textile factories and factories in Austria, Switzerland, France, Spain, Turkey, and Tunisia. According to statistics for 1985 to 1990, production of rayon staple remained fairly stable. Spolana was the monopolistic producer of rayon staple in Czechoslovakia.

Spolana also manufactured the following industrial chemical products: sulphuric acid, hydrochloric acid, sodium hydroxide, chlorine, sodium hypochloride, sodium sulphate, ammonium sulphate, and caprolactam. Like the rayon-staple production, the industrial chemical products area was relatively stable from 1985 to 1990.

Agrochemicals was Spolana's most diversified product area; over forty kinds of products were manufactured. These products were based on both proprietary and licensed products. Trade partners, whose licensed trademarks were used by Spolana, included firms in England and Switzerland.

Other products produced by Spolana included a line of sweeteners, specialty hormones, and various other chemical products. According to Spolana, the production of sweeteners decreased significantly from 1989 to 1990 due to processing problems. Specialty hormones were produced for pharmaceutical and veterinary customers.

Spolana's products could be placed into three categories: standard mass-production chemical products, nonstandard products with industry-specific utility properties, and technologically advanced products.

TABLE 13.4   Percentage Defects at Spolana

Year	Defects
1984	0.004
1985	0.005
1986	0.009
1987	0.011
1988	0.004
1989	0.010
1990	0.010
1991	0.008

Source: Spolana, 1992.

Spolana's goal for mass-production products was to stabilize the production processes to improve productivity and quality. The market for mass-production products was fairly static in 1991, with many producers worldwide.

Nonstandard products with industry-specific utility properties were developed for further processing at the customers' facilities. The strategic goal with these products was to meet the needs and expectations of the individual customers as fully as possible.

The technologically advanced products competed in a dynamic environment where innovation was required to compete effectively. Two of the chemicals in this category were remophan and sualin. Remophan, used for veterinary purposes, was a very successful export. Sualin is an artificial sweetener, a combination of aspartam and saccharin.

At the time of this study, Spolana was selling its exported products at below-average prices but at 1.9 times the price of similar domestic products. Innovation to develop higher-quality products was needed to reach average prices, but Spolana had discovered that the costs of innovation were often prohibitive. Due to the costs of innovation, the company bought licenses from and engaged in production with foreign firms to produce products developed out of the country. For example, Spolana purchased a license from Imperial Chemical Industries (ICI), an English company, and signed a contract for joint production. Through the agreement, ICI invested considerable capital into the assembly line and shared valuable technological information.

In comparison to other Czechoslovak companies, Spolana had a long tradition of improving the quality of its products. For example, Spolana had used statistical process control (SPC) for over twenty-five years. Table 13.4 shows data on the percentage of defects from 1984 to 1991. The low rates of defects clearly demonstrate that Spolana was quite capable of producing high-quality products and contradict other countries' perceptions that Czechoslovak companies like Spolana manufactured products inferior to those of their foreign counterparts.

The problem at Spolana and other Czechoslovak companies was in how quality control was used. According to the head of the Quality Control Department, Mr. Kubr, the work force at Spolana had the technical knowledge and skills but were lacking in management skills to effect changes in procedures.

One of the major problems at Spolana prior to the revolution was that the organizational structure did not empower the quality-control department to properly implement change. Kubr's position as head of quality control was an example of how the structure had changed. Kubr reported directly to the director of Spolana, as can be seen in Figure 13.1. As a result, all of the other departments had to seriously consider quality-management requirements because of the support from top management.

The main problems of managing quality at Spolana were identified through interviews with management as follows:

- No reward or recognition system for workers was implemented to support TQM. (Rewards were given to technicians for innovations.)
- Workers lived in an atmosphere of fear. The quality-control manager believed that if TQM requirements were not fulfilled, then the worker responsible should be fired.
- Top management did not understand the need to update and change production processes in order to improve productivity and quality.
- Top management believed that cultural differences prevented the company from adopting many foreign philosophies, such as Japanese management philosophies.
- Customer and supplier involvement were not deemed as very necessary in producing higher-quality products.

At the time of this study, resolution of these problems was taking place. For example, all suppliers were asked to reach ISO (International Standards Organization) 9000 by the end of 1992, and close collaboration with customers has become prevalent for products in Categories 2 and 3.

Kaučuk Case Study

Kaučuk manufactured refinery products such as liquid fuels, plastics, and rubber. The fuels produced at Kaučuk were leaded gasoline and a high-quality jet fuel. The main rubber product was a high-quality Indian rubber, which required certification in order to sell to most customers. Foreign customers such as Perilli Tire Company of Italy and Continental of Germany had certified the Indian rubber to be of high quality. In discussions with Mr. Pacha, Kaučuk's quality-control manager, we discovered that both foreign companies were surprised by the high-quality rubber. Their surprise indicates once again that foreign companies had a misconception about the quality of Czechoslovak products and processes.

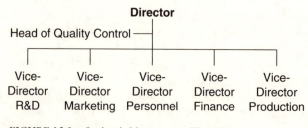

FIGURE 13.1   Spolana's Management Hierarchy.

In 1992 Kaučuk had the goal of reaching ISO 9000 by the middle of 1993, while still meeting customers' standards at the lowest cost. At that time, the company had approximately 2,600 employees. In addition, facilities were thirty years old and technologically inadequate according to industry standards. For example, no storage tanks existed for the fuel that was produced; therefore, the production of fuels was directly subject to fluctuations in demand. Production as a result of demand is, in essence, a pull production system; Kaučuk was implementing just-in-time manufacturing techniques and philosophies.

At Kaučuk, a quality-control group was formed to replace a quality-control management department that was responsible for the quality of products in the company divisions. In the new system, divisions were responsible for intraproduction and postproduction control. The development of the group was a reaction by top management to Kaučuk's losing markets. The group improved quality through training, measuring customer satisfaction, developing suppliers, and by comparing competitors' products.

Training employees in process-control techniques and quality-control management was an important function of the quality-control group. The group had five specialists in statistical quality control who could train other employees. The managers in the quality-control group were well-educated. For example, familiarity with the works of authors Edwards Deming, J. M. Juran, and Phillip Crosby was evident in discussions with Pacha, the quality-control manager. The group had developed educational material specifically for training purposes. In addition to training employees, the group had the power to evaluate workers to determine whether their skills were being best utilized in the positions they currently held.

Another task of the quality-control group was to gauge the satisfaction and needs of customers. To help meet this objective, technicians regularly visited customers to check their satisfaction and needs. The group was also developing an objective method for measuring customer satisfaction. The only measurement already available was sales, which only provided only a reactionary understanding of customer needs and expectations.

Development of suppliers at Kaučuk demonstrated the influence that Edwards Deming had had on Pacha. Kaučuk was currently using only evaluations and audits of suppliers to determine whether suppliers were meeting Kaučuk's requirements, which indicated that Kaučuk was in the early stages of supplier development.

Through comparison of the specifications and tolerances of its products with competitors' products, Kaučuk had been able to improve quality. This method, however, can lead to complacency in innovation; effort is directed at merely matching the quality levels of competitors. At Kaučuk, this strategy of comparison had created a situation in which Kaučuk was developing products while competitors were already in mass production. In addition, information on competitors' products could be difficult to obtain.

Despite the efforts of the quality-control group, many of the quality-management problems that were revealed in the Spolana case study were also present at Kaučuk. The following problems were identified:

- According to the Kaučuk quality-control group, top management discussed quality but did not act upon what was said.
- The quality-control group had not been given the power or standing in the company to enforce changes. For example, none of the quality-control managers were in top management.
- As at Spolana, employees were motivated by fear of losing their jobs, but in this case they were apprehensive because a continuing loss of market share could lead to layoffs.
- Employees strongly resisted training in quality-control procedures such as SPC. The resistance was mainly due to years of obligatory ideological training prior to the revolution.
- Prior to the revolution, promotions were not solely based upon the capability of the individual. As a result, the distribution of Spolana's greatest resource, its skilled labor force, did not fully benefit the company.

Analysis

The concept behind TQM is that to achieve high quality and to stay competitive, it is necessary to make an organizationwide commitment to quality.[3] In reviewing the quality-management problems at Spolana and Kaučuk, it was clear that both companies needed to improve their organizationwide commitment. The main problem was primarily one of marketing the value of quality to all employees from top management on down.

Although top management at both Spolana and Kaučuk appeared to believe they were supportive of improving quality, they could have done much more. At Kaučuk, top management supported quality management in theory but appeared to be unwilling to provide the necessary resources. At Spolana, top management was more supportive, as demonstrated by the quality-control manager reporting directly to top management.

Fear provided the greatest motivation for workers in both Spolana and Kaučuk. Whenever fear is a motivational factor, workers will try to eliminate the fear. At Spolana, a worker could get fired for producing low-quality work. As a result, defects were hidden and difficult to trace. At Kaučuk, the fear was the result of a diminishing market share that might force layoffs. The fear at Kaučuk could have served as a good motivational tool; the fear at Spolana was destructive.

Neither Spolana nor Kaučuk fully utilized teamwork for solving quality-management problems. The various functions of the companies such as human resource planning, production, marketing, and information processing were not integrated to achieve the common goal of high quality. Quality management at Spolana and Kaučuk was too isolated from the interfunctional areas to produce excellent results. Due to the tremendous marketing task of eliminating misconceptions regarding the quality of Czech products, the marketing departments in Spolana and Kaučuk needed to be solidly integrated into every phase of bringing a product to the market.

Neither Spolana nor Kaučuk had objective measurements of the costs of quality. Quantification of the costs of quality would have been a tremendous plus for identifying and prioritizing the most important problems and for selling quality-control programs to top management.

The knowledge of SQC was very good at both Spolana and Kaučuk. ANSI/ASQC defines quality control as the operational techniques and activities used to fulfill requirements of quality.[4] The aim of quality control is to assure satisfactory quality, and this assurance is provided through SQC. According to our interviews with quality-control managers, Czechoslovak companies were proficient with SQC; however, quality standards, not quality itself, had increased.

Both companies needed to eradicate incorrect perceptions by foreign customers about the levels of quality that existed. This problem had been partly created by the Western media, which had continually reported that former Soviet-bloc countries created poor-quality products. Clearly the statistics on percentage defects and the surprise of foreign firms as to the high quality of certain Czechoslovak products demonstrated that misperceptions did persist.

Prescription for Change

Ideally, quality management has the following attributes:

- Top management regards quality as essential to the company's success.
- Prevention is the main quality activity.
- Except in the most unusual cases, problems are prevented.
- The reported cost of quality is the same as the actual cost of quality.
- Quality improvement is a regular and continuing process.

The prescription for reaching this ideal state is to develop an overall plan, empower quality-control personnel, demonstrate commitment, and involve all functional areas.

Develop an Overall Plan

The first requirement to bridge the gap between the ideal state and the existing state of quality management at Spolana and Kaučuk is the development of a plan. The plan must have the following general elements: organizational mission, environmental survey, clear specification of objectives, action steps, plan evaluation, and control mechanism. For example, the organizational mission should address questions such as:

- What should the quality mission of the company be?
- What are the key qualities as seen by the clients?
- As to the key qualities, what is the company's state of competitiveness?
- What opportunities does the company have for quality improvement and for cost reduction?
- What can the company do to make better use of its resources?
- What are the threats on the horizon?

Empower Quality-Control Personnel

Once a plan has been developed, quality-control personnel should be empowered to enforce program implementations. As pictured in the organizational hierarchy diagram for Spolana, the head of quality control reported directly to top management. As a result, the quality-control department at Spolana had the power to initiate and follow through with quality-control programs.

The empowerment should not create fear within the organization. As reported in the Boston Globe on December 23, 1986, Russia sentenced three female factory managers to two years in a labor camp and fined them $14,000 for producing poor-quality clothes at a government factory.[5] This is not the way to create an atmosphere where employees work together for the continual improvement of quality. Employees must feel comfortable enough so that bottom-up communication exists along with top-down communication. For example, an employee who fears failing may hide problems and send a poor product down the line to another workcenter rather than stopping the process and solving the problem.

Demonstrate Commitment

Once empowerment has been provided, the quality-control department and top management must demonstrate their commitment to improving quality. The goal of demonstrating commitment is to convince employees that change is needed. The following activities can greatly aid in demonstrating the commitment to quality:[6]

- Conduct employee opinion surveys.
- Conduct customer-satisfaction surveys.
- Jointly develop definitions of quality with employees, suppliers, and customers.
- Set specific goals.
- Create rewards for commitment to quality.
- Focus on quality in corporate communications.
- Periodically or randomly work with employees on their jobs.
- Create a quality-control phone line so that employees can immediately contact quality control about issues.
- Create a suggestion box and reply to all ideas with respect for the employee.
- Create legends, tell stories.
- Create an atmosphere of "blameless error."
- Make decisions based on quality, not on cost containment.
- Measure the costs of quality.
- Explain trade-offs between cost and quality.
- Be honest.

Demonstrating commitment to quality is, in essence, internal marketing. The relationship of quality improvement to increases in productivity should be explained. Deming and Crosby have both shown that as quality increases, so does productivity. In his book *Out of Crisis*, Deming talks about the chain reaction of improving quality: Costs decrease because of less rework, fewer mistakes, and better use of machine time and materials, which improve productivity. Improved productivity and quality increase market share and raise the competitive advantage.[7] The same concepts are reflected in Crosby's book *Quality is Free*.[8]

Involve All Functional Areas

Once the commitment of top management and the quality-control department has been demonstrated, the various departments will be more open to change. The next step is to create interfunctional teams to address quality-control issues and problems. "Quality function deployment" (QFD) has proven beneficial in enhancing interfunctional integration.

QFD is a management approach that is a set of planning and communications routines designed to break down functional areas and encourage teamwork. QFD originated in 1972 at Mitsubishi's Kobe shipyard site. QFD focuses and coordinates skills within an organization, first to design, then to manufacture and market goods that customers want to purchase and will continue to purchase.[9]

Summary

TQM's success in companies like Spolana and Kaučuk will not require teaching in statistical process control or statistical quality control. Much to the surprise of foreign manufacturers, the companies discussed in this case were quite knowledgeable on these subjects. In addition, the quality of the products the companies produce is better than an observer from a foreign competitor's country would expect. Perhaps the greatest misconception and revelation is the skill and knowledge level of the average worker.

Despite all of these promising revelations, at the time of this study Czechoslovak companies were not competing very well on an international level. The two primary reasons for the failure have been identified as misconceptions of foreign customers about the quality levels of Czechoslovak products and the lack of Czechoslovak companies specifically meeting the needs of foreign customers (a definition of quality). The goal of the prescription given in the previous section is to provide a format for dealing with both reasons for failure. The primary ingredients in the prescription are simply the following:

1. Develop a plan.
2. Provide quality-control management with the power to achieve that plan.
3. Earn the commitment of all employees to achieve the plan.
4. Achieve the plan through interfunctional teams that specifically address quality-control issues and problems.

The prerevolution days are gone when the engineering department designs the product, the production department produces it, quality-control people inspect it, and the government distributes it. Czechoslovak companies were forced to adjust to a new postrevolution competitive manufacturing environment from a prerevolution environment that hindered the management of quality. The adjustment required companies to adopt quality-management techniques quickly and effectively.

Notes

1. Pandu Tadikamalla, "Quality, Productivity, and Competitive Position," *Competing* (January 1990).

2. *Spolana Annual Report,* 1990.

3. Tadikamalla, "Quality, Productivity, and Competitive Position."

4. American National Standards Institute/American Society of Quality Control. *Quality Systems Technology.* American National Standard A3-1987 (Milwaukee, WI: ANSI/ASQC, 1987).

5. "Building Quality into Your Leadership Style." *Boston Globe,* December 23, 1986.

6. Christopher Hart, "Building Quality into Your Leadership Style," (Harvard Business School, 1988).

7. W. Edwards Deming, *Out of Crisis* (Cambridge, MA: MIT Center for Advanced Engineering Study, 1986).

8. Phillip Crosby, *Quality is Free* (New York, NY: McGraw-Hill, 1979).

9. J. R. Hauser and D. Clausing, "The House of Quality," *Harvard Business Review* (May-June 1988).

PART FOUR

Conclusion

CHAPTER FOURTEEN

———————— ■ ————————

Lessons Learned

DANIEL S. FOGEL

Vaclav Havel, in his book *Summer Meditations,* wrote, "Clearly, nothing can get along without the participation of powers as unscientific as healthy common sense and the human conscience."[1] Through this book we came to realize, like Havel, that often common sense and experience rule over scientific data. We have tried in this book to help the reader gain an awareness of the challenges facing companies in the former Czechoslovakia through a variety of examples of enterprises undergoing change in an economic arena that appears to escape scientific definition.

This book is designed for students, businesspeople, faculty, and the general public interested in gaining a more thorough knowledge of Central and Eastern Europe and the former Soviet Union. In these case studies, we have depicted actual situations in which companies are operating. These situations are ones we have experienced personally.

The introductory chapters are designed to give readers an understanding of the economic conditions of Central and Eastern Europe. The chapters contain several lessons about the former Czechoslovak economic reform. In the 1930s, Czechoslovakia was one of the fifteen most developed countries in the world. It survived World War II relatively unscathed, with most of its property, plant, and infrastructure intact, and by 1948 it had more or less regained its prewar income level. Yet, forty years of central planning and close political and economic ties with the Soviet Union led Czechoslovakia to relative economic decline.

From World War II to the 1960s, deteriorating economic performance and obvious inefficiencies of the economic system led to several radical attempts at reformation, especially in the 1960s. These attempts were brought to an abrupt end with the events of the Prague Spring of 1968. During the following two decades, "normalization" was reintroduced with strict central planning. Inspired by perestroika in the Soviet Union and by reform attempts in

Poland and Hungary, Czechoslovak leaders took various steps after 1986 to lay the groundwork for the far-reaching market and economic reforms that the former Czechoslovakia embarked on in 1990.

After the Velvet Revolution of November 1989, Czechoslovakia abandoned the inefficient system of central planning and aimed to create the systemic and macroeconomic conditions for a return to the path of economic growth that would allow it eventually to catch up with the industrialized countries. To this end, it dismantled the institutions supporting the central planning apparatus and strove to reintroduce a market economy. The country's leaders initiated a process of forging close links with the international economic and financial community. In several respects, the initial conditions for systemic transformation in the Czech and Slovak republics were less favorable than in some other Central and Eastern European countries:

- The private sector at the beginning of 1990 was almost nonexistent.
- The legal and institutional frameworks for a market economy were lacking.
- Economic activity was still concentrated in large units, with large-scale enterprises dominating the industrial landscape and monopoly trade organizations organizing the distribution of goods.
- The closed character of the economy and the tradition of tight central planning were also reflected in the low number of active joint ventures.
- Prices were almost completely controlled in 1989, except for a few luxury items, on wholesale as well as retail levels.
- Czechoslovakia was more dependent on socialist trade than were other Central and East European countries, except for Bulgaria.

Thus, the former Czechoslovakia was, at the outset of its systemic transformation, an economy almost completely dominated by central planning and had little experience with markets and almost no legal and institutional basis for a market economy. Yet the following were several favorable macroeconomic conditions of the Czechoslovak economy up to 1992 that may facilitate reform:

- Inflation never emerged as a serious problem, averaging less than 2 percent from 1980 to 1989.
- The monetary overhang in 1989 was relatively small.
- Hard-currency debt in 1989 was only 15 percent of GDP.
- Net government debt in 1989 was small, less than 1 percent of GDP.

The basic challenges that the government faced in pursuing economic reform may be summarized in four points:

1. The countries' legal frameworks and basic institutions, defined previously by strict central planning, must be completely overhauled so that a market economy may emerge and function.
2. Macroeconomic stability must be maintained.
3. The reform program must combine structural transformation and macroeconomic policies to minimize transition costs and to sustain public support.
4. The Czech and Slovak republics must deal with their new independence while maintaining control over economic matters.

The period in question in this book is characterized by cautious optimism combined with a rapid drop in production, a sharp increase in unemployment, and an unstable political situation. Furthermore, the book's cases were written at a time when the split between the Czechs and Slovaks was not anticipated. The populist leader of the Movement for a Democratic Slovakia, Vladimir Meciar, was not in the political arena. Václav Havel, president of the former Czechoslovakia, was firmly entrenched in his job, and Václav Klaus, then minister of finance, was an increasingly popular figure as his plans for privatization became more well known.

One key to understanding these cases is to understand the classical socialist system in the Czech and Slovak republics. Most important to this understanding is that the political structure, particularly the power of the ruling Communist party, was key to society's functioning. The party dominated all facets of Czech and Slovak life, exercising its power with reference to the official ideology of, among others, Marxism and Leninism.

The one-party rule in Czechoslovakia, "imbued by the official ideology," led to the dominance of the state and to quasi-state ownership.[2] The party nationalized banking, industry, and transportation and eventually eliminated private ownership in all economic areas including agriculture. The party's power and its need to control all aspects of society was incompatible with private ownership and individual sovereignty.

The dominance of the party, with its ideology and the dominance of state-owned property, led to bureaucratic coordination through the elimination of free enterprise, autonomous actors in the market, and competition. Decision-making and information were centralized, and the party created a dominance of hierarchical dependence and vertical integration.

The structure, size distribution, and businesses of enterprises in socialist economies of the former Czechoslovakia were not driven by profit motives. The firms were driven by the behavior of bureaucrats in state agencies and managers in state firms. Such behavior was motivated by a desire to maximize control over resources or to minimize risk of penalty due to noncompliance with a mandated economic plan.[3]

Also, the costs associated with transacting business with other firms was very high in the centrally planned economy. An efficient response within such a system was the formation of large enterprises or centrally controlled networks of firms. The establishment of a system of private property rights, market-driven prices, open labor markets, and a legal system compatible with market activity is changing the cost of carrying out market transactions and thus will change the managers' behavior in firms.[4]

Given these systemic factors, the interest and motivation of actors become evident. For example, managers engaged in plan bargaining exercised paternalistic behavior toward subordinates and viewed prices as inconsequential to enterprise decisions. The government created mechanisms and incentive systems forcing managers to produce for export purposes because managers of production failed to develop a strong, intrinsic interest in gaining access to foreign hard-currency markets.

These conditions had devastating effects on the Czech and Slovak economies. They produced forced growth, labor shortages at the same time that employed workers often had little to do, and a chronic shortage economy. Thus, the introduction of the reform in the republics, punctuated by the Velvet Revolution, has resulted in several penchants in the economic, social, and political domains. These penchants affect managerial behavior.

First, political liberalization is evident. The Communist party has fallen out of favor and elections have occurred with some regularity. Every case in this book reflects a response to political freedom. Each manager or organization is able to react to the new economic situation because of the liberalization of the political system. Second, the private sector has been revived. This revival has been coincidental with the guarantees for private property and the ability of citizens and foreign investors to enforce those rights in the courts. Also, the private sector is greatly influenced by direct foreign investment.

Of special interest to understanding the evolution of the private sector are the cases on marketing. Lusico (formerly called Copy Service) is operating in a highly competitive transitory market. It has a number of domestic and foreign competitors. With new capital and management, the company formed a new marketing strategy.[5] Lusico quickly learned the need to respond to market conditions by formulating a strategic plan that anticipated more competition. Unlike many of its counterparts in other industries, it developed a marketing strategy to find new opportunities and to define its mission.

We also see from this case how easy it is for companies to focus only on sales and service rather than on broader marketing issues. We learn many things from this case about the typical new private company in the former Czechoslovakia trying to make the transition to a market economy.

Hoy and Pivoda in their case about Ecofluid show us an in-depth look at an entrepreneur trying to develop his own business. Entrepreneurs in an economy such as the former Czechoslovakia must develop support mechanisms on their own, unlike in Western cultures. These supports include distribution channels, marketing mediums, and sources of capital and labor. The Ecofluid chapter shows how private companies are formed in the former Czechoslovakia. We see an interesting strategy to start the company, a strategy not often found in Western countries. The Machrle brothers used the Academy of Sciences and various universities and institutes as their places for innovation. They gained both scientific experience and organizational skills through conducting research in universities and trying out their ideas in France and Italy. We can generalize from this case to understand that innovation in the former Czechoslovakia probably will come (and continues as such) from academia and not from the private or corporate sectors.

The Machrles' contacts are important to the success of their company. These contacts were developed prior to starting a business. In fact, this may be the one determining factor of a successful new venture. If we can generalize from this case, successful new Czech and Slovak ventures are characterized by founders who have many loose connections with individuals and organizations that existed prior to the reform rather than a few newly developed connections. These multiple and well-developed connections pay off in access to markets, capital, employees, and other resources.

The success of these new ventures comes from a fit between the competitive advantage, the way the organization is designed, and the personality and skills of the owners. But, as we know from other cases in this book, early success of private companies does not predict future success. Markets are fickle and connections change quickly in transition economies. The Ecofluid case is an ideal opportunity to explore the risks of adopting a growth strategy in a highly uncertain market.

A third penchant during the reform is that the governments will pursue energetic privatization of state-owned property. The unique methods of using vouchers has caught the attention of the international community. The companies represented in these cases have all participated in the privatization process, usually with the involvement of a foreign partner.

The Ferox Děčín case reveals company manager Radek Malec's struggle with the new realities of the market economy, privatization, and a new partner. The stress and personal sacrifice he endures is instructive. It also gives us insight into the changes a general manager must make to be effective in the new market economy with an active privatization program. We see a person who used to have a wider scope of responsibility yet now has less authority than his Western counterpart. This manager handles the uncertainty of the country's economic and social changes through his "three-pillar approach": (1) privatization, (2) improvisation, and (3) long-term strategy. Each of these pillars is a new approach to running a business. The focus on privatization is particularly instructive. We see two partners who have had extensive and positive previous contact. Yet, the future may be different when the U.S. company

Air Products and Chemicals, Inc., assumes control of this Czech company. Certainly, Malec's job will change from his free-wheeling and autonomous operating mode.

The Ferox case also points out cultural differences between Western and Czechoslovak partners. Western managers see rules as reflecting a well-organized operation; in a command economy, managers see the same rules as stupid and unfair. Similarly, under communism, managers who improvise and develop a personal involvement with all levels of the organization are seen as humane and effective, but in Western organizations they appear capricious and self-indulgent.

The case also illustrates some sources of the negative impressions of each partner in cross-cultural operations. Most of the conflicts detailed in the Ferox case are related to the organization, but they are interpreted as personal and are expressed in negative terms: Czechs lack integrity; Americans are naive; Germans pay bribes to get what they want; and Westerners think all problems can be solved by just throwing money at them. These negative evaluations are exacerbated by language differences and by the very real fear Czechs have of losing their jobs and homes. At the same time, they have less than the full attention of the distant U.S. corporate management, which has, of course, a much larger international business to run. However, Ferox is an atypical joint venture in that a great deal of time and cultural sensitivity were brought to bear on doing business together. The success of Ferox and Air Products is a result of these interpersonal aspects of the negotiations and business management.

Glavunion, another example of privatization in the former Czechoslovakia, is a relatively large company that is trying to privatize with the involvement of foreign partners. Glavunion is trying to maintain its position in the domestic market while trying to modernize itself to meet the demands of the Western market. The selected foreign partner will ultimately become the primary financier of its modernization.

In this case, as in the Ferox case, we learn that earlier privatization efforts in the former Czechoslovakia usually involve a foreign partner. To attract these partners, Czech and Slovak companies must do more than declare an intent for joint cooperation. They must also adhere to the foreign partner's requirements, including restrictions on the organization's management and hiring and firing practices, as well as to a new organizational culture. This case illustrates the complex levels of competing agendas that result from joint ventures for privatization.

Electro-Products Limited illustrates the difficulties of cross-cultural partnerships. Josef Novak, the newly appointed head of a small marketing and marketing analysis group at EPL, must deal with the relationship between EPL and LIEM, a large European-based electronic manufacturer and marketer. EPL thought LIEM would offer assistance and training to EPL in a friendly way in order to help EPL develop its marketing capability. Instead, LIEM is acting like an aggressive competitor in EPL's market. This behavior occurs even though, under the EPL-LIEM contract, EPL has exclusive control over the sales and distribution of its products in the republics.

The problems EPL faces are more complicated than that of dealing with a partner. We see an interesting array of problems related to the internal organization of a Czech company and its inability to work forcibly with its foreign partner. The company is incapable of developing new market strategies quickly enough to be competitive. In brief, the case illustrates that Czech managers underestimate the need to have a well-managed company prior to pursuing a foreign partner.

A fourth penchant in the reform process is that prices have been liberalized to the extent that they can be used as market information and now provide a framework for decisions made by consumers and producers. This change places more responsibility on the shoulders of managers.

We get glimpses of executives running their companies in the case about the Harvard Group and its controversial founder, Victor Koženy. Koženy represents the epitome of both an entrepreneur and a carpet-bagger. He is smart, quick to meet market demands, and actively taking advantage of his competitive edge within the former Czechoslovakia. Through his actions we see some of the problems associated with emerging markets. Few rules exist, and those with special access to market information can gain advantages within the new markets. For example, his firm was responsible for conducting valuations on firms that would be privatized within two years of the valuation. Koženy's company had this information and was not obligated to share it with anyone else. He also opened a mutual fund that acquired, at one time, up to 40 percent of the Czechoslovak vouchers for purchasing shares in firms—the same firms for which he conducted valuations. Do Koženy's actions present a legal problem?

Another lesson we learned from the Harvard Capital Group case is the effect of rapid change on an emerging company in reform economies. We can expect most firms to organize in a similar fashion to that of the Harvard Group; creating a separate division every time a new market opportunity is conceived and acted upon. Well known to the Western world, this organization strategy helps to create flexibility in response and is appropriate for this particular environmental setting.

Thus, we learn a great deal from this case about the different management systems in the West and in the former Czechoslovakia. This case complements the information from the Nath and Jirasek case. These points about interpersonal sensitivity may come into play in the Czechoslovak Management Center case. The resolution may be not only a strategic point but an opportunity to consider carefully the partners involved and their abilities to work together.

The Czechoslovak Management Center case illustrates the difficulty of establishing a new institution within an emerging economy. On the one hand, new institutions need the freedom to develop on their own. In CMC's case, the center needed freedom to develop curriculum, hire faculty at competitive wages, and establish its own admission standards. This independence came at a price, namely that CMC could potentially become disenfranchised from other organizations in its industry, mostly universities. This independence may leave CMC out of funding possibilities, out of faculty opportunities, and may be unrealistic for future development. The question posed by this case is, Does an evolving institution (in an environment such as the former Czechoslovakia) eventually need to integrate with existing institutions? If yes, when might this happen and under what circumstances?

The key lesson from the CMC case is that new institutions, even those servicing a need identified as critical to national goals, must become self-sustaining. This can be accomplished by affiliating with an existing, stable organization. Also, the CMC case shows the difficulty of depending on foreign aid to create a viable institution. CMC must raise its own money through tuition, direct funding, and more dependence on local faculty. No institution can survive with only direct aid—it must create revenues from customers.

A final penchant during the reform is toward macrotensions that have built up in the economy, such as inflation, money supply, foreign trade, and employment. These factors are no longer suppressed or enhanced artificially. These economic factors are influenced mainly by government taxation, spending, and market forces.

Given these cases, and the trends we see in the former Czechoslovak republics, what lessons have we learned about firms' responses to the Czechoslovak transition? I see several major lessons that can be used as tentative hypotheses of how companies respond to a transition economy. Here are seven:

1. Companies are trying to understand how to react under two systems: the declining socialist system and the evolving market system. Companies in this transition state will be seen as building up their ability to gather information or to reduce the needs for information by streamlining their companies. Thus, conflicting behaviors are attributed more to systemic uncertainty than to managers not having skills or incentives to adapt.

2. Individuals within organizations are generally unprepared for the personal sacrifice for simultaneous major economic, social, and political change. In particular, they need the skills and knowledge to survive. We would expect a similar lack of preparedness in the West.

3. Several reasons exist for managers reacting the way they do: They do not know how to seek foreign partners; they are satisfied with what they achieved; they learned certain lessons that influence present decisions;

they are getting pressure from their constituents; and they have assessed their environment as being too uncertain to support change.

4. Companies in the former Czechoslovakia are faced with dilemmas in entering the market economy. These dilemmas include the complicating factor of having foreign partners involved in the privatization of firms and strategic planning.

5. Transitions within the companies cannot be studied from a pure economics framework. We must understand the political and social transformations and the human interpretation of these transformations.

6. Long-term strategies are replacing ad hoc management styles and improvisation or deference to authority.

7. Organizations strive to fit with their environment. Yet, enterprises in the Czech and Slovak republics also are trying to be different to be competitive. This paradox is accentuated by the uncertainty prevalent throughout the society.

My goal in writing this book has been to present the various issues and difficulties in companies trying to make the transition from a command economy to a market economy. These cases are actual situations designed to illustrate at least one key point.

The reader would do best to make these cases as personal as possible. Try to imagine yourself in the place of each manager as he or she makes decisions that could define the company's future survival. We welcome your involvement in the cases. We also welcome your feedback on how we can improve our cases and presentation to you, your students, or your colleagues.

Notes

1. Vaclav Havel, *Summer Meditations* (New York: Alfred A. Knopf, 1992), 67.

2. J. Kornai, *The Socialist System* (Princeton, NJ: Princeton University Press, 1992).

3. A. Blair, L. Feick, F. Giarratani, and M. Spiro, *Regional Economies in Transition* (London: Ashgate, forthcoming).

4. Ibid.

5. Its original success was short-lived. One could argue that Lusico would have been successful initially in spite of itself. Any company would have done well offering a reasonable service to businesspeople during the early period of the Czechoslovak transition and the involvement of private companies.

Acronyms

AIF	Advance Investment Fund
AM	Asset Management
ANSI/ASQC	American National Standards Institute/American Society of Quality Control
CCS	Credit Control Services
CEECs	Central and East European Countries
CES	Credit Evaluation Services
CIA	Central Intelligence Agency
CIS	Commonwealth of Independent States
CMC	Czechoslovak Management Center
CMEA	Council for Mutual Economic Assistance
COMECON	Council for Mutual Economic Assistance
ČSA	Czechoslovak Airlines
CSP	Corporate Security Products
CTU	Czech Technical University
ECU	European currency unit
EPL	Electro-Products Limited
GATT	General Agreement on Tariffs and Trade
GDP	gross domestic product
GDR	German Democratic Republic
GMP	Graduate Management Program
HC&C	Harvard Capital and Consulting
HG	Harvard Group
IATA	International Air Traffic Association
ICI	Imperial Chemical Industries
IMC	International Management Center
IMF	International Monetary Fund
INLECO	International Legal Consulting
IPO	initial public offering
ISB	Investors' Stock Brokerage
ISO	International Standards Organization
MIT	Massachusetts Institute of Technology
NMP	net material product
OECD	Organization for Economic Cooperation and Development
PHARE	Poland and Hungary: Assistance for Reconstructing the Economy
PPP	purchasing power parity
PSE	Prague School of Economics
QFD	quality function deployment

SPC	statistical process control
SQC	statistical quality control
SU	Sklo Union State Company
SWOT	strengths, weaknesses, opportunities, and threats
TEMPUS	Trans European Mobility Plan for Universities and Students
TQM	total quality management

About the Book and Editor

Since 1989, east-central Europe has plunged headlong into reform efforts, and firms large and small have been forced almost overnight to adapt to the demands of a market economy. This book of case studies on business development in the Czech and Slovak Republics illustrates how various industries and specific companies are responding to the challenges of privatization.

After an introduction surveying the economic transition throughout the region, the book provides an overview of the former Czechoslovakia's unique approaches to economic and social reform. The heart of the work rests with the case studies, which were jointly authored by U.S. and Czech academics. They address a range of problems unleashed by reform, including pricing strategies, layoffs, management styles, methods of privatization, marketing, and start-up costs.

Professionals and students focusing on international business, marketing, and organizational behavior will find these case studies timely and cogent.

Daniel S. Fogel is director of the Center for International Enterprise Development, associate dean, and professor of business administration at the University of Pittsburgh.